When Race & Prejudice Is Policy: Prejudicial & Discriminatory Laws, Decisions and Policies in U. S. History

by

Edward Rhymes Ph.D.

Bloomington, IN Milton Keynes, UK

authorHOUSE

AuthorHouse™
1663 Liberty Drive, Suite 200
Bloomington, IN 47403
www.authorhouse.com
Phone: 1-800-839-8640

AuthorHouse™ UK Ltd.
500 Avebury Boulevard
Central Milton Keynes, MK9 2BE
www.authorhouse.co.uk
Phone: 08001974150

This book is a work of non-fiction. Unless otherwise noted, the author and the publisher make no explicit guarantees as to the accuracy of the information contained in this book and in some cases, names of people and places have been altered to protect their privacy.

First published by AuthorHouse 01/02/07

ISBN: 978-1-4259-8721-3 (e)
ISBN: 978-1-4259-8718-3 (sc)

Printed in the United States of America
Bloomington, Indiana

This book is printed on acid-free paper.

Table of Contents

FOREWORD

As we as a nation are beginning to grasp for some definitive meaning for the word "American," as many institutions of higher learning are beginning to offer more courses concerning race & race relations, ethnicity and culture. As many teachers on every level have started to interpret history through the clear lenses of objectivity and not through the unreliable spectacles of nationalism and prejudice, I wanted to add my voice to the massive refrain of authors who have written volumes concerning prejudice and racism.

I believe that these writers understood that for a democratic government to be guilty of injustice and inequality is not only a transgression that many other societies and governments have been guilty of, but an outright betrayal of the principles that this government was supposed to be founded upon.

There are many who may balk at the delving into the history of the political and social sins of America. They say that "those things happened a long time ago" and the examination of the past "only stirs up trouble."

I will first answer the "it happened a long time ago" argument. I agree whole heartedly with Dr. Martin Luther King Jr. when he said: "there is nothing magical in the flow of time. Time is neutral; it can be used either constructively or destructively." Many people have the erroneous belief that "time heals all wounds," but a wound without proper medical care and attention, left uncleaned, doesn't get better over time but worse. And the infection can become deadly if the wound is serious enough.

It is what we do with time that determines its impacts and benefits. As to the statement of the examination of the past "only stirs up trouble," I say that sweeping also stirs up dirt and dust, but when all is said and done the floor should be cleaner. One should always be apprehensive of a peace that comes at the expense of the truth.

As a sociologist I have tried to view myself as a "social physician," and one the first things any physician wants to know about a patient is the medical history of their family. I have never heard of any patient telling a doctor that by doing this they would only stir up trouble. On the contrary, most (if not all) patients know that, to better serve them, the physician must be made aware of the history. That by knowing the medical history of the patient's family a physician can not only better treat the medical problems that patient may presently have, but also what preventive measures to take as well.

If a patient dares to ignore the medical history of their family and the precautions prescribed by their physician, they court danger and disaster. Along these same lines, I believe, that any country that ignores the ills of their political and social history and refuses to take the necessary precautions to treat those ills, it too courts danger and disaster.

I am neither naïve nor arrogant enough to believe that by the revealing of certain truths it will make *justice inevitable*, but it is my hope to make *injustice inexcusable*.

INTRODUCTION

This text was written in light of the irrefutable truth, that in a historically racist social system, the laws will reflect, protect and sustain values that are consistent with racism. The historical testimony of this is too compelling to be ignored. Most people have very little social or historical perspective, knowing next to nothing about how racism and prejudice have played a leading role in the formulation of this nation's laws and policies (while at the same time erroneously believing that America has always been impartial in administering justice).

In reading about these laws and policies it should be abundantly clear to the honest and unbiased mind that it is racism and discrimination that is the norm in America's legislation. This is made manifest when comparing the speed and vehemence in which discriminatory statutes are implemented to the retarded and apathetic pace that laws aimed at ensuring equity and justice are enacted and enforced. For example we see the lightning speed in which the internment/concentration camps for Japanese Americans that were set up following the bombing of Pearl Harbor on December 7, 1941. It took all of four months when the establishment of the first internment/concentration camp occurs in March of 1942. Altogether different was what took place after Brown v. the Board of Education. The Brown decision was delivered in 1954, but we do not see substantial action towards desegregation until the Supreme Court's decision in 1971's Swann v. Charlotte-Mecklenburg (17 years later).

Another example is the hurried passage of the Patriot Act in October 26, 2001 (a law which I believe is on the whole discriminatory and smacks of racism) just a little over a month after the September 11th attacks. In stark contrast the 13th, 14th and 15th amendments passed after the Civil War, took about 100 years to become a *legal* reality with the Civil Rights Act of 1965.

To impress upon the reader these actualities in American history and society, I endeavored to write each section with three major components in mind. First, historical overview. No law that significantly impacts a specific group in a society or country can be separated from that same group's history within that same culture. Most important aspects of political and social history are the result of long-standing arrangements and past experiences.

Second, the social and political climate leading to the law or policy. Although, as was stated previously, the overall history of a group is indirectly connected to discriminatory laws and policies, there are also certain immediate factors that impact the passage of these same statutes (i.e. the Depression of the 1870's and it's relation to the Chinese Exclusion Act of 1882).

Third, the aftermath of the law and/or policy. As an educator I have witnessed a disturbing detachment and indifference concerning the very laws and policies treated in this book. I have watched students discuss these decrees as historical curiosities, while being ignorant and indifferent to their social and historical significance. To quote noted anthropologist John Henrik Clarke: "What happened 500 years ago, 50 years ago or 5 minutes ago, impacts what happens 5 minutes from now, 50 years from now and 500 years from now. All of history is a current event."

In writing this book I wanted to stay rooted in historical truth and to pontificate as little as possible. By this I do not mean to insinuate that I am without opinion on the subject of racism (I regard it as a sin and a cancer, as well as America's greatest unresolved moral dilemma). However, in my experience, the agents of bigotry and error are not overturned by opinion, but by the truth.

With that in mind there still may be some who will view this as a scathing indictment against America. While I do not deny that the writings contained in this volume may appear to be highly critical, it is history, not I, that points the finger of rebuke.

OVERVIEW OF COLONIAL AMERICA'S LAWS & POLICIES

This section will focus largely on the colonial laws and policies (although laws and policies implemented after the colonies gained their independence will be treated as well). Also, the focus will be on the legislation and policies that impacted, primarily, Native and African Americans.

If American colonial law is to be understood, then we must first look to English laws and customs. It was English law that ruled the American colonies in their infancy and it was English customs that determined the attitudes of the colonists towards the Native & African-American peoples. It is also worthy of note that since the English newcomers identified themselves as being "Christian," they also sought to find some sort of religious and or spiritual justification for their actions and behavior.

HISTORICAL OVERVIEW

Attitudes Towards Native Americans

Englishmen did not arrive at Jamestown, Virginia, in 1607, or at Plymouth, Massachusetts, in 1620, with minds devoid of images and preconceptions of the native occupiers of the land. A mass of reports and stories concerning the Indians of the New World, many of them based upon the Spanish and Portuguese experiences in Mexico, Peru, and Brazil, were available in printed form or by word of mouth for curious Englishmen crossing the Atlantic. From this literature ideas and fantasies concerning the Indians gradually entered the English consciousness.

These early accounts seem to have created a split image of the Indian in the English mind. On the one hand, the native was imagined to be a savage, hostile, beast-like creature that inhabited the animal kingdom rather than the kingdom of men. In 1585, prospective adventurers to the New World could read one

1

description of the natives of North America which depicted them as naked, lascivious individuals who cohabited "like beasts without any reasonableness." Another account described them as men who "spake such speech that no men could understand them, and in their demeanor like to brute beastes."[1] But Englishmen also entertained another more positive version of the New World native. Richard Hakluyt, the great propagandist for English colonization, described the Indians in 1585 as "simple and rude in manners, and destitute of the knowledge of God or any good laws, yet of nature gentle and tractable, and most apt to receive the Christian Religion, and to subject themselves to some good government." Many other reports spoke of the native in similarly optimistic terms.

This dual vision of the native matched the two-sided image of the New World refracted through the prism of the sixteenth-century European mind. In some ways prospective colonists fantasized the New World as a Garden of Eden, a land abounding with precious minerals, health foods, and exotic wildlife. The anti-image was of a barbarous land filled with a multitude of unknown dangers, a "howling wilderness" capable of dragging man down to the level of beasts.

Attitudes Towards African Americans

We sometimes imagine that such oppressive laws concerning slavery were put quickly into full force by greedy landowners. But that's not the way slavery was established in colonial America. It happened gradually—one person at a time, one law at a time, even one colony at a time.

One of the places we have the clearest views of this reality, is the colony of Virginia. In the early years of the colony, many Africans and poor whites—most of the laborers came from the English working class—stood on the same ground. Black and white women worked side-by-side in the fields. Black and white men who broke their servant contract were equally punished.

All were indentured servants. During their time as servants, they were fed and housed. Afterwards, they would be given what were

2

known as "freedom dues," which usually included a piece of land and supplies, including a gun. Black-skinned or white-skinned, they became free.

Historically, the English only enslaved non-Christians, and not, in particular, Africans. And the status of slave (Europeans had African slaves prior to the colonization of the Americas) was not one that was life-long. A slave could become free by converting to Christianity. The first Virginia colonists did not even think of themselves as "white" or use that word to describe themselves. They saw themselves as Christians or Englishmen, or in terms of their social class. They were nobility, gentry, artisans, or servants.

[handwritten margin note: Black & white were not defining characteristics]

One of the few-recorded histories of an African in America that we can glean from early court records is that of "Antonio the negro," as he was named in the 1625 Virginia census. He was brought to the colony in 1621. At this time, English and Colonial law did not define racial slavery; the census calls him not a slave but a "servant." Later, Antonio changed his name to Anthony Johnson, married an African-American servant named Mary, and they had four children. Mary and Anthony also became free, and he soon owned land and cattle and even indentured servants of his own. By 1650, Anthony was still one of only 400 Africans in the colony among nearly 19,000 settlers. In Johnson's own county, at least 20 African men and women were free, and 13 owned their own homes.

There were several key factors in the evolution and formation of prejudicial laws and policies in British colonial America. There are three, which I believe to be, of particular importance to this study. They are: (1) The English Pattern of Conquest, (2) English Concept of Land Ownership, and (3) Religious Endorsement.

[handwritten margin note: British Colonial America]

The English Pattern of Conquest

In contrast to the Spaniards who frequently intermarried with the native populations of Mexico, Central America and South America, the English followed a pattern of driving away the peoples they defeated. This pattern shows itself in England's conquest of Ireland.

The English practiced a systematic discrimination against the Irish people with the Statutes of Kilkenny in the 1300's, the Penal Laws of the late 17th century and Oliver Cromwell's large scale land confiscation policy in the mid 1600's.

The Statutes of Kilkenny's purpose was to prevent further assimilation of the English colonizers with the Irish natives, by legal and religious penalties. The settlers were forbidden to use the Irish language. They were also forbidden to use Irish names, marry into Irish families, use the Irish mode of dress, adopt any Irish laws and play the Irish game of hurling. But the English crown, embroiled in a costly military campaign in Scotland and the Hundred Years War (1338-1453) against France, had little time for Irish affairs and the statutes remained inoperative.

The Penal Laws were a set of legal codes put into place by Ireland's English rulers following the Treaty of Limerick in the late 17th century. Also called the "Popery Laws," the Penal Laws were based on the fears of an English Protestant ruling class: they were meant to both protect the Protestant religion and eliminate the native Roman Catholic Irish as a threat. Although the Penal Laws were largely unenforced during the 18th century, they remained on the books and were still legally binding until Catholic Emancipation in 1829.

The first of Penal Laws went into effect a scant three years after the signing of the Treaty, in which the Irish were guaranteed "that the Irish in Ireland should, in their lives, liberties and property be equally protected" and "protected in the free and unfettered exercise of their religion."

This first law was called the *Act for the Better Securing of the Government against Papists*. Under this law, no Papist (Catholic) could have any "gun, pistol, or sword, or any other weapon of offense or defense, under penalty of fine, imprisonment, pillory (locking ones head and hands in a wooden rack for public ridicule), or public whipping." It further stated that any magistrate could show up at the house of any Irish person no matter what time of the day or night and search for weapons legally.

This was followed, circa 1697, with the *Act for banishing all Papists exercising any ecclesiastical jurisdiction, and regulars of the Popish clergy, out of this Kingdom*, also called *"The Bishop's Banishment Act."* The law required all Catholic clergy to leave Ireland by May 1st, 1698 under the penalty of transportation (indentured servitude) for life. It further stated that if any returned, they would be hanged, drawn, and quartered.

But this was just the start of the restrictions. Further laws were passed over time that severely limited the ability of a Catholic to do anything. These included laws that:

- Forbade Catholics from exercising their religion
- Forbade Catholics from receiving a Catholic education
- Forbade Catholics from entering a profession
- Forbade Catholics from holding Public Office
- Forbade Catholics from engaging in trade or commerce
- Forbade Catholics from living in a corporate town or within five miles of one
- Forbade Catholics from owning a horse worth more than 5 pounds
- Forbade Catholics from buying or leasing land
- Forbade Catholics from voting
- Forbade Catholics from receiving a gift or inheritance of land from a Protestant
- Forbade Catholics from renting any land that was worth more than thirty shillings
- Forbade Catholics from gaining any profit from his land over a third of the land's value
- Forbade Catholics from being the guardian of a child
- Fined Catholics for not attending Protestant services
- Forbade Catholics from sending their children abroad for an education

By these laws the Catholics were deprived of all civil life, reduced to the condition of ignorance and dissociated with the soil. Catholic schoolmasters and priests became hunted men and women. The laws were simply designed to repress the native Irish who were for the most part Catholic.

Conditions and the treatment of the Irish degraded to the point where a Protestant could beat or kill any Catholic without fear of recrimination. By these means, the Protestant residents of Ireland successfully controlled the other 80% of the Irish population, the Catholics.

Puritan leader Lord Protector Oliver Cromwell had ordered all Irish landowners to leave their holdings and relocate west of the Shannon River. The area of Connaught to which the former landholders were assigned was barren and totally unsuitable for the amount of farming that was needed to sustain a population as lame as that which was forced there.

All confiscated land was given to those who supported Cromwell's Irish campaign, from financial backers to volunteer soldiers. Those Irish who owned no land prior to the conflict, and were still alive, were allowed to remain as a servant force for the new English settlers. Those who opposed Cromwell's conquest of Ireland were killed or deported, but the saddest part of it all was the fate of the Irish children. Many, orphaned as a result of the fighting, were sent to England's colonies in the Indies and America as slaves.

The English brought this pattern of colonization with them to North America. Viewing the Native Americans as being "like the wild Irish," the English settlers had no desire to intermarry with the Native Americans they defeated. Their conquest over the native peoples was total and absolute.

English Concept of Land Ownership

Although its control had waned by the time the first settlers from England had arrived in North America, the remnants of the old medieval feudal system were very much a part of English life. This reality greatly impacted the attitudes of the early English settlers towards the Native Americans (and later African Americans). Land ownership and control was the foundation upon which the whole system rested. And this ownership and control extended to those who inhabited that land.

Beginning with the Jamestown settlement of 1607 and intensifying with the great Puritan migration of the 1630's, Englishmen coming to the New World thought less about Indian trade, the Northwest Passage, and fabled gold mines and more about land. As the dreams of El Dorado evaporated, English attention centered on the less glamorous goal of permanent settlement. Now land became all-important, for without land how could there be permanent settlement? The Indian, who had been important when trade and exploration were the keys to overseas involvement, became an inconvenient obstacle. One Englishman went to the heart of the difficulty in 1609: "By what right or warrant can we enter into the land of these Savages, take away their right-full inheritance from them, and plant ourselves in their places, being unwronged or unprovoked by them?" It was a cogent question to ask, for Englishmen, like other Europeans, had organized their society around the concept of private ownership of land. They regarded it, in fact, as an important characteristic of their superior culture. Colonists were not blind to the fact that they were invading the land of another people, who by prior possession could lay sole claim to the whole of mainland America. The resolution of this moral and legal problem was accomplished by an appeal to logic and to higher powers. The English claimed that they came to share, not appropriate, the trackless wilderness. The Indians would benefit because they would be elevated far above their present condition through contact with a richer culture, a more advanced civilization, and most importantly, the Christian religion. Samuel Purchas, a clerical promoter of English expansion, gave classic expression to this idea: "God in wisedome ... enriched the Savage Countries that those riches might be attractive for Christian suters, which there may sowe spirituals and reape temporals." Spirituals, to be sown, of course, meant Christianity; temporals to be reaped meant land. Purchas went on to argue that to leave undeveloped a sparsely settled land populated only by a few natives was to oppose the wishes of God who would not have showed Englishmen the way to the New World if he had not intended them to possess it. Moreover,

7

if the English did not occupy North America, Spain would; and the Indians would then fall "victim" to Catholicism.

Land was the key to English settlement after 1620. It was logical to assume in these circumstances that the Native would not willingly give up the ground that sustained him, even if the English offered to purchase land, as they did in most cases. For anyone as property conscious as the English, the idea that people would resist the invasion of their land with all the force at their disposal came almost as a matter of course. Thus the image of the hostile, "savage Indian" began to triumph over that of the receptive, "friendly Indian." Their own intentions had changed from establishing trade relations to building permanent settlements. A different conception of the Native American was required in these altered circumstances.

What we see here is a subconscious attempt to manipulate the world in order to make it conform to the English definition of it. The evidence also suggests that the English stereotype of the hostile savage helped to alleviate a sense of guilt which inevitably arose when men whose culture was based on the concept of private property embarked on a program to dispossess another people of their land. To type-cast the Native American as a brutish savage was to solve a moral dilemma. If the Indian was truly cordial, generous, and eager to trade, what justification could there be for taking his land? But if he was a savage, without religion or culture, perhaps the colonists' actions were defensible. The English, we might speculate, anticipated hostility and then read it into the Native's character because they recognized that they were embarking upon an invasion of land to which the only natural response could be violent resistance. Having created the conditions in which the Native American could only respond violently, the Englishman defined the native as brutal, beastly, savage, and barbarian and then used that as a justification for what he was doing.

Religious Endorsement

Slavery was rationalized because Africans were not Christian, therefore labeled "heathens" and considered sub-human. The Promised Land theology of the book of Joshua with its model of military conquest was used to justify the wars against indigenous peoples, the "Canaanites" of the New World. The Puritans who came to the New World saw themselves as God's elect, called to establish the New Israel. Frontier individualism and the optimism of progress through expansion and wealth led to the political slogan "Manifest Destiny," which reflected Christian or Protestant ascendancy, a biblical interpretation that encouraged an attitude of the moral and economic superiority of white Christians over all others, and justified the taking of land.

"We shall be as a City upon a Hill, the eyes of all people are upon us...," the Puritan John Winthrop wrote. The Puritans who disembarked in Massachusetts in 1620 believed they were establishing the New Israel. Indeed, the whole colonial enterprise was believed to have been guided by God. "God hath opened this passage unto us," Alexander Whitaker preached from Virginia in 1613, "and led us by the hand unto this work."

Promised Land imagery figured prominently in shaping English colonial thought. The pilgrims identified themselves with the ancient Hebrews. They viewed the New World as the New Canaan. They were God's chosen people headed for the Promised Land. Other colonists believed they, too, had been divinely called. The settlers in Virginia were, John Rolf said, "a peculiar people, marked and chosen by the finger of God."

This self-image of being God's Chosen People called to establish the New Israel became an integral theme in America's self-interpretation. During the revolutionary period, it emerged with new force. "We cannot but acknowledge that God hath graciously patronized our cause and taken us under his special care, as he did his ancient covenant people," Samuel Langdon preached at Concord, New Hampshire in 1788. George Washington was the "American Joshua," and "Never was the possession of arms used with more glory, or in a better cause, since the days of Joshua, the son of Nun," Ezra Stiles urged in Connecticut in 1783. In 1776, Benjamin Franklin and Thomas Jefferson wanted Promised Land images for the new nation's Great Seal. Franklin proposed Moses dividing the Red (Reed) Sea with Pharaoh's army being overwhelmed by the closing waters. Jefferson urged a representation of the Israelites being led in the wilderness by the pillar of fire by night and the cloud by day. Later, in his second inaugural address (1805), Jefferson again recalled the Promised Land. "I shall need...the favor of that Being in whose hands we are, who led our fathers, as Israel of old, from their native land and planted them in a country flowing with all the necessities and comforts of life."

The sense of divine election and the identification of the Americas with ancient Canaan were used to justify expelling America's Indigenous Peoples from their land. The colonists saw themselves as confronting "satanic forces" in the Native Americans. They were Canaanites to be destroyed or thrown out.

This view of Native Americans was challenged by a Mohawk chief named Joseph Brant (Thayendanegea) in a letter to King George III of England: "Our wise men are called Fathers and they truly sustain that character. Do you call yourselves Christians? Does the religion of Him who you call your Savior inspire your spirit and guide your practices? Surely not. It is recorded of him that a bruised reed he never broke. Cease then to call yourselves Christians, lest you declare to the world your hypocrisy. Cease too to call other nations savage, when you are tenfold more the children of cruelty than they...."

COLONIAL LAWS & POLICIES

Note: These laws deal directly with African Americans (free & slave). Most of the governmental legislation that discriminated against the Native American in particular, would come after the colonies won their independence from England.

1619

Maryland Segregation Policy: Recommended that African Americans be socially excluded.

1639

Virginia: Passes the first law that excludes "Negroes" from the normal protections of the government.

1642

Virginia Fugitive Slave: Authorized the branding an "R" on the face of a runaway slave.

1641

Massachusetts: Legalizes slavery (Virginia followed in 1661, Maryland in 1664).

1642

Virginia: Enacts a law that fines those who help slaves escape (The Virginia law, penalizes people sheltering runaways 20 English pounds worth of tobacco for each night of refuge granted. Slaves are branded after a second escape attempt).

1660

Connecticut Military Law: Barred African Americans from military service.

1662

Virginia: passed law that made African-Americans' servitude for life. Also stated that the status of the mother determined whether a child was born free or slave.

1664

Maryland Marriage Law: Prohibited marriage between African Americans and whites (this law was in effect for over 300 years).

1667

Virginia: Christian baptisms would no longer affect the bondage of blacks or Indians, preventing enslaved workers from improving their legal status by changing their religion.

1682

Virginia: A law establishing the racial distinction between servants and slaves was enacted.

1686

Carolina Trade Law: Barred African Americans from all trades.

1691

Virginia Marriage Law: Prescribed banishment from the colony for any white woman marrying an African-American man.

1705

Massachusetts Anti-Miscegenation Law: Criminalized interracial marriages.

1705

New York Runaway Slave Law: Prescribed execution for recaptured runaway slaves.

1705

Virginia Public Office Law: Prohibited African Americans from holding or assuming any public office.

1710

Virginia Meritorious Manumission Policy: Rewarded slaves with freedom for informing on other slaves.

1715

North Carolina Anti-Interracial Marriage Law: Forbade and criminalized marriages between whites and African-Americans.

1721

Delaware Anti-Miscegenation Law: Forbade marriage between African-American men and white women.

1722

Pennsylvania Morality Law: Condemned African-American males for sexual acts with white women.

1723

Virginia Anti-Assembly Law: Forbade the assembly of African Americans with one another.

1740

South Carolina Consolidated Slave Act: Made it illegal for slaves to own or raise farm animals.

1775

Virginia Runaway Law: Allowed sale and execution of slaves attempting to escape.

1775

North Carolina Manumission Law: Forbade freeing slaves except for meritorious service.

1784

Connecticut Military Law: Forbade African Americans from serving in the militia.

1790

First Naturalization Law: Congress restricts U.S. citizenship to whites only.

SOCIAL & POLITICAL CLIMATE LEADING TO THE RACIALIZATION OF SLAVERY

Slavery was unknown in the British Isles when the first English colonists arrived in North America in the late 1500's. Moreover, the very idea of slavery was contrary to English law. Thus, although slavery could be found throughout the Spanish and Portuguese settlements of the Americas, the English did not adopt the institution immediately.

In the early years of the English colonies, the landowning and elite English colonists in Virginia, Maryland, and elsewhere relied on indentured servants; who contracted their services for a limited term of years-for their labor supply. In 1619 the first Africans arrived in Virginia aboard a Dutch ship. The Virginia colonists treated these Africans as indentured servants, and some eventually gained their freedom. Throughout the 1620's the legal system in Virginia seems not to have discriminated against blacks. For example, a record from

14

1624 notes that "John Phillip, A Negro" was allowed to testify in a lawsuit involving two whites (a right that would later be rescinded for blacks).

However, by 1640 the legal system had begun to single out Africans for distinctly different treatment. In that year a Virginia court sentenced a black indentured servant named John Punch to "serve his said master or his assigns for the time of his natural Life here or elsewhere." No white indentured servant in Virginia ever received such a sentence. At about this time court records and wills indicate that other blacks were being treated as slaves. The legal system was not uniformly hostile to blacks in the 17th century. For example, as late as 1672 a Virginia court freed Edward Mozingo, ruling that he had been brought to the colony as an indentured servant, had served his full term of years, and was entitled to his freedom. A year later the court ruled in favor of a freedom claim by "Andrew Moore, A Servant Negro."

However, Mozingo and Moore were the exceptions to the growing support for slavery by the Virginia courts and legislature. In 1659 and 1660 the Virginia legislature recognized the existence of slaves in the colony by providing an import tax for "foreigners [who] shall import negro slaves." Two years later the legislature provided that if white servants ran away with slaves, the whites would have to serve extra time to make up for the time that the slaves were absent because the slaves could not have any more time added to their service. This law had the practical effect of separating white indentured servants (who still made up the majority of agricultural workers in the English colonies) from black slaves. White workers, who frequently ran away, could no longer afford to share their plans or their hopes of liberty with their black coworkers. This was the beginning of a conscious attempt by the leaders of Virginia and other colonies to drive a wedge between black and white workers. In 1662 the Virginia legislature passed its most important early statute on slavery. This act declared that "all children born in this country shall be held bond or free only according to the condition of the mother." This legal rule, known as *partus sequitur ventrem* (the offspring follows the mother), was based on Roman law and was a complete reversal of existing English common law. In England the status of a child, even an illegitimate child, was based on the status of the father. But under this rule children in Virginia would follow the status of the mother. Every other English colony in North America eventually adopted this rule.

This law had two practical results. First, it meant that the children of black women throughout the American South would usually be slaves, even if their fathers were free. Second, this law facilitated sexual relations between male owners and female slaves. At this time in the colonies, fathers of children born outside of marriage were frequently prosecuted, both to bring public shame on them and to ensure their support for their children. However, this law took away any fear of such prosecution for sex with slaves. Any children born of such a relationship would be slaves, owned by the owner of the slave mother. The state would have no interest in investigating who the father was, because the master would happily pay for the costs of raising another slave. Thus this law encouraged the sexual exploitation of slave women.

Another compelling event in colonial America and the enslavement of Africans in America was Bacon's Rebellion. Bacon's Rebellion demonstrated beyond question the lack of a sufficient intermediate stratum to stand between the ruling plantation elite and the mass of the European-American and African-American laboring people, free and bond. It began in April 1676 as a difference between the elite and the sub-elite planters over "Indian policy," but by September it had become a civil war against the social order established by the plantation bourgeoisie. When Bacon's forces besieged, captured, and burned the colonial capital city of Jamestown and sent Governor Berkeley, scurrying into exile across Chesapeake Bay, the rebel army was composed mainly of European-American and African-American bond-laborers and freedmen recently "out of their time." Although Bacon's rebellion failed, it exposed the growing power of the colony's lower classes. The colony's elite devised a divide and conquer strategy which made the white lower classes the intermediate stratum and effectively regulated the African American to slavery.

Sexual exploitation of Slave women

In 1669 the Virginia legislature declared that masters or overseers would not be criminally liable if a slave died while being punished. In 1680 the legislature further declared that any white could kill a slave believed to be a fugitive. The same law provided the severe penalty of 30 lashes for any slave who "shall presume to lift up his hand in opposition" to any white. A 1691 law directed sheriffs to "kill and destroy" slaves hiding out in the woods and further guaranteed that the colony would recompense a master for the value of the dead slave. This law put the military force and the economic power of the colony behind the emerging institution of slavery.

By 1700 slavery was an integral and significant part of the Virginia economy. White indentured servants still outnumbered slaves, but indentured servitude was clearly being eclipsed by slavery. In 1705 Virginia enacted its first comprehensive statute on slavery, "An Act Concerning Servants and Slaves." Combining many earlier acts, the law required that slaves be taxed as property and registered by their owners, explained when runaways or rebellious slaves "may be killed," and described what other punishments might be inflicted on slaves. The law made clear that blacks were a pariah race whose members could not marry whites or associate with them. The law equated blacks with slaves, although in fact hundreds of blacks in the colony were free.

By 1750 all of the Southern colonies and most of the Northern ones had adopted slave codes similar to those of Virginia. In the process they managed to create an entirely new area of law, unknown in England, to support slavery in the colonies. While colonial legislatures tinkered with these codes, they remained basically the same until the American Revolution (1775-1783).

Slavery was particularly important in the Southern colonies because they relied on large-scale agriculture, although Rhode Island, New York, New Jersey, and Pennsylvania all had significant numbers of slaves as well. The laws of all the colonies were similar. Slaves had virtually no legal rights. They could be executed in most places for numerous crimes that were not capital offenses for whites. Their testimony was restricted in legal cases and could not be used for or against whites. Trials of slaves were usually by special courts. They could not own property, could not possess guns or dogs, could not move about without the consent of their owner, and could not be legally married. Throughout the South, killing a slave was not murder; it was usually considered simply a destruction of property. It was not considered a crime to kill a slave who was resisting white authority, rebelling, or even, in some circumstances, running away. In Virginia, the colony with the largest slave population, and elsewhere in the South, it was even illegal for a master to manumit (voluntarily free) a slave.

Slavery was legal in all of the 13 colonies that revolted against Great Britain in the American Revolution. It was also legal in Canada, where, with the exception of Upper Canada (present-day Ontario), it remained legal until Britain abolished slavery throughout its remaining colonies in 1834. Thereafter Canada generally served as a safe haven for runaway slaves from the United States, who fled by means of the Underground Railroad.

(handwritten margin note: North tried to end slavery during revolution)

The American Revolution, however, undermined the basis of slavery through the articulation of the principle "all men are created equal" in the Declaration of Independence. During and after the war Northern patriots took seriously this new ideology and took steps to end slavery. Massachusetts (1780), and New Hampshire (1784), ended slavery outright in their new state constitutions. Vermont had abolished slavery in its 1777 constitution, which was officially recognized when it became the 14th state in 1791. Pennsylvania (1780), Connecticut (1784), Rhode Island (1784), New York (1799), and New Jersey (1804) adopted "gradual emancipation statutes," which provided that the children of all slave women would be born free (although subject to indentured service until adulthood), and that no new slaves could be brought in from other states. Upper Canada adopted a similar law in 1793. New York accelerated this process by ending all slavery on July 4, 1827. By the 1840's Pennsylvania and Connecticut had also eliminated the last vestiges of slavery.

The Revolution also had some effect on slavery in the South. For example, in 1791 North Carolina made it a capital offense to murder a slave. The preamble to this statute, which was later declared unenforceable for technical reasons, acknowledged the ideological changes brought about by the Revolution. In 1782 Virginia allowed for the voluntary manumission of slaves by masters. As a result, the free black population of the state grew from about 2,000 to about 30,000 between 1782 and 1806, when Virginia modified the law by requiring newly freed slaves to leave the state. Other Southern states eased restrictions on voluntary manumission. However, none of the Southern states considered actually ending slavery. On the contrary, most Southerners assumed that one of the benefits of the Revolution was the new states' increased right to pass laws that strengthened slavery within their territory.

From the first day of substantive debate at the Constitutional Convention in 1787 until the final signing of the finished Constitution, slavery was a central issue. On the first day of debate the issue of slavery nearly derailed the convention as the delegates considered a proposal to have representation based on population. The discussion had hardly begun when the question of counting or not counting slaves for purposes of representation led to bitter debate. Despite this controversy, the finished Constitution protected slavery in a variety of ways.

The three-fifths clause (Article I, Section 2, Paragraph 3) provided for counting three-fifths of all "other Persons" (slaves) for purposes of representation in Congress, although such people of course could not vote. At the end of the convention Elbridge Gerry of Massachusetts refused to sign the Constitution, at least in part because the three-fifths clause gave the South increased representation and political power because of its slaves.

The slave trade clause (Article I, Section 9, Paragraph 1) prohibited Congress from banning the "Migration or Importation of such Persons as any of the States now existing shall think proper to admit" before the year 1808. Awkwardly phrased and designed to confuse readers, this clause prevented Congress from ending the African slave trade before 1808 but did not require Congress to ban the trade after that date. The clause was a significant exception to the general power granted to Congress to regulate all commerce.

The Electoral College clause (Article II, Section 1, Paragraph 2) provided for the indirect election of the President through an electoral college based on Congressional representation. This provision incorporated the three-fifths clause into the Electoral College, giving whites in slave states a disproportionate influence in the election of the President. In 1800 the electoral votes based on slaves provided the margin of victory for the slaveholding candidate, Thomas Jefferson, over John Adams, who had never owned a slave.

The fugitive slave clause (Article IV, Section 2, Paragraph 3) prohibited the states from emancipating a "Person held to Service or Labour in one State…and escaping into another (a fugitive slave) and required that runaways be returned to their owners if claimed. Oddly, no Northerners commented on this clause during the debates over ratification. By the 1830s, however, it had emerged as the most controversial clause connected to slavery.

NATIVE & AFRICAN AMERICAN ALLIANCES

After arriving in the Americas, Europeans turned first to Native Americans as a source of forced labor. They introduced African slaves to the region only after calculating the difficulty of coercing large numbers of Native Americans into their labor systems. Africans who fled from slavery frequently mixed with Native Americans to avoid being captured. Native Americans who escaped from slavery could evade the colonists through their knowledge of the surrounding areas, and some of them returned to help free enslaved Africans.

Wherever they established slavery in the Americas, Europeans feared the revolutionary potential of alliances between Native Americans and Africans. The first slave rebellion on North American soil took place along the Carolina coast in 1526 and was organized and executed by a coalition of Africans and Native Americans. Europeans especially feared communities of escaped slaves, known as maroon societies or *quilombos*, that arose in frontier areas and that often allied with Native Americans. These communities established themselves outside the boundaries of

European settlement, where they sometimes allied with local Native Americans.

Despite the limited number of these maroon communities, they provoked strong reactions among the Europeans, who sought to keep the African and Native American peoples separated and mutually hostile if possible. They taught Africans to fight Native Americans and bribed Native Americans to hunt escaped Africans. Further sowing division between the peoples, whites introduced African slavery into the Five Civilized Tribes, as the indigenous peoples of southeastern North America were known.

By the time of the Revolutionary War (1775-1783), the United States government had ended the enslavement of Native Americans. However, the government still attempted to enlist Native Americans in enforcing the slavery of Africans. Until the onset of the Civil War in the early 1860's, the government negotiated treaties with indigenous peoples that included promises by the Native Americans to return escaped slaves. However, the peoples who had such clauses in their treaties with the American government largely ignored them, harboring many fugitive slaves and returning few.

CONTRASTING NATIVE & AFRICAN AMERICANS

Of course not every settler who came to America in the early seventeenth century harbored deeply negative thoughts about Africans and Indians. Probably few of the Pilgrims and Puritans who colonized New England or few of the settlers in Virginia had met face to face with natives of Africa or North America or even thought very systematically about the culture and character traits of such people. But Africans and Indians did impress English adventurers of the late sixteenth and early seventeenth centuries in certain ways, and these impressions were recorded in books that literate men read or knew about. Thus, ideas and attitudes concerning red and black men were entering the collective English consciousness at just that time when England was making its first attempts to compete with Spain, Portugal, Holland, and France for possession of the New World. These first impressions would change under the pressure of circumstances in the New World. But the colonists first met these

21

men from other continents with ideas and notions already in their heads, though the images were vague and half formed. It is only with an understanding of these early attitudes and knowledge of early Anglo and Native American relations that we can comprehend the connection between prejudice and slavery. No doubt the early English image of the African as a heathen, primitive creature made it easier for Englishmen to cast him into slavery.

However, the Native American also was depicted in unfavorable terms, as were the Irish and even the dregs of white English society. But among those seen in such a light, it was the Africans who were most vulnerable to economic exploitation because only they could be wrenched from their homeland in great numbers, often with the active participation of other Africans. Moreover, they were unusually helpless once transported to a distant and unfamiliar environment where they were forced into close association with a people whose power they could not contest. Certainly an underlying and still forming prejudice against people with black skin was partially responsible for the subjugation of Africans. But the chronic labor shortage in the colonies and the almost total failure to mold the Native American into an agricultural labor force were probably more important factors.

The effect of slavery on racial attitudes is less complicated. Once institutionalized in the American colonies, slavery cast the African American in such a lowly role that the initial bias against him could only be confirmed and vastly strengthened. It was hardly possible for one people to enslave another without developing strong feelings against them. While initially unfavorable impressions of Africans and economic conditions which encouraged their exploitation led to the mass enslavement of men with black skins, it required slavery itself to harden negative racial feelings into a deep and almost unshakable prejudice which continued to grow for centuries to come. A labor system was devised which kept the African in America at the bottom of the social and economic pyramid. By mid-eighteenth century, when black codes had been legislated to ensure that slaves were totally and unalterably caught in the web of perpetual servitude, no further opportunity remained to prove the white stereotype wrong. Socially and legally defined as less than a man, kept in a degraded and debased position, virtually without power in his relationships with his white master, the African became a truly servile, ignoble, degraded creature in the perception of white men. In the long evolution of racial attitudes in America nothing was of greater importance than the enslavement of Africans in a land where freedom, equality, and opportunity were becoming the foundations of a new social order.

Whereas the white colonist almost always encountered the black man as a slave after about 1660, and thus came to think of him as a slave-like creature by nature, the English settler met the Indian, (especially after 1675 when the last large-scale Indian wars occurred, until the nineteenth century) far less frequently. When he did interact with the Native American, it was rarely in a master-slave context. The English settler learned how difficult it was to enslave the native in his own habitat. Thus, if the Native American had survived the coming of white civilization, he usually maintained a certain freedom to come and go, and, more significantly, the capacity to attack and kill the white encroacher. Though he was hated for this, it earned him a grudging respect. The Anglo and Native American relationship in the eighteenth century was rarely that of master and slave, with all rights and power concentrated on one side. In fact, the Native American and the white man were involved in a set of power relationships in which each side, with something to offer the other, maneuvered for the superior position. That the Native American was the ultimate loser in almost all these interchanges should not obscure the fact that for several hundred years the Anglo American confronted the native as an adversary rather than a chattel.

The Anglo and Native American economic relationship illustrates the point. In almost every colony the Native-American trade was of importance to the local economy in the early stages of development. Trade implied a kind of equality; each side bargained in its own interest; and in each exchange agreement had to be reached between buyer and seller. The long-term effect of the trade was attritional for the Native Americans because it fostered a dependence upon alcohol and the implements of European civilization, especially the gun. But even while their culture was transformed by this contact with a technologically advanced society, and even though they often were exploited by unscrupulous traders, the Native Americans maintained considerable power in the trade nexus. Just as the provincial government of South Carolina could bring a recalcitrant tribe to terms by threatening to cut off trade, the Iroquois tribes of New York could obtain advantages from the English by threatening to transfer their allegiance and their trade to the French. New York and Pennsylvania competed for decades for the Native American trade of the Susquehanna River Valley, a fact of which the Native Americans were well apprised and able to use to their own advantage.

In land transactions, though the Native American was again the ultimate loser, power was also divided between red and white. The Native American, unlike the African, possessed a commodity indispensable to the English settlers. Throughout the colonial period, provincial governments acknowledged an obligation to purchase rather than appropriate land. For several hundred years the two cultural groups negotiated land purchases, signed treaties, registered titles, and determined boundaries. These transactions had symbolic as well as legal meaning for they served as reminders that the Indian, though often despised and exploited, was not without power.

As in matters of land and trade, so it was in political relationships. Between 1652 and 1763, North America was a theater of war in four international conflicts involving the English, French, Spanish, and Dutch. In each of these wars the Native Americans played a significant role since the contending European powers vied for alliances with them and attempted to employ them against their enemies. Whether it was the English and French competing for the support of the Iroquois in New York or the English and Spanish wooing the Creeks of the Carolina region, the Indians were entitled to the respect, which only an autonomous and powerful group could command.

Thus throughout the colonial period, Native Americans alternately traded, negotiated, allied, and fought with the English. In each case power was divided between the two parties and shifted back and forth with time, location, and circumstances. Though he was exploited, excluded, and sometimes decimated in his contacts with

European civilization, the Native American maneuvered from a position of strength which the African, devoid of tribal unity, unaccustomed to the environment, and relatively defenseless, never enjoyed. The African in America was rarely a part of any political or economic equation. He had only his labor to offer the white man and even that was not subject to contractual agreement. He was never in a position to negotiate with the colonist and was only occasionally capable of either retaliating against his oppressors or escaping from them.

This relative powerlessness of the African in America, as compared with the Native American, could not help but effect attitudes. Unlike the native, the African was uniquely unable to win the respect of the white man because his situation was rarely one where respect was required or even possible. Tightly caught in a slave-master relationship, with virtually all the power on the other side, the African could only sink lower and lower in the white man's estimation. Meanwhile, the Indian, though hated, was often respected for his fighting ability, his dignity, solemnity, and even his oratorical ability. American colonists may have scoffed at the Enlightenment portrait of the "noble savage," but nonetheless, the Native American had gained the reputation as a force to be reckoned with. In contrast, the African in America was, for the most part, the object of ridicule, disrespect and disregard.

THE AFTERMATH

Where does one begin when speaking of the aftermath of the laws and policies aimed against African & Native Americans? If I were to go into any great detail regarding this subject, it would create material for several other books. To avoid confusion as well as unnecessary verbiage, I will attempt to be clear and concise.

The Native American

The colonial wars and attitudes against the Native American peoples would later lead to laws such as The Indian Removal Act of 1830, (this will be treated more fully in another section) which led to the displacement and deaths of thousands of Native Americans.

According to the current anthropological debate, approximately seven million people indigenous to the borders of the United States of America and Canada died in the formation of these two countries. Factors leading to the Native-American demise included warfare, genocide, internment, displacement and slavery.

For brief periods after the American Revolution, the United States adopted a policy toward Native Americans known as the "conquest" theory. In the Treaty of Fort Stansix of 1784, the Iroquois had to cede lands in western New York and Pennsylvania. Those Iroquois living in the United States (many had gone to Canada where the English gave them refuge) rapidly degenerated as a nation during the last decades of the eighteenth century, losing most of their remaining lands and much of their ability to cope. The Shawnees, Miamis, Delawares, Ottawans, Wyandots, and Potawatomis watching the decline of the Iroquois formed their own confederacy and informed the United States that the Ohio River was the boundary between their lands and those of the settlers. It was just a matter of time before further hostilities ensued.

The "Indian Removal" policy was implemented to "clear" land for white settlers. Removal was more than another assault on American Indians' land titles. Insatiable greed for land remained a primary consideration, but many people now believed that the removal was the only way of saving Native Americans from extermination. As long as the Native Americans lived in close proximity to non-Native American communities, they would be decimated by disease, alcohol, and poverty. The Indian Removal Act began in 1830. Forced marches at bayonet-point to relocation settlements resulted in high mortality rates. The infamous removal of the Five Civilized Tribes—the Choctaws, Creeks, Chickasaws, Cherokees, and Seminoles—is a bleak page in United States history. By the 1820's the Cherokees, who had established a written constitution modeled after the United States Constitution, a newspaper, schools, and industries in their settlements, resisted removal. In 1938 the federal troops evicted the Cherokees. Approximately four thousand Cherokees died during the removal process because of poor planning by the United States Government. This exodus to Indian Territory is known as the Trail of Tears. More than one hundred thousand

American Indians eventually crossed the Mississippi River under the authority of the Indian Removal Act.

Strategies of targeting Native-American children for assimilation began with violence. Forts were erected by Jesuits, in which indigenous youths were incarcerated, indoctrinated with non-indigenous Christian values, and forced into manual labor. Schooling provided a crucial tool in changing not only the language but the culture of impressionable young people. In boarding schools students could be immersed in a 24 hours bath of assimilation. The founder of the Carlisle Indian Industrial School in Pennsylvania, Capt. Richard H. Pratt, observed in 1892 that Carlisle has always planted treason to the tribe and loyalty to the nation at large. More crudely put, the Carlisle philosophy was, "Kill the Indian to save the man." At the boarding schools children were forbidden to speak their native languages, forced to shed familiar clothing for uniforms, cut their hair and were subjected to harsh discipline. Children who had seldom heard an unkind word spoken to them were all too often verbally and physically abused by their white teachers. In short, this was full scale cultural aggression—the uprooting or destruction of a race and its culture.

The children, forcibly separated from their parents by soldiers often never saw their families until later in their adulthood, after their value-system and knowledge had been supplanted with colonial thinking. When these children returned from boarding schools they no longer knew their native language, they were strangers in their own world; there was a loss, a void of not belonging in the native world, or the white man's world. In the movie "Lakota Women," these children are referred to as "Apple Children (red on the outside, white on the inside)." They did not know where they fit in and they were unable to assimilate into either culture. This confusion and loss of cultural identity led to suicide, drinking and violence.

During the 1950's, the Native Americans were hit hard again by the U.S. government, which then adopted an official policy of "terminating" tribes. Termination involved taking away all federal support (e.g., health services and education) and closing the reservations. Frequently, tribal members were then relocated to urban areas. By 1990, more than 50% of Native Americans had little choice but to move to urban areas of the United States.

The African American

From the time Massachusetts legalized slavery in 1641, African Americans have endured discrimination, prejudice and racism in America on a mass scale. The shift to the racialization of slavery in the colonies effectively changed the definition of slavery. It had once been a practice, it became an institution. An institution that controlled practically every aspect of the life of not only the African American slave, but that of the free African American as well. Who you could marry, where you could live, what you could own, what trade you could learn, whether you could learn to read or write, (all the things that the poorest and humblest person of European descent could enjoy) were considered out of bounds for the African American.

The colonial laws led to the ultimate dehumanization of an entire continent of people of varying nations and cultures. They were not considered human beings with intelligence, hopes, ambitions or culture, but savages and uncivilized barbarians fit only to be chattel.

In America, with only a few early exceptions, all slaves were Africans, and almost all Africans were slaves. This placed the label of inferiority on black skin and on African culture. In other societies, it had been possible for a slave who obtained his freedom to take his place in his society with relative ease. In America, however, when a slave became free, they were still obviously an African. The taint of supposed inferiority clung to him.

Not only did white America become convinced of white superiority and black inferiority, but it endeavored to impose these racial beliefs on the Africans themselves. Slave masters gave a great deal of attention to the education and training of the model slave. According to Norman Coombs, there were five steps in molding the character of such a slave: strict discipline, a sense of his own inferiority, belief in the master's superior power, acceptance of the master's standards, and, finally, a deep sense of his own helplessness and dependence.

28

At every point this education was built on the belief in white superiority and black inferiority. Besides teaching the slave to loathe his own history and culture, the master strove to instill his own value system into the African's viewpoint.

The slave in America was systematically exploited for the gathering of wealth. Being a slave in a democratic society, he was put outside of the bounds of that society. Finally, because his slavery was racially defined, his predicament was incurable. Although he might escape from slavery, he could not flee from the color of his skin.

Conclusion

It is my belief that the enslavement of Africans in the Americas and the assault against the Native Americans should be considered a holocaust. For the African American, even though the intention was to keep them alive (dead slaves were valueless), the functional outcome of the capture and transportation through the "middle passage" resulted in an estimated 10 million dead in about two centuries. For the Native American the horror of displacement, disease and systematic extermination affected the death of millions and immeasurable pain and suffering on those who remained.

THE INDIAN REMOVAL ACT OF 1830

HISTORICAL OVERVIEW

Of all the U.S. laws and policies that will be addressed in this book, no law or policy carries quite the expansive history as this one. The Native-Americans occupied, what is now called the United States of America, first. Unlike the African who was shipped and sold into slavery here or the Chinese and Japanese who immigrated here, The Native-Americans' history pre-dated the arrival of the European settlers by countless centuries.

On May 26, 1830, the Indian Removal Act of 1830 was passed by the Twenty-First Congress of the United States of America. After four months of strong debate, Andrew Jackson signed the bill into law. Land greed was a big reason for the federal government's position on Indian removal. This desire for Native-American lands was also abetted by the "Native-American" hating mentality that was peculiar to some American frontiersman.

Native-American Societies

During the period of European colonization, Native American societies within the present continental United States varied markedly. Despite this diversity, however, almost all the tribes were integrated through interconnecting political, economic, social, and religious obligations provided by extended families or kinship groups. During the next three centuries some of these societies were forced to alter many of their original structures, but others were able to preserve some of their traditional forms. All, however, retained considerable kinship ties, and within both the traditional and the acculturated modern societies, the extended family structures still form the basis for tribal cohesion.

In the Northeast most Indian people lived in small bands that came together in the summer to form larger villages. The people planted corn and other vegetables, which were cultivated by women, and they enjoyed a series of ceremonies marking the ripening of crops and the rhythm of the seasons. Some tribes (such as Senecas and Hurons) relied heavily upon agriculture, whereas others (Ottawas, Kickapoos) depended more upon hunting or fishing. During the seventeenth and eighteenth centuries almost all became dependent upon the fur trade, and by 1750 much of their economic activity focused upon procuring pelts for the Europeans. Their growing association with Europeans and colonists also encouraged a centralization of political power, since whites preferred to deal with a single "chief" rather than a series of band or kinship leaders. Protestant and Catholic missionaries proselytized among the tribes, and some groups were converted. Others integrated Christian doctrines with their traditional beliefs to form new syncretic faiths.

By the early nineteenth century most of these northeastern tribes had been forced to sell their lands, and during the 1830s and 1840s they were moved to new territory west of the Mississippi. Today many of their descendants live in Oklahoma where they have continued the acculturation process. Others (Senecas, Chippewas, Menominees) remain on reservations or tribal lands within their old homelands, where they retain many of their cultural patterns.

The southeastern tribes were more dependent upon agriculture, and many had been heavily influenced by the Mississippian culture, a complex, pre-Columbian way of life characterized by considerable political stratification, culture-wide religious organizations, large burial mounds, and relatively large population centers. Although most adherents of the Mississippian culture were gone by the early 1700s, the southeastern tribes remained a sedentary village people held together through a network of primarily matrilineal clans. Like the northeastern tribes, they marked their calendar with a series of feasts and religious ceremonies. Although many southeastern people (Creeks, Cherokees, Choctaws) participated in the British deerskin trade, their adherence to agriculture and later herding (Choctaws) made them less dependent than the northeastern tribes upon the Anglo-Americans.

31

By 1800 intermarriage between white traders and members of the Five Southern, or "Civilized" Tribes (Cherokees, Choctaws, Chickasaws, Creeks, Seminoles—called "civilized" by whites because they had adopted many white cultural patterns) had produced mixed-blood leaders who championed further acculturation. By the 1820s, for example, many mixed-blood Cherokee leaders were raising cotton or other cash crops on large farms or plantations worked by black slaves. The Cherokees had a tribal government modeled after the federal system, with a bicameral council, an elected chief, and tribal courts. Sequoyah, a Cherokee living in Arkansas, had developed a Cherokee syllabary, and the tribe published a newspaper and books in the language. Although the other southern tribes were less acculturated than the Cherokees, they too had adopted many facets of white culture.

During the 1830s and 1840s, however, the southern tribes were forced to relinquish their lands and remove to Oklahoma. Intra-tribal arguments over the removal treaties created political divisions within the tribes, and this fragmentation continued to plague the tribes in the West. There the Five Southern Tribes reestablished their tribal governments, and for some the pace of acculturation quickened. Today, many Cherokees, Choctaws, Creeks, Chickasaws, and Seminoles continue to adhere to traditional values, but others, while maintaining their tribal identities, have become integrated into the American mainstream.

In the early contact period two types of tribal societies shared the Great Plains. Ensconced along the banks of major rivers, sedentary tribes such as the Mandans, Pawnees, and Hidatsas lived in villages of large earthen lodges. They tended fields of maize, beans, squash, and sunflowers, supplementing their diet with bison and other animals hunted on the plains. The village people followed a rich ceremonial life that included such rituals as the Okipa (Mandan) and the Morning Star ceremony (Pawnee), which involved the personal sacrifice of the individual for the benefit of the tribe. Kinship networks entailing a series of obligations and support systems provided the village people with social and political cohesion. Since these communities produced and stored agricultural surpluses, their villages prior to the mid-eighteenth century were major trading and political centers.

The plains during this early period were also inhabited by small numbers of wandering pedestrian hunters who would form groups to stalk bison or combine to drive herds of the animals over cliffs or "kill-sites." Carrying their small skin lodges with them, they lived a nomadic existence in search of the herds and may have spent the winter camped on the fringes of the plains or in sheltered river valleys.

The introduction of the horse in the eighteenth century had a profound impact upon both societies. For the nomads, the effect was beneficial. Horses enabled them to cover great distances, and hunters could locate and kill the bison more easily. Women's tasks were made easier, too, since horses served as beasts of burden. Because horse-drawn travois could drag heavier lodge skins and longer tipi poles, lodges increased in size and larger quantities of food and household possessions could be kept. More time was now available for creative activity, and skin painting, beadwork, and other artistic endeavors flourished. In addition, the tribes' ceremonial life was enlarged and elaborated; the Sun Dance became the most important communal religious experience on the plains.

The sedentary village people accepted horses, but they refused to adopt a nomadic way of life and now became the target of raids by the bison hunters. As the nomadic tribes (Sioux, Kiowas, Arapahoes, among others) flourished, the village people declined, and by the first decades of the nineteenth century the nomads dominated the plains. Indeed, this was their golden era, and their rich and abundant way of life became a cultural magnet, attracting other tribes to share in their lifestyle.

Tragically, by the last quarter of the nineteenth century, most of these Plains Indians were confined to reservations and subjected to forced acculturation programs by the federal government. Encouraged to abandon their traditional way of life and to become yeoman farmers in a region that would not sustain agriculture, most of the Plains tribes, like other Indian peoples of this period, suffered from disease and a declining birthrate. Recently their populations have increased, and although many of the reservation communities remain economically depressed, they are wellsprings of traditional culture. Many groups have resurrected tribal languages and religious traditions. Others are active in the Native American Church, a pan-Indian religious organization that has incorporated religious traditions from several tribes with Christian doctrines and the use of peyote. Tribal identities among the Plains peoples remain particularly strong.

Many of the Native-American people living in the desert Southwest have also been able to retain much of their traditional culture. In the seventeenth century, Spanish immigrants into the region were welcomed by pueblo-dwelling villagers who had built adobe settlements along the Rio Grande watershed. Descendants of the Anasazi people, a widespread pre-Columbian cultural complex extending across the Southwest, the pueblo dwellers were agriculturists steeped in a religious ceremonialism that permeated their lives and was closely associated with the geographic features that marked their homelands. Their villages were governed by gender- and age-graded religious societies whose leaders formed a theocracy. Their followers were admonished to live in harmony both with their gods and with their fellow villagers. They wove cotton cloth and produced an abundance of highly decorated earthen pottery. Their villages attracted Spanish missionaries, and some of the Pueblo people converted to Christianity. But their steadfast adherence to many traditional beliefs forced the priests to incorporate them into Roman Catholic ritual. Still residing in their ancestral villages, the modern Pueblo communities remain cohesive units retaining much of their rich ceremonialism. Although many residents work outside their communities, others produce traditional patterns of jewelry and ceramics that are much in demand. Among the Pueblo tribes, the Hopis of northern Arizona remain one of the most traditional Native-American communities in the continental United States.

The Athabascan-speaking people, Apaches and Navajos, compose the other major southwestern group. Unlike the Pueblos they originally were a hunting and gathering people who supplemented their food supply through horticulture. Ranging across the Southwest, the Apaches lived in brush- and hide-covered wickiups. In the seventeenth century, their acquisition of horses increased mobility and probably diminished their already limited reliance upon horticulture.

The Navajos, their close relatives, lived in a similar fashion until they acquired horses and sheep in the same period. Adopting a more sedentary mode of life, the Navajos developed transhumant economic patterns: they followed their flocks and herds into the uplands during the summer and removed them to protected valleys during the winter. They erected hexagonal, dirt-covered hogans as residences and began to plant larger fields of beans and corn and small orchards of peach trees. After migrating westward into the canyon and mesa lands of northeastern Arizona, the Navajos grazed their animals on lands radiating out from Canyon de Chelly, a long, Y-shaped, steep-sided canyon near the modern Arizona-New Mexico border. Prospering in their new environment, the Navajos became successful herdsmen, harvesting wool to be woven into cloth. They also became skilled silversmiths. During the nineteenth century they acquired a very large reservation in their homeland where they still reside, scattered across the desert in small communities or individual dwellings. Clan identification remains important and many Navajos still follow traditional cultural patterns. Most are bilingual (Navajo and English), and in recent decades the question of energy development upon the reservations has stirred considerable interest in Navajo politics. The Navajos are the nation's largest Native-American tribe.

During the early colonial period California held a larger Native-American population than any other region, with the population concentrated along the coast and in the great interior valleys. Characterized by relatively small tribes or political units, the native peoples spoke many tongues and manifested a variety of cultural patterns. Most, however, were hunters, fishers, and gatherers, who often relied heavily upon the seasonal catches of salmon or the gathering of acorns. In the eighteenth century the tribes along the southern coast were forced into the Spanish mission system, and during the latter half of the nineteenth century the interior tribes were almost annihilated by the influx of Anglo-American settlers. During the twentieth century, however, economic opportunities in California attracted large numbers of Native-American migrants, with both the Los Angeles basin and the San Francisco Bay region supporting relatively large urban Indian communities.

North of California, along the coast of Washington and Oregon, seafaring fishermen, Chinook and Salish, harvested a large variety of marine life and developed one of the most successful hunting and gathering cultures in the world. They lived in large wooden plank structures amid such material abundance that they developed institutional mechanisms, like the potlatch, for the redistribution of wealth. (Potlatches were ceremonies in which individuals gave away much of their wealth in return for the esteem and veneration of their fellow tribespeople.) Skilled woodworkers, they exhibited a fine artistry in intricately carved masks, wooden beams, and totem poles, the last reflecting the clan affiliation of the inhabitants in the extended family residences. These coastal dwellers suffered considerably from diseases introduced during the nineteenth century, but many small reservation communities persisted. Some still rely upon fishing while others have relocated in Seattle, Portland, and other cities in the region.

Native-American & White relationships

From the beginning, Native Americans had helped the colonists, providing them with land, giving them agricultural advice and engaging them in trade-trade that helped many Puritan merchants flourish. However, as Native-Americans saw their own people killed by European diseases and their lands claimed, they recognized that the rapid spread of the settlers meant an end to their way of life. This conflict of cultures and interests led to some of the most intense fighting between settlers and Native-Americans in the early English colonies.

Disputes between the Puritans and Native Americans arose over two issues—land and religion. For every acre a colonial farmer needed to farm, a Native American needed twenty for hunting, fishing and agriculture. To Native-Americans no one owned the land---it was there for everyone to use. Native Americans saw land treaties with Europeans more as agreements in which they received gifts, blankets, guns, tools or whatever, in exchange for sharing the land for a limited time. Europeans, however, saw treaties as a one time agreement in which Native Americans permanently sold their land to the new owners.

Similar conflicts arose over religion. Puritans considered Native-Americans heathens, people without a faith. At first, puritans sought to convert them, which many Native Americans resisted. Over time, as hostility between the two groups grew, many Puritans began to view the Native Americans as agents of the devil who presented a constant threat to their godly society. Rather than convert the Native Americans, the New England colonists set out to remove or destroy native societies. For their part, Native Americans began to develop a similarly hard view toward their white trespassers.

Native-American Wars and Conflicts

Suspicion and hostility, stemming from technological and cultural differences as well as mutual feelings of superiority, have permeated relations between Indians and non-Native Americans in North America. Intertribal antagonisms among the Indians, and nationalistic rivalries, bad faith, and expansionist desires on the part of non-Indians exacerbated these tensions. The resulting white-Native American conflicts often took a particularly brutal turn and ultimately resulted in the near-destruction of the indigenous peoples.

Warfare between Europeans and Native Americans was common in the seventeenth century. In 1622, the Powhatan Confederacy nearly wiped out the struggling Jamestown colony. Frustrated at the continuing conflicts, Nathaniel Bacon and a group of vigilantes destroyed the Pamunkey Indians before leading an unsuccessful revolt against colonial authorities in 1676. Intermittent warfare also plagued early Dutch colonies in New York. In New England, Puritan forces annihilated the Pequots in 1636-1637, a campaign whose intensity seemed to foreshadow the future. Subsequent attacks inspired by Metacom (King Philip) against English settlements sparked a concerted response from the New England Confederation.

Employing Indian auxiliaries and a scorched-earth policy, the colonists nearly exterminated the Narragansetts, Wampanoags, and Nipmucks in 1675-1676. A major Pueblo revolt also threatened Spanish-held New Mexico in 1680.

Native-Americans were also a key factor in the imperial rivalries among France, Spain, and England. In King William's (1689-1697), Queen Anne's (1702-1713), and King George's (1744-1748) wars, the French sponsored Abnaki and Mohawk raids against the more numerous English. Meanwhile, the English and their trading partners, the Chickasaws and often the Cherokees, battled the French and associated tribes for control of the lower Mississippi River valley and the Spanish in western Florida. More decisive was the French and Indian War (1754-1763). The French and their Native-American allies dominated the conflict's early stages, turning back several English columns in the north. Particularly serious was the near-annihilation of Gen. Edward Braddock's force of thirteen hundred men outside of Fort Duquesne in 1755. But with English minister William Pitt infusing new life into the war effort, British regulars and provincial militias overwhelmed the French and absorbed all of Canada.

But eighteenth-century conflicts were not limited to the European wars for empire. In Virginia and the Carolinas, English-speaking colonists pushed aside the Tuscaroras, the Yamasees, and the Cherokees. The Natchez, Chickasaw, and Fox Indians resisted French domination, and the Apaches and Comanches fought against Spanish expansion into Texas. In 1763, an Ottawa chief, Pontiac, forged a powerful confederation against British expansion into the Old Northwest. Although his raids wreaked havoc upon the surrounding white settlements, the British victory in the French and Indian War combined with the Proclamation of 1763, which forbade settlement west of the Appalachian Mountains, soon eroded Pontiac's support.

Most of the Native Americans east of the Mississippi River now perceived the colonial pioneers as a greater threat than the British government. Thus northern tribes, especially those influenced by Mohawk chief Thayendanegea (Joseph Brant), generally sided with the Crown during the American War for Independence. In 1777, they joined the Tories and the British in the unsuccessful offensives of John Burgoyne and Barry St. Leger in upstate New York. Western Pennsylvania and New York became savage battlegrounds as the conflict spread to the Wyoming and Cherry valleys. Strong American forces finally penetrated the heart of Iroquois territory, leaving a wide swath of destruction in their wake.

In the Midwest, George Rogers Clark captured strategic Vincennes for the Americans, but British agents based at Detroit continued to sponsor Tory and Indian forays as far south as Kentucky. The Americans resumed the initiative in 1782, when Clark marched northwest into Shawnee and Delaware country, ransacking villages and inflicting several stinging defeats upon the Native Americans. To the south, the British backed resistance among the Cherokees, Chickasaws, Creeks, and Choctaws but quickly forgot their former allies following the signing of the Treaty of Paris (1783).

By setting the boundaries of the newly recognized United States at the Mississippi River and the Great Lakes, that treaty virtually ensured future conflicts between whites and resident tribes. In 1790, Miami chief Little Turtle routed several hundred men led by Josiah Harmar along the Maumee River. Arthur St. Clair's column suffered an even more ignominious defeat on the Wabash River the following year; only in 1794 did Anthony Wayne gain revenge at the Battle of Fallen Timbers. Yet resistance to white expansion in the Old Northwest continued as a Shawnee chief, Tecumseh, molded a large Indian confederation based at Prophetstown. While Tecumseh was away seeking additional support, William Henry Harrison burned the village after a stalemate at the Battle of Tippecanoe in 1811.

Indian raids, often encouraged by the British, were influential in causing the United States to declare war on Great Britain in 1812. The British made Tecumseh a brigadier general and used Indian allies to help recapture Detroit and Fort Dearborn (Chicago). Several hundred American prisoners were killed following a skirmish at the River Raisin in early 1813. But Harrison pushed into Canada and won the Battle of the Thames, which saw the death of Tecumseh and the collapse of his confederation. In the Southeast, the Creeks gained a major triumph against American forces at Fort Sims, killing many of their prisoners in the process. Andrew Jackson led the counterthrust, winning victories at Tallasahatchee and Talladega before crushing the Creeks at Horseshoe Bend in 1814.

Alaska and Florida were also the scenes of bitter conflicts. Native peoples strongly contested the Russian occupation of Alaska. The Aleuts were defeated during the eighteenth century, but the Russians found it impossible to prevent Tlingit harassment of their hunting parties and trading posts. Upon the Spanish cession of Florida, Washington began removing the territory's tribes to lands west of the Mississippi River. But the Seminole Indians and runaway slaves refused to relocate, and the Second Seminole War saw fierce guerrilla-style actions from 1835 to 1842. Osceola, perhaps the greatest Seminole leader, was captured during peace talks in 1837, and nearly three thousand Seminoles were eventually removed. The Third Seminole War (1855-1858) stamped out all but a handful of the remaining members of the tribe.

In the United States, the removal policy met only sporadic armed resistance as whites pushed into the Mississippi River valley during the 1830s and 1840s. The Sac and Fox Native Americans were crushed in Black Hawk's War (1831-1832), and tribes throughout the region seemed powerless in the face of the growing numbers of forts and military roads the whites were constructing. The acquisition of Texas and the Southwest during the 1840s, however, sparked a new series of Indian-white conflicts. In Texas, where such warfare had marred the independent republic's brief history, the situation was especially volatile.

On the Pacific Coast, attacks against the native peoples accompanied the flood of immigrants to gold-laden California. Disease, malnutrition, and warfare combined with the poor lands set aside as reservations to reduce the Native-American population of that state from 150,000 in 1845 to 35,000 in 1860. The army took the lead role in Oregon and Washington, using the Rogue River (1855-1856), Yakima (1855-1856), and Spokane (1858) wars to force several tribes onto reservations. Sporadic conflicts also plagued Arizona and New Mexico throughout the 1850s as the army struggled to establish its presence. On the southern plains, mounted warriors posed an even more formidable challenge to white expansion. Strikes against the Sioux, Cheyennes, Arapahos, Comanches, and Kiowas during the decade only hinted at the deadlier conflicts of years to come.

The Civil War saw the removal of the Regulars and an accompanying increase in the number and intensity of white & Native-American conflicts. The influence of the Five Southern or "Civilized" Tribes of the Indian Territory was sharply reduced. Seven Indian regiments served with Confederate troops at the Battle of Pea Ridge (1862). Defeat there and at Honey Springs (1863) dampened enthusiasm for the South, although tribal leaders like Stand Waite continued to support the confederacy until the war's end. James H. Carleton and Christopher ("Kit") Carson conducted a ruthlessly effective campaign against the Navahos in New Mexico and Arizona. Disputes on the southern plains culminated in the Sand Creek massacre (1864), during which John M. Chivington's Colorado volunteers slaughtered over two hundred of Black Kettle's Cheyennes and Arapahos, many of whom had already attempted to come to terms with the government. In Minnesota, attacks by the Eastern Sioux prompted counterattacks by the volunteer forces of Henry H. Sibley, after which the tribes were removed to the Dakotas. The conflict became general when John Pope mounted a series of unsuccessful expeditions onto the plains in 1865.

Regular units, including four regiments of black troops, returned west following the Confederate collapse. Railroad expansion, new mining ventures, the destruction of the buffalo, and ever-increasing white demand for land exacerbated the centuries-old tensions. The mounted warriors of the Great Plains posed an especially thorny problem for an army plagued by a chronic shortage of cavalry and a government policy that demanded Indian removal on the cheap.

Winfield S. Hancock's ineffectual campaign in 1867 merely highlighted the bitterness between whites and Indians on the southern plains. Using a series of converging columns, Philip Sheridan achieved more success in his winter campaigns of 1868-1869, but only with the Red River War of 1874-1875 were the tribes broken. Major battlefield encounters like George Armstrong

Custer's triumph at the Battle of the Washita (1868) had been rare; more telling was the army's destruction of Indian lodges, horses, and food supplies, exemplified by Ranald Mackenzie's slaughter of over a thousand Indian ponies following a skirmish at Palo Duro Canyon, Texas, in 1874.

To the north, the Sioux, Northern Cheyennes, and Arapahos had forced the army to abandon its Bozeman Trail forts in Red Cloud's War (1867). But arable lands and rumors of gold in the Dakotas continued to attract white migration; the government opened a major new war in 1876. Initial failures against a loose Native-American coalition, forged by leaders including Crazy Horse and Sitting Bull, culminated in the annihilation of five troops of Custer's cavalry at the Little Bighorn. A series of army columns took the field that fall and again the following spring. By campaigning through much of the winter, harassing Indian villages, and winning battles like that at Wolf Mountain (1877), Nelson A. Miles proved particularly effective. The tribes had to sue for peace, and even Sitting Bull's band returned from Canada to accept reservation life in 1881. Another outbreak among the Sioux and Northern Cheyennes, precipitated by government corruption, shrinking reservations, and the spread of the Ghost Dance, culminated in a grisly encounter at Wounded Knee (1890), in which casualties totaled over two hundred Indians and sixty-four soldiers.

Less spectacular but equally deadly were conflicts in the Pacific Northwest. In 1867-1868, George Crook defeated the Paiutes of northern California and southern Oregon. In a desperate effort to secure a new reservation on the tribal homelands, a Modoc chief assassinated Edward R. S. Canby during an abortive peace conference in 1873. Canby's death (he was the only general ever killed by Native Americans) helped shatter President Ulysses S. Grant's peace policy and resulted in the tribe's defeat and removal. Refusing life on a government-selected reservation, Chief Joseph's Nez Percés led the army on an epic seventeen-hundred-mile chase through Idaho, Wyoming, and Montana until checked by Miles just short of the Canadian border at Bear Paw Mountain (1877). Also unsuccessful was armed resistance among the Bannocks, Paiutes, Sheepeaters, and Utes in 1878-1879.

To the far southwest, Cochise, Victorio, and Geronimo led various Apache bands in resisting white and Hispanic encroachments, crossing and recrossing the border into Mexico with seeming impunity. Many an officer's record was scarred as repeated treaties proved abortive. Only after lengthy campaigning, during which army columns frequently entered Mexico, were the Apaches forced to surrender in the mid-1880s.

The army remained wary of potential trouble as incidental violence continued. Yet, with the exception of another clash in 1973 during which protesters temporarily seized control of Wounded Knee, the major Native-American & white conflicts in the United States had ended. Militarily, several trends had become apparent. New technology often gave the whites a temporary advantage. But this edge was not universal; Indian warriors carrying repeating weapons during the latter nineteenth century sometimes outgunned their army opponents, who were equipped with cheaper (but often more reliable) single-shot rifles and carbines. As the scene shifted from the eastern woodlands to the western plains, white armies found it increasingly difficult to initiate fights with their Indian rivals. To force action, army columns converged upon Indian villages from several directions. This dangerous tactic had worked well at the Battle of the Washita but could produce disastrous results when large numbers of tribesmen chose to stand and fight, as at the Little Bighorn.

Throughout the centuries of conflict, both sides had taken the wars to the enemy populace, and the conflicts had exacted a heavy toll among noncombatants. Whites had been particularly effective in exploiting tribal rivalries; indeed, Indian scouts and auxiliaries were often essential in defeating tribes deemed hostile by white governments. In the end, however, military force alone had not destroyed Indian resistance. Only in conjunction with railroad expansion, the destruction of the buffalo, increased numbers of non-Native-American settlers, and the determination of successive governments to crush any challenge to their sovereignty had white armies overwhelmed the tribes.

THE LAW/POLICY:

May 28, 1830

Chapter CXLVIII

An Act to provide for an exchange of lands with the Indians residing in any of the states or territories, and for their removal west of the river

Be it enacted by the Senate and House of Representatives of the United States of America, in Congress assembled, That it shall and may be lawful for the President of the United States to cause so much of any territory belonging to the United States, west of the river Mississippi, not included in any state or organized territory, and to which the Indian title has been extinguished, as he may judge necessary, to be divided into a suitable number of districts, for the reception of such tribes or nations of Indians as may choose to exchange the lands where they now reside, and remove there; and to cause each of said districts to be so described by natural or artificial marks, as to be easily distinguished from every other.

Sec. 2 And be it further enacted, That it shall and may be lawful for the President to exchange any or all of such districts, so to be laid off and described, with any tribe or nation of Indians now residing within the limits of any of the states or territories, and with which the United States have existing treaties, for the whole or any part or portion of the territory claimed and occupied by such tribe or nation, within the bounds of any one or more of the states or territories, where the land claimed and occupied by the Indians, is owned by the United States, or the United States are bound to the state within which it lies to extinguish the Indian claim thereto.

Sec. 3 And be it further enacted, That in the making of any such exchange or exchanges, it shall and may be lawful for the President solemnly to assure the tribe or nation with which the exchange is made, that the United States will forever secure and guarantee to them, and their heirs or successors, the country so exchanged with them; and if they prefer it, that the United States will cause a patent or grant to be made and executed to them for the same: Provided always, That such lands shall revert to the United States, if the Indians become extinct, or abandon the same.

Sec. 4 And be it further enacted, That if, upon any of the lands now occupied by the Indians, and to be exchanged for, there should be such improvements as add value to the land claimed by any individual or individuals of such tribes or nations, it shall and may be lawful for the President to cause such value to be ascertained by appraisement or otherwise, and to cause such ascertained value to be paid to the person or persons rightfully claiming such improvements. And upon the payment of such valuation, the improvements so valued and paid for, shall pass to the United States, and possession shall not afterwards be permitted to any of the same tribe.

Sec. 5 And be it further enacted, That upon the making of any such exchange as is contemplated by this act, it shall and may be lawful for the President to cause such aid and assistance to be furnished to the emigrants as may be necessary and proper to enable them to remove to, and settle in, the country for which they may have exchanged; and also, to give them such aid and assistance as may be necessary for their support and subsistence for the first year after their removal.

Sec. 6 And be it further enacted, That it shall and may be lawful for the President to cause such tribe or nation to be protected, at their new residence, against all interruption or disturbance from any other tribe or nation of Indians, or from any other person or persons whatever.

Sec. 7 And be it further enacted, That it shall and may be lawful for the President to have the same superintendence and care over any tribe or nation in the country to which they may remove, as contemplated by this act, that he is now authorized to have over them at their present places of residence: Provided, That nothing in this act contained shall be construed as authorizing or directing the violation of any existing treaty between the United States and any of the Indian tribes.

Edward Rhymes Ph.D.

Sec. 8 And be it further enacted, That for the purpose of giving effect to the provisions of this act, the sum of five hundred thousand dollars is hereby appropriated, to be paid out of any money in the treasury, not otherwise appropriated.

IN LAYMEN'S TERMS:

Preamble: authorized the President to set up Indian districts west of the Mississippi.

Section 2: gave the President authority to negotiate and secure removal treaties from Native-American tribes.

Section 3: stated that the lands (the districts mentioned in the preamble) would always belong to the Native Americans (the particular Native-American nation that possessed it), if they did not abandon the land or die out.

Section 4: made provisions for compensation to pay the Native-American tribes for the improvements of lands left behind

Section 5: made provisions for removal (what we call moving expenses) costs and one year's allowance in their new lands west of the Mississippi.

Section 6: made provisions for federal protection of relocated Native Americans against any and all trespassers.

Section 7: emphasized that the change in residence of any Native-American nation, did not constitute a change in the President's authority over them.

Section 8: Congress allocated $500,000 for the carrying out of all the provisions contained in this law

SOCIAL & POLITICAL CLIMATE LEADING TO LAW/POLICY

Early in the 19th century, while the rapidly-growing United States expanded into the lower South, white settlers faced what they considered an obstacle. This area was home to the Cherokee, Creek, Choctaw, Chickasaw and Seminole nations. These Indian nations, in the view of the settlers and many other white Americans, were standing in the way of progress. Eager for land to raise cotton, the settlers pressured the federal government to acquire Native-American territory.

How the Native-American removal issue was observed can be summarized into three viewpoints: (1) Those who were appeared to be in sympathy (but also patronizing and condescending in their views) with Native Americans, but were in favor of removal (2) Those who hated the Native Americans and were greedy for land, who were (of course) in favor of removal (3) Opponents of removal

Those who appeared to be in sympathy with Native Americans, but were in favor of removal thought the removal would protect them from unscrupulous white traders and whiskey dealers. They also surmised that the Native Americans needed more time to move towards "civilization" at their own pace and removal would give them the opportunity to do so. There were prominent men who had a record of being in support of the Native Americans. Men such as: Thomas McKenney, head of the Office of Indian Affairs (OIA); William Clark, the Indian Superintendent of St Louis; Lewis Cass, former Gov. of Mich., who were in favor of removal.

Those who were greedy for land and hated Native Americans felt the Native Americans were in the way of progress and were hopelessly barbaric and could not be civilized (the "civilized"-as in the Five Civilized Tribes-Southeastern Native Americans were in the minority in their opinion). The cotton-explosion meant great demand for lands—should be used as God intended, i.e., market based, mono-crop agriculture (in this idea we see a total disregard for Native-American achievement in such types of agriculture—as was stated earlier in this section, the Native-Americans agricultural guidance to the early settlers was instrumental in their survival and prosperity—they were just viewed as "savage" hunters).

The opponents of removal believed that the existing treaty rights of the Native Americans should be respected. The American Board of Commissioners of Foreign Missions urged church groups to deluge Congress with cries for justice for the Native Americans—they did

The federal government wanted the states' western lands for white settlement. In 1802 Georgia made a pact with the federal government: in exchange for Georgia's western lands, the federal government would extinguish Native-American land titles within Georgia. In 1820 Georgia began to press the U.S. government to put this plan into action. President's Monroe and John Adams agreed that the exchange of Georgia's western lands and the removal of the Native Americans was probably the best plan, but did not act on their inclinations. It took Andrew Jackson to put this plan into action.

Andrew Jackson, from Tennessee, was a forceful proponent of Native-American removal. In 1814 he commanded the U.S. military forces that defeated a faction of the Creek nation. In their defeat, the Creeks lost 22 million acres of land in southern Georgia and central Alabama. The U.S. acquired more land in 1818 when, spurred in part by the motivation to punish the Seminoles for their practice of harboring fugitive slaves, Jackson's troops invaded Spanish Florida.

From 1814 to 1824, Jackson was instrumental in negotiating nine out of eleven treaties which divested the southern tribes of their eastern lands in exchange for lands in the west. The tribes agreed to the treaties for strategic reasons. They wanted to appease the government in the hopes of retaining some of their land, and they wanted to protect themselves from white harassment. As a result of the treaties, the United States gained control over three-quarters of Alabama and Florida, as well as parts of Georgia, Tennessee, Mississippi, Kentucky and North Carolina. This was a period of voluntary Indian migration, however, and only a small number of Creeks, Cherokee and Choctaws actually moved to the new lands. It should be noted, however, that although Jackson negotiated land treaties with the Native Americans, he was not a proponent of Native-American rights. In a letter to James Monroe in 1817 he declared that the Native Americans had no status as sovereign nations. He further stated that: "I have long viewed treaties with Indians as an absurdity not to be reconciled with the principles of our government."

In 1823 the Supreme Court handed down a decision which stated that Indians could occupy lands within the United States, but could not hold title to those lands. This was because their "right of occupancy" was subordinate to the United States' "right of discovery." In response to the great threat this posed, the Creeks, Cherokee, and Chickasaw instituted policies of restricting land sales to the government. They wanted to protect what remained of their land before it was too late.

Although the five Indian nations had made earlier attempts at resistance, many of their strategies were non-violent. One method was to adopt Anglo-American practices such as large-scale farming, Western education, and slave-holding. This earned the nations the designation of the "Five Civilized Tribes." They adopted this policy of assimilation in an attempt to coexist with settlers and ward off hostility. But it only made whites jealous and resentful.

Other attempts involved ceding portions of their land to the United States with a view to retaining control over at least part of their territory, or of the new territory they received in exchange. Some Native-American nations simply refused to leave their land—the Creeks and the Seminoles even waged war to protect their territory. The First Seminole War lasted from 1817 to 1818. The Seminoles were aided by fugitive slaves who had found protection among them and had been living with them for years. The presence of the fugitives enraged white planters and fueled their desire to defeat the Seminoles.

The primary thrust of Jackson's removal policy was to encourage Native Americans to sell their homelands in exchange for new lands in Oklahoma and Arkansas. Such a policy, the president maintained, would open new farmland to whites while offering Indians a haven where they would be free to develop at their own pace. "There," he wrote, "your white brothers will not trouble you, they will have no claims to the land, and you can live upon it, you and all your children, as long as the grass grows or the water runs, in peace and plenty."

The Cherokee used legal means in their attempt to safeguard their rights. They sought protection from land-hungry white settlers, who continually harassed them by stealing their livestock, burning their towns, and squatting on their land. In 1827 the Cherokee adopted a written constitution declaring themselves to be a sovereign nation. They based this on United States policy; in former treaties, Indian nations had been declared sovereign so they would be legally capable of ceding their lands. Now the Cherokee hoped to use this status to their advantage. The state of Georgia, however, did not recognize their sovereign status, but saw them as tenants living on state land. The Cherokee took their case to the Supreme Court, which ruled against them.

The Cherokee went to the Supreme Court again in 1831. This time they based their appeal on an 1830 Georgia law which prohibited whites from living on Indian territory after March 31, 1831, without a license from the state. The state legislature had written this law to justify removing white missionaries who were helping the Indians resist removal. The court this time decided in favor of the Cherokee. It stated that the Cherokee had the right to self-government, and declared Georgia's extension of state law over them to be unconstitutional. The state of Georgia refused to abide by the Court decision, however, and President Jackson refused to enforce the law.

In Jackson's first annual address to Congress he declared that the U.S. would not support Cherokee sovereignty and called for the Native Americans to move. He asked Congress for legislation permitting the forcible removal of Native-American tribes. In this address he also argued that the Native Americans would never be able to assimilate, but were blocking the advance of citizen farmers and republican virtue. Further, he argued for the rights of states to conduct their own internal affairs without interference from the federal government. Removal was bitterly debated in Congress and the press (Daniel Webster and Henry Clay being the most outspoken Congressional members against Native-American removal). When the dust cleared and the clamoring grew silent, the removal forces had won and the Indian Removal Act was passed by Congress May 28, 1830.

THE AFTERMATH OF THE LAW/POLICY

In 1830, just a year after taking office, Jackson pushed a new piece of legislation called the "Indian Removal Act" through both houses of Congress. It gave the president power to negotiate removal treaties with Indian tribes living east of the Mississippi. Under these treaties, the Indians were to give up their lands east of the Mississippi in exchange for lands to the west. Those wishing to remain in the east would become citizens of their home state. This act affected not only the southeastern nations, but many others further north. The removal was supposed to be voluntary and peaceful, and it was that way for the tribes that agreed to the conditions. But the southeastern nations resisted, and Jackson forced them to leave.

Most white Americans thought that the United States would never extend beyond the Mississippi. Removal would save Indian people from the depredations of whites, and would resettle them in an area where they could govern themselves in peace. But some Americans saw this as an excuse for a brutal and inhumane course of action, and protested loudly against removal.

Their protests did not save the southeastern nations from removal, however. The Choctaws were the first to sign a removal treaty, which they did in September of 1830. Some chose to stay in Mississippi under the terms of the Removal Act. But though the War Department made some attempts to protect those who stayed, it was no match for the land-hungry whites who squatted on Choctaw territory or cheated them out of their holdings. Soon most of the remaining Choctaws, weary of mistreatment, sold their land and moved west.

For the next 28 years, the United States government struggled to force relocation of the southeastern nations. A small group of Seminoles was coerced into signing a removal treaty in 1833, but the majority of the tribe declared the treaty illegitimate and refused to leave. The resulting struggle was the Second Seminole War, which lasted from 1835 to 1842. As in the first war, fugitive slaves fought beside the Seminoles who had taken them in. Thousands of lives were lost in the war, which cost the Jackson administration approximately 40 to 60 million dollars—ten times the amount it had allotted for Indian removal. In the end, most of the Seminoles moved to the new territory. The few who remained had to defend themselves in the Third Seminole War (1855-58), when the U.S. military attempted to drive them out. Finally, the United States paid the remaining Seminoles to move west.

The Creeks also refused to emigrate. They signed a treaty in March, 1832, which opened a large portion of their Alabama land to white settlement, but guaranteed them protected ownership of the remaining portion, which was divided among the leading families. The government did not protect them from speculators, however, who quickly cheated them out of their lands. By 1835 the destitute Creeks began stealing livestock and crops from white settlers. Some eventually committed arson and murder in retaliation for their brutal treatment. In 1836 the Secretary of War ordered the removal of the Creeks as a military necessity. By 1837, approximately 15,000 Creeks had migrated west. They had never signed a removal treaty.

The Chickasaws had seen removal as inevitable, and had not resisted. They signed a treaty in 1832 which stated that the federal government would provide them with suitable western land and would protect them until they moved. But once again, the onslaught of white settlers proved too much for the War Department, and it backed down on its promise. The Chickasaws were forced to pay the Choctaws for the right to live on part of their western allotment. They migrated there in the winter of 1837-38.

The Cherokee, on the other hand, were tricked with an illegitimate treaty. In 1833, a small faction agreed to sign a removal agreement: the Treaty of New Echota. The leaders of this group were not the recognized leaders of the Cherokee nation, and over 15,000 Cherokees—led by Chief John Ross—signed a petition in protest. The Supreme Court ignored their demands and ratified the treaty in 1836. The Cherokee were given two years to migrate voluntarily, at the end of which time they would be forcibly removed. By 1838 only 2,000 had migrated; 16,000 remained on their land. The U.S. government sent in 7,000 troops, who forced the Cherokees into stockades at bayonet point. They were not allowed time to gather their belongings, and as they left, whites looted their homes. Then began the march known as the Trail of Tears, in which 4,000 Cherokee people died of cold, hunger, and disease on their way to the western lands

By 1837, the Jackson administration had removed 46,000 Native American people from their land east of the Mississippi, and had secured treaties which led to the removal of a slightly larger number. Most members of the five southeastern nations had been relocated west, opening 25 million acres of land to white settlement and to slavery.

Despite the semblance of legality—94 treaties were signed with Indians during Jackson's presidency—Native American migrations to the West almost always occurred under the threat of government coercion. Even before Jackson's death in 1845, it was obvious that tribal lands in the West were no more secure than Indian lands had been in the East. In 1851 Congress passed the Indian Appropriations Act, which sought to concentrate the western Native American population on reservations.

Why were such morally indefensible policies adopted? Because many white Americans regarded Indian control of land and other natural resources as a serious obstacle to their desire for expansion and as a potential threat to the nation's security. Even had the federal government wanted to, it probably lacked the resources and military means necessary to protect the eastern Indians from encroaching white farmers, squatters, traders, and speculators. By the 1830s, a growing number of missionaries and humanitarians agreed with Jackson that Indians needed to be resettled westward for their own protection. Removal failed in large part because of the nation's commitment to limited government and its lack of experience with social welfare programs. Contracts for food, clothing, and transportation were awarded to the lowest bidders, many of whom failed to fulfill their contractual responsibilities. Native-Americans were resettled on semi-arid lands, unsuited for intensive farming. The tragic outcome was readily foreseeable.

TRAIL OF TEARS

After the signing of the treaty, many saw their land and property sold before their own eyes. The "conveyances" promised turn out to be a forced march. At the point of a gun, the pace killed many of the old, exposure and bad food killed most. Rotten beef and vegetables were their provisions. Many walked the entire distance without shoes, barely clothed. What supplies were given had been rejected by the whites. This cannot directly be blamed on the government; nearly all of this was done by unscrupulous men, interested only in maximizing their profits. The government's fault lies in not being watchful of those taken into their charge. Many of the old and the children died on the road. At each allowed stop, the dead were buried. Hearing of this many escaped. They knew that as they signed the rolls, to be "removed", that this might as well be their death warrants. They took refuge in the hills, the swamps, and other places too inhospitable for the whites. Even as this occurred, those in charge reported their "peaceful progress" to Congress, who looked no further. About 4000 Cherokee died as a result of the removal. The route they traversed and the journey itself became known as "The Trail of Tears" or, as a direct translation from Cherokee, "The Trail Where They Cried" ("*Nunna daul Tsuny*").

After Relocation

At the end of the journey the "fertile lands, alive with game, lush with forests" turned out to be bone-dry and covered in alkali pits, and a strange black ooze (oil) that stank and caught fire easily. Blistering hot in the summer, freezing in the winter, this land was still their own. And then the whites decided they needed more land (greed played a major role in this "need" for more land. Greed for "black gold" or oil). Again, pressure was brought to bear on the

Native-American. By this time the Cherokee, Chickasaw, Cree, Kickapoo, Seminole, Wyandotte, Lenapi and Mohawk had their reservations shrunk around them. The Choctaw had only been the first to be removed, the government desirous of more land, had removed nearly all. The Mississippi Band of the Choctaw had temporarily avoided displacement, but had their land stripped down to 500 acres, but within five years none of that land was in Native-American hands. Already Arkansas had begun to be settled by whites, who ignored the treaties. Even those who fled to California were being displaced by miners, farmers and ranchers. The discovery of gold galvanized the vise forming around the Indian people, so that expansion from the East was equaled by expansion from the West.

Plains Indians Wars

During the period of the 1860's, Americans and plains Indians clashed as Americans attempted to force Native Americans onto reservations. The battles are highlighted by the *Battle of Little Bighorn*, where Lt. Col. George Armstrong Custer and his regiment of 250 where all killed by approximately 4500 Sioux and Cheyenne warriors and the battle at *Wounded Knee* where thousands of Cheyenne men, women and children were slaughtered by the American Calvary. Wounded Knee represented the end of any real armed resistance on the part of the Native American.

The Dawes Act

Another act was passed by Congress that had a profound and damaging impact on the Native-American nations was the Dawes Act of 1887. Congressman Henry Dawes, author of the act, once expressed his faith in the civilizing power of private property with the claim that to be civilized was to "wear civilized clothes...cultivate the ground, live in houses, ride in Studebaker wagons, send children to school, drink whiskey [and] own property."

The act provided for the following:

1. Each Native-American family head be allotted a 160 acre farm out of reservation lands.

2. Each new land owner who abandoned tribal practices and adopted the "habits of civilized life" would be granted American citizenship.

3. "Surplus" reservation lands would be made available to sell to white settlers.

The United States Government had been trying unsuccessfully to register Native Americans for over a hundred years. The infamous Dawes Act of 1887 was the first such effort on a large-scale. The purported aim of the Act was to protect Indian property rights during the Oklahoma Land Rush. By registering, Indians were told; they would be allotted 160 acres of land per family in advance of the Land Rush and thus be restituted for 100 years of genocide against them.

The purpose of the Dawes Act, ostensibly to protect Indian welfare, was viewed with suspicion by many Native-American hurt by government's clumsy relocation efforts of the past. Indians who had refused to submit to previous relocations refused to register on the Dawes Rolls for fear that they would be caught and punished.

To get on the Dawes Rolls, Native Americans had to "anglicize" their names. Rolling Thunder thus became Ron Thomas and so forth. This bit of "melting pot" deception allowed agents of the government, sent to the frontier to administer the Act, to slip the names of their relatives and friends onto the Dawes Rolls and thus reap millions of acres of land for their friends and associates.

"melting pot" deception

The abuses of the Dawes Act were revealed and set forth in the Miriam Report of 1928. A Group of 1001 Native Americans and prominent citizens were charged by Congress to look into widespread allegations of corruption and abuse of the Dawes Act. The 800 page report documented massive fraud and misappropriation by the very government agents sent to administer the Act. It was found in one state alone that Indian held land, which totaled 138 million acres in 1887 at the time the Dawes Act was signed into l aw, had been reduced to 47 million acres of land by 1934 when the Act was repealed.

The Miriam Report led to the repeal of the Dawes Act however; repeal did not mean that land obtained through fraud was restored. The Indian Reorganization Act of 1934, written specifically to indemnify Native Americans for the abuses of the Dawes Act simply "grandfathered in" the existing deeds.

THE FUGITIVE SLAVE ACT OF 1850

HISTORICAL OVERVIEW

Fugitive Slave Laws: laws passed by the Congress of the United States in 1793 and 1850 providing for the return of runaway slaves to their owners.

Before the American colonies won independence from Great Britain, several legislatures in Southern colonies passed laws providing for the return of runaway slaves. Under some of these laws, slaves who resisted arrest could be killed, and their owners would be reimbursed by the government. Other laws levied penalties against people who protected runaways and offered rewards to those who caught them. However, these laws had little effect outside the colonies that passed them, leaving those in other colonies free to harbor escaped slaves.

In 1787 the Congress of the Confederation passed the Northwest Ordinance, which banned slavery from the Northwest Territory but allowed slaves who fled to the territory to be caught and returned to their owners. However, the ordinance did not require governments or settlers to cooperate in the capture and return of runaways. Two years later the Constitution of the United States took effect, with a clause in Article IV, Section 2 that said runaway slaves and indentured servants "shall be delivered" to their masters when requested. The U.S. Constitution did not, however, specifically require governments to help return fugitives.

The U.S. Congress intended the Fugitive Slave Act of 1793 to resolve the ambiguities present in previous legislation. Slave catchers were permitted to capture a runaway slave in any state or territory and needed only to prove orally to a federal or state judge that the person was an escaped slave. The slave was not guaranteed a trial by jury, and the judge's decision was final. Anyone sheltering an escaped slave could be fined $500, a stiff penalty at the time.

The law met with opposition in many, though not all, Northern states, several of which responded by passing laws to protect free blacks and fugitive slaves. These laws, known as personal liberty laws, required a slave catcher to produce additional evidence that his quarry was a runaway and often gave the accused the rights to appeal and to a trial by jury. In some states, the laws also made it easier to extradite a runaway slave once his or her slave status was proven. Generally, however, the Fugitive Slave Act was unevenly enforced and increased acrimony between North and South.

In 1842 the Supreme Court of the United States held in **Prigg v. Pennsylvania** that the Northern states' personal liberty laws unconstitutionally interfered with the Fugitive Slave Act. The Court said that while states did not have to enforce the federal law, they could not interfere with it. **Prigg** prompted many Northern states to amend their statutes, directing judges and law enforcement officers to do nothing about fugitive slaves. The only recourse left to slave-catchers was to abduct runaways themselves or take them before federal judges, who were not bound by the state statutes.

THE LAW

Section 1: *Be it enacted by the Senate and House of Representatives of the United States of America in Congress assembled*, That the persons who have been, or may hereafter be, appointed commissioners, in virtue of any act of Congress, by the Circuit Courts of the United States, and Who, in consequence of such appointment, are authorized to exercise the powers that any justice of the peace, or other magistrate of any of the United States, may exercise in respect to offenders for any crime or offense against the United States, by arresting, imprisoning, or bailing the same under and by the virtue of the thirty-third section of the act of the twenty-fourth of September seventeen hundred and eighty-nine, entitled "An Act to establish the judicial courts of the United States" shall be, and are hereby, authorized and required to exercise and discharge all the powers and duties conferred by this act.

Section 2: *And be it further enacted*, That the Superior Court of each organized Territory of the United States shall have the same power to appoint commissioners to take acknowledgments of bail and affidavits, and to take depositions of witnesses in civil causes, which is now possessed by the Circuit Court of the United States; and all commissioners who shall hereafter be appointed for such purposes by the Superior Court of any organized Territory of the United States, shall possess all the powers, and exercise all the duties, conferred by law upon the commissioners appointed by the Circuit Courts of the United States for similar purposes, and shall moreover exercise and discharge all the powers and duties conferred by this act.

Section 3: *And be it further enacted*, That the Circuit Courts of the United States shall from time to time enlarge the number of the commissioners, with a view to afford reasonable facilities to reclaim fugitives from labor, and to the prompt discharge of the duties imposed by this act.

Section 4: *And be it further enacted*, That the commissioners above named shall have concurrent jurisdiction with the judges of the Circuit and District Courts of the United States, in their respective circuits and districts within the several States, and the judges of the Superior Courts of the Territories, severally and collectively, in term-time and vacation; shall grant certificates to such claimants, upon satisfactory proof being made, with authority to take and remove such fugitives from service or labor, under the restrictions herein contained, to the State or Territory from which such persons may have escaped or fled.

Section 5: *And be it further enacted*, That it shall be the duty of all marshals and deputy marshals to obey and execute all warrants and precepts issued under the provisions of this act, when to them directed; and should any marshal or deputy marshal refuse to receive such warrant, or other process, when tendered, or to use all proper means diligently to execute the same, he shall, on conviction thereof, be fined in the sum of one thousand dollars, to the use of such claimant, on the motion of such claimant, by the Circuit or District Court for the district of such marshal; and after arrest of such fugitive, by such marshal or his deputy, or whilst at any time in his custody under the provisions of this act, should such fugitive escape, whether with or without the assent of such marshal or his deputy, such marshal shall be liable, on his official bond, to be prosecuted for the benefit of such claimant, for the full value of the service or labor of said fugitive in the State, Territory, or District whence he escaped: and the better to enable the said commissioners, when thus appointed, to execute their duties faithfully and efficiently, in conformity with the requirements of the Constitution of the United States and of this act, they are hereby authorized and empowered, within their counties respectively, to appoint, in writing under their hands, any one or more suitable persons, from time to time, to execute all such warrants and other process as may be issued by them in the lawful performance of their respective duties; with authority to such commissioners, or the persons to be appointed by them, to execute process as aforesaid, to summon and call to their aid the bystanders, or posse comitatus of the proper county, when necessary to ensure a faithful observance of the clause of the Constitution referred to, in conformity with the provisions of this act; and all good citizens are hereby commanded to aid and assist in the prompt and efficient execution of this law, whenever their services may be required, as aforesaid, for that purpose; and said warrants shall run, and be executed by said officers, anywhere in the State within which they are issued.

Section 6: *And be it further enacted,* That when a person held to service or labor in any State or Territory of the United States, has heretofore or shall hereafter escape into another State or Territory of the United States, the person or persons to whom such service or labor may be due, or his, her, or their agent or attorney, duly authorized, by power of attorney, in writing, acknowledged and certified under the seal of some legal officer or court of the State or Territory in which the same may be executed, may pursue and reclaim such fugitive person, either by procuring a warrant from some one of the courts, judges, or commissioners aforesaid, of the proper circuit, district, or county, for the apprehension of such fugitive from service or labor, or by seizing and arresting such fugitive, where the same can be done without process, and by taking, or causing such person to be taken, forthwith before such court, judge, or commissioner, whose duty it shall be to hear and determine the case of such claimant in a summary manner; and upon satisfactory proof being made, by deposition or affidavit, in writing, to be taken and certified by such court, judge, or commissioner, or by other satisfactory testimony, duly taken and certified by some court, magistrate, justice of the peace, or other legal officer authorized to administer an oath and take depositions under the laws of the State or Territory from which such person owing service or labor may have escaped, with a certificate of such magistracy or other authority, as aforesaid, with the seal of the proper court or officer thereto attached, which seal shall be sufficient to establish the competency of the proof, and with proof, also by affidavit, of the identity of the person whose service or labor is claimed to be due as aforesaid, that the person so arrested does in fact owe service or labor to the person or persons claiming him or her, in the State or Territory from which such fugitive may have escaped as aforesaid, and that said person escaped, to make out and deliver to such claimant, his or her agent or attorney, a certificate setting forth the substantial facts as to the service or labor due from such fugitive to the claimant, and of his or her escape from the State or Territory in which he or she was arrested, with authority to such claimant, or his or her agent or attorney, to use such reasonable force and restraint as may be necessary, under the circumstances of the case, to take and remove such fugitive person back to the State or Territory whence he or she may have escaped as aforesaid. In no trial or hearing under this act shall the testimony of such alleged fugitive be admitted in evidence; and the certificates in this and the first [fourth] section mentioned, shall be conclusive of the right of the person or persons in whose favor granted, to remove such fugitive to the State or Territory from which he escaped, and shall prevent all molestation of such person or persons by any process issued by any court, judge, magistrate, or other person whomsoever.

Section 7: *And be it further enacted,* That any person who shall knowingly and willingly obstruct, hinder, or prevent such claimant, his agent or attorney, or any person or persons lawfully assisting him, her, or them, from arresting such a fugitive from service or labor, either with or without process as aforesaid, or shall rescue, or attempt to rescue, such fugitive from service or labor, from the custody of such claimant, his or her agent or attorney, or other person or persons lawfully assisting as aforesaid, when so arrested, pursuant to the authority herein given and declared; or shall aid, abet, or assist such person so owing service or labor as aforesaid, directly or indirectly, to escape from such claimant, his agent or attorney, or other person or persons legally authorized as aforesaid; or shall harbor or conceal such fugitive, so as to prevent the discovery and arrest of such person, after notice or knowledge of the fact that such person was a fugitive from service or labor as aforesaid, shall, for either of said offences, be subject to a fine not exceeding one thousand dollars, and imprisonment not exceeding six months, by indictment and conviction before the District Court of the United States for the district in which such offence may have been committed, or before the proper court of criminal jurisdiction, if committed within any one of the organized Territories of the United States; and shall moreover forfeit and pay, by way of civil damages to the party injured by such illegal conduct, the sum of one thousand dollars for each fugitive so lost as aforesaid, to be recovered by action of debt, in any of the District or Territorial Courts aforesaid, within whose jurisdiction the said offence may have been committed.

Section 8: *And be it further enacted,* That the marshals, their deputies, and the clerks of the said District and Territorial Courts, shall be paid, for their services, the like fees as may be allowed for similar services in other cases; and where such services are rendered exclusively in the arrest, custody, and delivery of the fugitive to the claimant, his or her agent or attorney, or where such supposed fugitive may be discharged out of custody for the want of sufficient proof as aforesaid, then such fees are to be paid in whole by such claimant, his or her agent or attorney; and in all cases where the proceedings are before a commissioner, he shall be entitled to a fee of ten dollars in full for his services in each case, upon the delivery of the said certificate to the claimant, his agent or attorney; or a fee of five dollars in cases where the proof shall not, in the opinion of such commissioner, warrant such certificate and delivery, inclusive of all services incident to such arrest and examination, to be paid, in either case, by the claimant, his or her agent or attorney.

The person or persons authorized to execute the process to be issued by such commissioner for the arrest and detention of fugitives from service or labor as aforesaid, shall also be entitled to a fee of five dollars each for each person he or they may arrest, and take before any commissioner as aforesaid, at the instance and request of such claimant, with such other fees as may be deemed reasonable by such commissioner for such other additional services as may be necessarily performed by him or them; such as attending at the examination, keeping the fugitive in custody, and providing him with food and lodging during his detention, and until the final determination of such commissioners; and, in general, for performing such other duties as may be required by such claimant, his or her attorney or agent, or commissioner in the premises, such fees to be made up in conformity with the fees usually charged by the officers of the courts of justice within the proper district or county, as near as may be practicable, and paid by such claimants, their agents or attorneys, whether such supposed fugitives from service or labor be ordered to be delivered to such claimant by the final determination of such commissioner or not.

Section 9: *And be it further enacted*, That, upon affidavit made by the claimant of such fugitive, his agent or attorney, after such certificate has been issued, that he has reason to apprehend that such fugitive will be rescued by force from his or their possession before he can be taken beyond the limits of the State in which the arrest is made, it shall be the duty of the officer making the arrest to retain such fugitive in his custody, and to remove him to the State whence he fled, and there to deliver him to said claimant, his agent, or attorney. And to this end, the officer aforesaid is hereby authorized and required to employ so many persons as he may deem necessary to overcome such force, and to retain them in his service so long as circumstances may require. The said officer and his assistants, while so employed, to receive the same compensation, and to be allowed the same expenses, as are now allowed by law for transportation of criminals, to be certified by the judge of the district within which the arrest is made, and paid out of the treasury of the United States.

Section 10: *And be it further enacted*, That when any person held to service or labor in any State or Territory, or in the District of Columbia, shall escape therefrom, the party to whom such service or labor shall be due, his, her, or their agent or attorney, may apply to any court of record therein, or judge thereof in vacation, and make satisfactory proof to such court, or judge in vacation, of the escape aforesaid, and that the person escaping owed service or labor to such party. Whereupon the court shall cause a record to be made of the matters so proved, and also a general description of the person so escaping, with such convenient certainty as may be; and a transcript of such record, authenticated by the attestation of the clerk and of the seal of the said court, being produced in any other State, Territory, or district in which the person so escaping may be found, and being exhibited to any judge, commissioner, or other office, authorized by the law of the United States to cause persons escaping from service or labor to be delivered up, shall be held and taken to be full and conclusive evidence of the fact of escape, and that the service or labor of the person escaping is due to the party in such record mentioned. And upon the production by the said party of other and further evidence if necessary, either oral or by affidavit, in addition to what is contained in the said record of the identity of the person escaping, he or she shall be delivered up to the claimant. And the said court, commissioner, judge, or other person authorized by this act to grant certificates to claimants or fugitives, shall, upon the production of the record and other evidences aforesaid, grant to such claimant a certificate of his right to take any such person identified and proved to be owing service or labor as aforesaid, which certificate shall authorize such claimant to seize or arrest and transport such person to the State or Territory from which he escaped. Provided that nothing herein contained shall be construed as requiring the production of a transcript of such record as evidence as aforesaid. But in its absence the claim shall be heard and determined upon other satisfactory proofs, competent in law.

Approved, September 18, 1850.

IN LAYMEN'S TERMS

Section 1: Gave the same authority to appointed commissioners (those responsible for the apprehension of runaway slaves) that federal or local judges and magistrates had. This authority was in the areas of arrest, imprisonment and the setting of bail for offenders.

Section 2: Gave power to the Superior Court of each U.S. state to appoint commissioners for execution of this act.

Section 3: Gave the U.S. Circuit Courts authority to increase the number of commissioners, as well as the ability to increase the provision of facilities to hold those accused of being fugitive slaves.

Section 4: Granted commissioners with the same jurisdiction as that of federal Circuit and District courts, as well as states' Supreme Courts. Also gave commissioners the authority to return those found guilty of being fugitive slaves to their former masters.

Section 5: Officers charged with arresting a "fugitive" could be fined up to $1,000 for refusing to help and could also be charged for the value of the "fugitive slave" who escaped while in their custody.

Section 6: Outlines the procedures involved in granting certificates that gave commissioners the legal right to apprehend those thought to be fugitive slaves. Those apprehended could not speak in their own defense in court.

Section 7: Stated that any private citizen found giving aid, shelter, food or any other assistance to any deemed a "fugitive slave," was guilty of obstruction and liable for up to 6 months imprisonment and a $1,000 fine.

Section 8: Stated that commissioners received $10 for every person found guilty of being a fugitive slave and $5 for every apprehended person found not guilty of being a fugitive slave.

Section 9: Stated that after a person was found guilty of being a fugitive slave, it was the responsibility of the commissioner to ensure the return of the individual to their former master. Also, if this "fugitive slave" was rescued by force, this same commissioner was also responsible for their recapture. However, the commissioner had the authority to deputize ANY (with or without their consent) and as many individuals as he wished in order to procure the recapture.

Section 10: Stated the means of providing proof or evidence that someone was a fugitive slave, as well as how the courts would authenticate such evidence.

SOCIAL & POLITICAL CLIMATE LEADING TO THE LAW/POLICY

By the 1820's more than 100 antislavery societies were advocating that African Americans be resettled in Africa. In 1817, the American Colonization Society had been founded to encourage African-American emigration. These early antislavery societies generally were based on the belief that African Americans were an inferior race that could not coexist with white society. Most free blacks, on the contrary, considered America their home, and only about 1,400 blacks emigrated to Africa between 1820 and 1830.

African Americans increasingly were joined by whites in openly criticizing slavery. Much of the white support for abolition came from preachers like Charles G. Finney, who termed slavery "a great national sin." The most radical white abolitionist was the young editor named William Lloyd Garrison. Active in religious reform movements in Massachusetts, Garrison began a publishing career in 1828 as editor of an antislavery paper. Three years later he established his own paper, *The Liberator*, to deliver an uncompromising message: immediate emancipation with no payment to slaveholders.

Before Garrison's call for immediate emancipation of slaves, support for that position had been limited. Beginning in the 1830's, however, Garrison's words began to find a willing audience. Garrison founded the New England Anti-Slavery Society in 1832 and then helped found the national American Anti-Slavery Society the following year. He enjoyed widespread black support; three out of four early subscribers to *The Liberator* were African Americans. Garrison's uncompromising, and sometimes inflammatory style often incensed those ardently opposed to abolition. Even whites who supported the cause of abolition opposed Garrison when he attacked churches and the government for failing to condemn slavery. Garrison alienated whites even more when he associated with David Walker, whom some whites also viewed as a radical.

David Walker, a free black North Carolinian who had moved to Boston, urged African Americans to rise up and take their freedom by force. In his *Appeal to the Colored Citizens of the World,* published in 1829, Walker advised African Americans to fight for freedom rather than to wait for slave owners to end slavery. The majority of free African Americans expressed less extreme views than Walker but still formed scores of antislavery societies by the end of the 1820's.

In 1850, most of the nation's 434,000 free African Americans worked as day laborers for white employers in the South, but some held jobs as artisans, craftsmen, or seamstresses. In the North, free blacks faced a segregated society and job discrimination that opened only the lowest-paying jobs to them. It was from this racist and prejudiced soil that the noble flower Frederick Douglass sprung from. Frederick Douglass stands out as one of the most influential figures in 19th century American (as well as World) history. His rise out of slavery and consequent work was instrumental and pivotal in the struggle for abolition and human rights.

Born into slavery in 1817, Douglass had been taught to read and write by the wife of one his owners. Her husband ordered her to stop teaching Douglass, however, because reading "would forever unfit him to be a slave." Douglass, by other means, continued to learn and studied even harder. Years later, after a disagreement with his owner, Douglass decided to escape. Borrowing the identity of a free black sailor and carrying official papers, he stepped onto a train. When Douglass reached New York, he breathed his first breaths of freedom. Garrison and Douglass formed a brief alliance, but separated because Douglass believed that abolition could be accomplished without violence. In 1847 Douglass began his own antislavery paper and named it the *North Star*.

In stark contrast to Douglass' non-violent stance, was the rebellion of Nat Turner in August of 1831. Nat Turner, a plantation slave in Virginia's Southampton County, organized a bloody rebellion that left many dead and strengthened the resolve of Southern whites to defend slavery and control their slaves. During the course of this insurrection, Turner and a band of 50 followers, attacked four plantations and killed about 70 white inhabitants. By the fifth attack, an alarm alerted whites who captured and killed 16 members of

Turner's band. Turner, however, wasn't captured until several weeks later and then he was promptly tried and hanged.

As a result of Nat Turner's rebellion, many slave owners pushed their state legislatures to pass laws that would further restrict the liberties of African Americans, slave and free. These slave and black codes included laws such as the 1833 Alabama statute that forbade free and enslaved blacks from preaching the gospel unless a "respectable" slave owner was present. In 1835 North Carolina became the last Southern state to deny the right to vote to free blacks. In some states, free blacks lost the right to own guns, purchase alcohol, assemble in public and testify in court. Slaves could no longer own property, learn to read or write, or work independently as carpenters or blacksmiths in some Southern states.

Also, during this time, Southern Christian churches gradually shifted their positions on slavery. While some ministers had attacked slavery in the early 1800's, by the 1830's most agreed that slavery and Christianity could coexist. The myth of the "happy slave" became more prominent during this period (a sign of white denial and fear, as well as a smokescreen for Northern abolitionists). Despite these rationalizations in favor of slavery, abolitionists continued to press for emancipation. Abolitionists and antislavery societies flooded Congress with petitions to end slavery, but Southern congressmen countered in 1836 by securing the adoption of a gag rule. The gag rule prevented discussion in Congress of abolitionist petitions, which meant citizens submitting petitions had been deprived of the right to have them heard. Former President John Quincy Adams, a representative from Massachusetts, fought against the gag rule, even as the focus of the argument shifted from abolishing slavery to the constitutional right to petition Congress. The gag rule stood until 1845.

The North was industrializing rapidly as factories turned out ever-increasing amounts of products, from textiles and sewing machines to farm equipment and guns. Railroad tracks (with more than 20,000 miles of track laid during the 1850's) were reaching across the section. They carried wheat, iron ore, and other raw materials eastward and manufactured goods and settlers westward. Small towns like Chicago matured into cities almost overnight, due to the sheer volume of goods and people arriving by railroad. Telegraph wires being strung along the railroad tracks tied the North together, providing a network of instant communication.

Immigrants fleeing from famine and poverty in Europe, mostly from Ireland and Germany, entered the industrial workplace in growing numbers. Many immigrants became factory workers, while others moved westward to try to fulfill their version of "The American Dream" as farmers and miners. In any case they soon became voters--- with a strong opposition to slavery. In their eyes, slaves represented unfair labor competition because they could perform work that otherwise could be done by free workers. For example, in Boston in 1850, nearly half of all Irish immigrants worked in unskilled jobs. These people often competed with African Americans for jobs. They feared the expansion of slavery for two reasons. First, it might bring slave labor in direct competition with free labor, or people who work for wages. Second, it threatened to reduce the status of white workers who could not successfully compete with slaves. Opposition to the expansion of slavery, however, did not mean that the Irish were sympathetic with the plight of the African-American slave. For instance, in 1850 in New York City, Irish immigrants marched to the polls shouting that African Americans should "go back to Africa, where they belong."

Unlike the North, the South remained a predominantly rural society, consisting mostly of plantations and small farms. The Southern economy relied on agriculture, especially cotton production, which became the dominant crop of the South since Eli Whitney's invention of the cotton gin in 1793. In fact, though one-third of the nation's population lived in the South in 1850, the South produced only 10 percent of the nation's manufactured goods. At the same time that Northern railroads were expanding, Southerners were slower to take advantage of technological advances in transportation, mostly using rivers to transport goods. In addition, the population of the South grew much more slowly than that of the North. Few immigrants settled in the South because African Americans, whether enslaved or free, filled most of the available jobs for artisans, mechanics and laborers.

The conflict over slavery, however, disturbed Southern society. Those few immigrants who did settle in the South presented significant opposition to slavery. For example German-Americans in Texas and Baltimore openly opposed slavery. German newspapers in these areas published editorials in favor of universal voting rights and freedom for African Americans. Furthermore, while African Americans dreamed of an end to slavery, many whites feared that any restriction of slavery would lead to a social and economic revolution. Senator John C. Calhoun of South Carolina believed that such a revolution would condemn blacks as well as whites "to the greatest calamity, and (the South) to poverty, desolation and wretchedness."

It was against the backdrop of the dual and contrasting (and often conflicting) societies of the North & South, that the Wilmot Proviso was introduced to Congress. On August 8, 1846, David Wilmot, a Democratic congressman for Pennsylvania, heightened tensions between the two sections. Wilmot added an amendment to a military appropriations bill that proposed that "neither slavery nor involuntary servitude shall ever exist" in any territory the United States might acquire as a result of the war with Mexico. In short, the Wilmot Proviso meant that California, as well as the territories of Utah and New Mexico, would be closed to slavery forever.

Northerners gradually came to support the Wilmot Proviso. Although most Northerners were not abolitionists, they were already at odds with the Southern congressman because of their refusal to vote for internal improvements, such as building canals and roads. They also feared that adding slave territory would give slave states more members in Congress and deny economic opportunity to free workers. Beginning with Ohio, and Michigan, nearly all of the Northern States passed resolutions endorsing the Wilmot Proviso.

Southerners opposed the Proviso, which some believed raised some complex constitutional issues. Slaves were property, Southerners claimed, and property was protected by the Constitution. Laws like the Wilmot Proviso, Southerners espoused, would undermine such constitutional protections. In addition, Southerners further argued

71

that territories belonged to all of the states in common and that Congress had not right to limit the spread of slavery there.

The House of Representatives approved the Proviso, but the senate rejected it. The Proviso then was attached to a different bill and once again was passed by the House, but rejected by the Senate. Adding fuel to this already volcanic situation was the statehood for California. As a result of the gold rush, California had grown so quickly in population that it skipped the territorial phase of becoming a state. From September to November of 1849, the Californians held a constitutional convention, during which they adopted a state constitution, elected a governor and legislature and applied for admission to the Union.

California's new constitution forbade slavery, a fact that outraged many Southerners. They had assumed that, because most of California lay south of the Missouri Compromise line (a series of laws enacted in 1820 to maintain the balance between slave and free states), it would be open to slavery. They hoped that the compromise struck in 1820 would apply to new territories, including California. President Zachary Taylor, although himself a slaveholder, supported California's admission as a free state because he believed the climate and terrain were not suited to slavery. More importantly, he felt that the South could counter abolitionism most effectively by leaving the slavery issue up to the individual territories rather than Congress. Southerners saw the move to block slavery as an attack on the Southern way of life—and began to question whether the South should remain in the Union.

Enter Henry Clay (chief architect of the Missouri Compromise of 1820) with a plan that he hoped would settle the issue. Once again, Henry Clay worked to shape a compromise that both the North and South could accept. Though ill, he visited his old rival Daniel Webster (Massachusetts) and obtained Webster's support. Eight days later, a visibly ill Clay rose to his feet to present to the Senate a series of resolutions later called the Compromise of 1850. This compromise, Clay hoped, would settle "all questions in controversy between the free and slave states, growing out of the subject of Slavery." Clay's compromise contained provisions to appease both the North and South. To please the North, California would be allowed to enter as a free state and the trading (but not slavery itself) of slaves would be banned in the District of Columbia. To please the South the Texas-Mexico boundary dispute would be settled and Texas would be paid $10 million to surrender its claim of New Mexico and a stricter fugitive slave law would be proposed. And a somewhat middle-of-the road decision would be made concerning Utah and New Mexico, which would allow each territory to decide whether they want to be a slave or free state. Despite the efforts of Clay (and Webster as well), the Senate rejected the proposed compromise in July. Tired, ill and disheartened, Clay withdrew from the conflict and left Washington. Stephen Douglas of Illinois stepped in and picked up the pro-compromise position. Douglas devised a different approach to the compromise than Clay's.

Clay had presented his compromise as an omnibus bill, meaning that all the resolutions had to be voted on as a package. Douglas realized that the compromise was doomed to failure if he offered it in the same fashion, because every member of Congress opposed at least one of its provisions. So to avoid another defeat of the compromise Douglas unbundled the package of resolutions and introduced them one at a time, hoping to obtain a majority vote for each measure individually. This strategy proved to be effective as the individual measures began to receive majority votes. Douglas' plan coupled with the deaths of President Zachary Taylor and Senator Calhoun (both of whom opposed the compromise) helped the Compromise of 1850 to be voted into law after eight months of effort. It would appear, for the time being; the future of the African slave in America was settled.

AFTERMATH & IMPACT OF LAW/POLICY

In the North the law encouraged widespread calls for civil disobedience. Large disturbances broke out in Boston, Massachusetts; Syracuse, New York; and Oberlin, Ohio. Coupled with the publication of Harriet Beecher Stowe's *Uncle Tom's Cabin* (1852), which dealt in part with a fugitive slave, the 1850 law made abolitionism and support for the Underground Railroad respectable, whereas before they had seemed radical. It was thought that the

Fugitive Slave Act would diminish the incentive for slaves to attempt escape. The rationale behind this was the slaves' realization that even if they managed to escape from their plantation, they could still be caught and returned by any citizen in the United States. Not only did the Fugitive Slave Act fail to diminish the activity of the Underground Railroad, it accelerated it. It is estimated that between 1850 and 1863, the Underground Railroad movement was responsible for helping approximately 70,000 slaves escape and journey safely northwards into Canada and subsequent freedom.

Many Northern states passed another round of personal liberty laws to protect free blacks and escaped slaves; others actively undermined the new law. This response was seen by many Southerners as proof that the North would go to any length, even subversion of the Constitution, to deprive the South of slavery (according to a vast number of historians, this law was also seen as a major catalyst in starting the Civil War).

A poignant and heart-wrenching quandary was formed in the wake of the Fugitive Slave Law: Which is worse? To be recaptured years after you have escaped to freedom or after having been free all your life and then being enslaved for the first time? This dilemma was played out time and time again after the passing of the Fugitive Slave Law. African-Americans during this time were regulated to four "legal" categories: (1) Free born (meaning they were born free and had been free all of their lives); (2) Emancipated or manumitted: (were once slaves but obtained their freedom, some were allowed to buy their own freedom, their owner decided to free them etc.); (3) Slave (those who were still, in the literal sense, chattel and currently in the possession of their owner); (4) Fugitive Slave (those who had escaped from slavery, but were still considered the legal "property" of their "owner"). Under this law practically no African-American was safe. The slave narratives from this time period address the apprehension that was present amongst African-Americans:

After escaping from slavery, Isaac Mason moved to Philadelphia where he became a hod carrier. He married but was forced to leave after the passing of the Fugitive Slave Act.

"I went to Philadelphia where I thought safety would be best secured. I worked there as a hod carrier. I had not been long settled before the Fugitive Slave Law came into full force. One day while climbing the ladder with a hod of bricks on my shoulder, I looked down at the passers by, which was not an uncommon thing to do, and who should I see but the son of the man Wallace. His business was soon found out and made known. He was searching for his runaway slaves, of whom I was one. I was advised to make my way into Massachusetts, and that without much delay. O the terror and curse of Slavery! We sold what we could, and what we could not dispose of had to be given away.

I had a letter of recommendation given to me, which I was to present to a Mr. Gibbs, of New York City, on my arrival there, enroute for Boston. He was a worker in the Underground Railroad scheme, and was a colored man. We left Philadelphia by boat, and had a pleasant sail to New York."

Solomon Northup was a free black man who was arrested by James H. Burch, a slave-dealer from Washington.

"The light admitted through the open door enabled me to observe the room in which I was confined. It was about twelve feet square – the walls of solid masonry. The floor was of heavy plank. There was one small window, crossed with great iron bars, with an outside shutter, securely fastened.

An iron-bound door led into an adjoining cell, or vault, wholly destitute of windows, or any means of admitting light. The furniture of the room in which I was, consisted of the wooden bench on which I sat, an old-fashioned, dirty box stove, and besides these, in either cell, there was neither bed, nor blanket, nor any other thing whatever. The door, through which Burch and Radburn entered, led through a small passage, up a flight of steps into a yard, surrounded by a brick wall ten or twelve feet high, immediately in rear of a building of the same width as itself.

'Well, my boy, how do you feel now?' said Burch, as he entered through the open door. I replied that I was sick, and inquired the cause of my imprisonment. He answered that I was his slave – that he had bought me, and that he was about to send me to New Orleans. I asserted, aloud and boldly, that I was a freeman – a resident of Saratoga, where I had a wife and children, who were also free, and that my name was Northup. I complained bitterly of the strange treatment I had received, and threatened, upon my liberation, to have satisfaction for the wrong. He denied that I was free, and with an emphatic oath, declared that I came from Georgia. Again and again I asserted I was no man's slave, and insisted upon his taking off my chains at once. He endeavored to hush me, as if he feared my voice would be overheard. But I would not be silent, and denounced the authors of my imprisonment, whoever they might be, as unmitigated villains."

Moses Grandy, *Life of a Slave* (1843)

"Our untiring friends, the abolitionists, once obtained a law that no colored person should be seized as a slave within the free states; this law would have been of great service to us, by ridding us of all anxiety about our freedom while we remained there; but I am sorry to say, that it has lately been repealed, and that now, as before, any colored person who is said to be a slave, may be seized in the free states and carried away, no matter how long he may have resided there, as also may his children and their children, although they all may have been born there. I hope this law will soon be altered again.

At present, many escaped slaves are forwarded by their friends to Canada where, under British rule, they are quite safe. There is a body of ten thousand of them in Upper Canada; they are known for their good order and loyalty to the British government; during the late troubles, they could always be relied on for the defence of the British possessions, against the lawless Americans who attempted to invade them."

These are but a few voices that speak concerning the direct impact this law made on the lives of countless African-Americans after its passage.

As I mentioned previously, many noted scholars point to the Fugitive Slave Law of 1850 as being a chief cause in the American Civil War. Its polarizing impact can't be overstated.

As a result of what the South considered Northern interference, the South moved inevitably toward secession, and the country, toward civil war. In 1863 the Fugitive Slave Laws were made largely irrelevant when President Abraham Lincoln issued the Emancipation Proclamation.

Fugitive Slave law = a chief cause of the civil war

THE CHINESE EXCLUSION ACT OF 1882

HISTORICAL OVERVIEW:

"The Chinese Exclusion Act...is the hinge on which all American immigration policy turned. Prior to the Exclusion Act there had been no significant restrictions of any kind on any immigration to the United States. There was no such thing as an illegal immigrant. After 1882...there are successive restrictions placed on all immigrants."— Professor Roger Daniels (from the book *Asian American*)

Beginning in the mid-19th century, Chinese immigration to America was influenced by both the "pull" of California's Gold Rush and the "push" created by China's impoverished conditions. Years of drought, floods, disease and famine ravaged China, a country already fraught with over-population and internal instability. European and American exploits into the region further exacerbated China's economic, political and social problems.

Chinese peasants, particularly in the rural Pearl River Delta area in the southeastern province of Guangdong, were desperate for relief. They began to migrate to urban centers in search of employment and survival. When these ventures proved insufficient, the Chinese migrated to Southeast Asia and the Pacific Region (Thailand, Singapore, Malaysia, Indonesia, and the Philippines). Word soon reached China that "Guam Saan," the "Gold Mountain" as the Chinese referred to America, was a land of opportunity for those seeking a better life.

Large numbers of Chinese began to migrate to the United States around 1850. The waves of newcomers from across the Pacific Ocean also included merchants seeking new business opportunities abroad. Upon reaching the western shores of America, many of the first Chinese immigrants joined the nation's gold rush. In 1848 the precious element was discovered in the hills of California. Soon miners from across the nation, as well as from Europe and South America, descended upon the area. By the mid-1850's, 24,000 Chinese (nearly two-thirds of the Chinese population in America by then) worked in the California mines. Most were independent prospectors who organized themselves into small groups and formed their own companies.

By the mid-1860's, gold mining profits began to dry up. As a result, many Chinese left the gold mines. Faced with few other employment opportunities, numerous Chinese workers turned to railroad construction.

In 1865 the first Chinese workers were hired by the Central Pacific Railroad, which was building a track east from Sacramento. By 1867, 12,000 Chinese were employed by the Central Pacific Railroad-nearly 90 percent of the company's work force. They performed not only the physical labor of laying track, but also the more technical jobs of operating power drills and handling the explosives used to blow holes through rocks and mountains.

Brutal work crews carved through hard earth from sunup to sundown in all ill conditions (including the dreadful winter of 1866-67) when snow storms and subzero temperatures battered the region for months. Dozens of workers died as snow drifts buried construction camps. That spring, workers found corpses of Chinese workers in an upright position still gripping shovels and picks. The winter deaths (along with the fact that they worked longer than their white counterparts and made less) pushed the "peaceable" Chinese over the edge. In the spring of 1867 about 5,000 Chinese went on strike for higher wages and an eight-hour work day. The company responded with a harsh hand. Management cut off the strikers' food supply and forced them back to work within a week.

After the failure of the strike, the Chinese workers resumed their labor on the railroad. In early afternoon of May 10, 1869, history was made at Promontory Point, Utah. The Central Pacific and Union Pacific railroads met, creating the first transcontinental railroad. Journalists noted the significant contribution of the Chinese. One magazine writer wrote, "The dream of Thomas Jefferson, and the desires of Thomas H. Benton's heart, have been wonderfully fulfilled, so far as the Pacific Railroad and the trade with the old world of the East is concerned. But even they did not prophesy that [the Chinese] should build the Pacificward end of the road."

With their work on the railroad completed, thousands of Chinese laborers joined their fellow countrymen already working in various towns throughout California. San Francisco, for example, saw its Chinese population swell from 2,719 in 1860 to 12,022 by 1870. The Chinese, who made their abode in the cities, worked in a variety of sectors. Some were shopkeepers and merchants, while others earned their pay as artisans. Many more worked numerous manufacturing jobs. During the 1860's, Chinese workers represented nearly 50 percent of the labor force involved in producing San Francisco's four key industrial products-shoes, woolens, tobacco and clothing.

Not all of the newcomers from China ended up in cities, however. A number of Chinese settled in California's rural areas, where they worked the land. Formerly farmers in China, these immigrants introduced innovative techniques and helped move the state's agriculture from wheat growing to fruit production. Some Chinese were able to farm their own land. Most, however, ended up as laborers on someone else's farm. By 1870 Chinese people accounted for almost 20 percent of California's farm labor.

In the towns across California, Chinese immigrants lived alongside each other in tight-knit communities known as Chinatowns. Like immigrants from European nations, the Chinese turned to each other as well as their traditional customs and practices in order to find comfort in a new and strange land. Chinese wedding and funeral customs were still observed as well as their traditional celebrations and holidays.

Whether they lived in cities or rural villages, the Chinese established social clubs and civic associations to help each other cope in the United States. These groups attended to a variety of immigrant's needs, from housing and employment, to sending letters to families in China and even shipping home bodies and bones of the deceased.

In San Francisco, the main associations merged into one organization known as the Chinese Six Companies. This group settled conflicts, provided entertainment, and organized health and other social services for the Chinese community and often interacted with public officials on behalf of the immigrants' interests.

THE LAW:

Forty-Seventh Congress. Session I. 1882

Chapter 126.-An act to execute certain treaty stipulations relating to Chinese.

Preamble.

Whereas, in the opinion of the Government of the United States the coming of Chinese laborers to this country endangers the good order of certain localities within the territory thereof: Therefore,

Be it enacted by the Senate and House of Representatives of the United States of America in Congress assembled, That from and after the expiration of ninety days next after the passage of this act, and until the expiration of ten years next after the passage of this act, the coming of Chinese laborers to the United States be, and the same is hereby, suspended; and during such suspension it shall not be lawful for any Chinese laborer to come, or, having so come after the expiration of said ninety days, to remain within the United States.

SEC. 2. That the master of any vessel who shall knowingly bring within the United States on such vessel, and land or permit to be landed, and Chinese laborer, from any foreign port of place, shall be deemed guilty of a misdemeanor, and on conviction thereof shall be punished by a fine of not more than five hundred dollars for each and every such Chinese laborer so brought, and may be also imprisoned for a term not exceeding one year.

SEC. 3. That the two foregoing sections shall not apply to Chinese laborers who were in the United States on the seventeenth day of November, eighteen hundred and eighty, or who shall have come into the same before the expiration of ninety days next after the passage of this act, and who shall produce to such master before going on board such vessel, and shall produce to the collector of the port in the United States at which such vessel shall arrive, the evidence hereinafter in this act required of his being one of the laborers in this section mentioned; nor shall the two foregoing sections apply to the case of any master whose vessel, being bound to a port not within the United States by reason of being in distress or in stress of weather, or touching at any port of the United States on its voyage to any foreign port of place: *Provided*, That all Chinese laborers brought on such vessel shall depart with the vessel on leaving port.

SEC. 4. That for the purpose of properly identifying Chinese laborers who were in the United States on the seventeenth day of November, eighteen hundred and eighty, or who shall have come into the same before the expiration of ninety days next after the passage of this act, and in order to furnish them with the proper evidence of their right to go from and come to the United States of their free will and accord, as provided by the treaty between the United States and China dated November seventeenth, eighteen hundred and eighty, the collector of customs of the district from which any such Chinese laborer shall depart from the United States shall, in person or by deputy, go on board each vessel having on board any such Chinese laborer and cleared or about to sail from his district for a foreign port, and on such vessel make a list of all such Chinese laborers, which shall be entered in registry-books to be kept for that purpose, in which shall be stated the name, age, occupation, last place of residence, physical marks or peculiarities, and all facts necessary for the identification of each of such Chinese laborers, which books shall be safely kept in the custom-house; and every such Chinese laborer so departing from the United States shall be entitled to, and shall receive, free of any charge or cost upon application therefore, from the collector or his deputy, at the time such list is taken, a certificate, signed by the collector or his deputy and attested by his seal of office, in such form as the Secretary of the Treasury shall prescribe, which certificate shall contain a statement of the name, age, occupation, last place of residence, personal description, and fact of identification of the Chinese laborer to whom the certificate is issued, corresponding with the said list and registry in all particulars. In case any Chinese laborer after having received such certificate shall leave such vessel before her departure he shall deliver his certificate to the master of the vessel, and if such Chinese laborer shall fail to return to such vessel before her departure from port the certificate shall be delivered by the master to the collector of customs for cancellation. The certificate herein provided for shall entitle the Chinese laborer to whom the same is issued to return to and re-enter the United States upon producing and delivering the same to the collector of customs of the district at which such Chinese laborer shall seek to re-enter; and upon delivery of such certificate by such Chinese laborer to the collector of customs at the time of re-entry in the United States, said collector shall cause the same to be filed in the custom house and duly canceled.

SEC. 5. That any Chinese laborer mentioned in section four of this act being in the United States, and desiring to depart from the United States by land, shall have the right to demand and receive, free of charge or cost, a certificate of indentification similar to that provided for in section four of this act to be issued to such Chinese laborers as may desire to leave the United States by water; and it is hereby made the duty of the collector of customs of the district next adjoining the foreign country to which said Chinese laborer desires to go to issue such certificate, free of charge or cost, upon application by such Chinese laborer, and to enter the same upon registry-books to be kept by him for the purpose, as provided for in section four of this act.

SEC. 6. That in order to the faithful execution of articles one and two of the treaty in this act before mentioned, every Chinese person other than a laborer who may be entitled by said treaty and this act to come within the United States, and who shall be about to come to the United States, shall be identified as so entitled by the Chinese Government in each case, such identity to be evidenced by a certificate issued under the authority of said government, which certificate shall be in the English language or (if not in the English language) accompanied by a translation into English, stating such right to come, and which certificate shall state the name, title, or official rank, if any, the age, height, and all physical peculiarities, former and present occupation or profession, and place of residence in China of the person to whom the certificate is issued and that such person is entitled conformably to the treaty in this act mentioned to come within the United States. Such certificate shall be prima-facie evidence of the fact set forth therein, and shall be produced to the collector of customs, or his deputy, of the port in the district in the United States at which the person named therein shall arrive.

SEC. 7. That any person who shall knowingly and falsely alter or substitute any name for the name written in such certificate or forge any such certificate, or knowingly utter any forged or fraudulent certificate, or falsely personate any person named in any such certificate, shall be deemed guilty of a misdemeanor; and upon conviction thereof shall be fined in a sum not exceeding one thousand dollars, an imprisoned in a penitentiary for a term of not more than five years.

SEC. 8. That the master of any vessel arriving in the United States from any foreign port or place shall, at the same time he delivers a manifest of the cargo, and if there be no cargo, then at the time of making a report of the entry of vessel pursuant to the law, in addition to the other matter required to be reported, and before landing, or permitting to land, any Chinese passengers, deliver and report to the collector of customs of the district in which such vessels shall have arrived a separate list of all Chinese passengers taken on board his vessel at any foreign port or place, and all such passengers on board the vessel at that time. Such list shall show the names of such passengers (and if accredited officers of the Chinese Government traveling on the business of that government, or their servants, with a note of such facts), and the name and other particulars, as shown by their respective certificates; and such list shall be sworn to by the master in the manner required by law in relation to the manifest of the cargo. Any willful refusal or neglect of any such master to comply with the provisions of this section shall incur the same penalties and forfeiture as are provided for a refusal or neglect to report and deliver a manifest of cargo.

SEC. 9. That before any Chinese passengers are landed from any such vessel, the collector, or his deputy, shall proceed to examine such passengers, comparing the certificates with the list and with the passengers; and no passenger shall be allowed to land in the United States from such vessel in violation of law.

SEC. 10. That every vessel whose master shall knowingly violate any of the provisions of this act shall be deemed forfeited to the United States, and shall be liable to seizure and condemnation on any district of the United States into which such vessel may enter or in which she may be found.

SEC. 11. That any person who shall knowingly bring into or cause to be brought into the United States by land, or who shall knowingly aid or abet the same, or aid or abet the landing in the United States from any vessel of any Chinese person not lawfully entitled to enter the United States, shall be deemed guilty of a misdemeanor, and shall, on conviction thereof, be fined in a sum not exceeding one thousand dollars, and imprisoned for a term not exceeding one year.

SEC. 12. That no Chinese person shall be permitted to enter the United States by land without producing to the proper officer of customs the certificate in this act required of Chinese persons seeking to land from a vessel. And any Chinese person found unlawfully within the United States shall be caused to be removed therefrom to the country from whence he came, by direction of the United States, after being brought before some justice, judge, or commissioner of a court of the United States and found to be one not lawfully entitled to be or remain in the United States.

SEC. 13. That this act shall not apply to diplomatic and other officers of the Chinese Government traveling upon the business of that government, whose credentials shall be taken as equivalent to the certificate in this act mentioned, and shall exempt them and their body and household servants from the provisions of this act as to other Chinese persons.

SEC. 14. That hereafter no State court or court of the United States shall admit Chinese to citizenship; and all laws in conflict with this act are hereby repealed.

SEC. 15. That the words "Chinese laborers", whenever used in this act, shall be construed to mean both skilled and unskilled laborers and Chinese employed in mining.

Approved, May 6, 1882.

IN LAYMEN'S TERMS:

Section 2: States that a person who owns a ship that brings Chinese laborers to the U.S. from any foreign place shall have to pay a fine of no more than $500. And also may imprisoned for up to one year.

Section 3: States that this act does not include Chinese laborers that were in the United States as of November 17, 1880. Or if a ship that has Chinese laborers must port because of a storm or other problems that all Chinese laborers on that ship must leave when that ship leaves.

Section 4: States that to confirm who is a legal Chinese laborer in the U.S., that previous citizen of the U.S. who are Chinese laborers will receive free of charge a certificate saying that they are a citizen of the U.S.

Section 5: States that any Chinese laborer listed from Section 4 of this act shall leave by land or water if they please and demand a certificate of identification.

Section 6: States that a Chinese person, not including a Chinese laborer, who wishes to enter may ask for a certificate of identity to enter and must present this certificate to the officer at the port of entry.

Section 7: States that any person who will falsely alter or substitute a name on a certificate of identification, or knowingly alter any fraudulent certificate, or wrongly impersonate the person on the certificate, will be convicted of a misdemeanor.

Section 8: States that any Chinese passengers on board a vessel must be claimed by the master of said ship.

Section 9: States that all Chinese passengers (in reference to Section 8) listed from above shall be checked out or examined and certificates must be compared with the list of passengers before being allowed to dock in the U.S.

Section 10: States that if the master of a vessel shall violate any of the provisions in this act, they forfeit their vessel to the United States government, and shall be liable to seizure and condemnation.

Section 11: States that any person trying to unlawfully sneak a Chinese person into the country will be fined up to $1000 and possibly imprisoned for up to one year.

Section 12: States that no Chinese persons may enter the United States without presenting the proper certificate to the proper official.

Section 13: States that this act does not include public officials of the Chinese government traveling in service to that government.

Section 14: States that no court of the state or the United States, shall admit any Chinese to citizenship.

Section 15: States that "Chinese laborers" in this act shall mean both skilled and unskilled laborers and Chinese working in mining.

SOCIAL AND POLITICAL CLIMATE LEADING TO LAW/POLICY:

The population of Chinese immigrants in America grew steadily from 1850 to 1880. By 1880 their number had grown to about 105,000 persons. The population of Chinese may have reached as many as 135,000 persons on the eve of the passage of the first federal law specifically excluding Chinese immigrants in 1882. In certain areas of the American West, Chinese immigrants constituted a substantial part of the population.

As mentioned previously the Chinese flocked to America in search of opportunities; most fled from their collapsing empire for economic reasons. The Gold Rush happened during a period of poverty in China. Upon their arrival in California, the Chinese newcomers soon became an exploited work force, especially since they were predominantly male. The wages they received, however, were still considerably higher than they could earn at home. But opposition in California was both immediate and strong. During the Gold Rush, thousands of Americans from the East, where they opposed European immigration, brought with them their attitudes of exclusion. And non-American whites (i.e. Irish, Russian), who had suffered from Eastern nativism, saw that in attacking the Chinese they elevated their own shaky status. As early as 1852, American miners in California protested the growing presence of Chinese laborers. California Governor John Bilger responded in that year by proclaiming to the state legislature: "Let us consider the vile coolies, who like craven beasts work the goldmines only to return to their native land and bring no profit to our state." As anti-Chinese sentiment grew, labor activists in San Francisco organized anti-Chinese clubs, and local and state lawmakers of all parties continually passed resolutions opposing Asian immigration.

Three measures that were born out of this unchecked legislative aggression against the Chinese were the 1854 Foreign Miner's Tax, The Chinese Police Tax Law of 1862 and the Page Law in 1875. The Foreign Miner's Tax called for the Chinese alone to pay a tax for gold mining in California (the Chinese were also forbidden from buying claims and had to work claims that had been discarded). The Chinese Police Tax imposed a monthly tax only on adults of the "Mongolian Race" who worked in the mines or were hired to work in most businesses. The fields of endeavor that were considered "Chinese" (production and manufacture of tea, rice, sugar, coffee) were exempt from this act.

In the resulting largely male, so-called "bachelor" Chinese community in America, a few Chinese men saw a business opportunity and imported Chinese women whom they pressed into prostitution. While prostitution was a general feature of the frontier West, the existence of Chinese prostitution gave Congress an excuse to pass the Page Law in 1875, specifically aimed at preventing Chinese women (including family members of Chinese immigrants (from entering the U.S. Not until 1970, almost 100 years later, following the major overhaul of immigration laws in 1965, did the Chinese community finally achieve a normal gender ratio of one man to one woman.

Accompanying these policy measures were numerous incidents of violence against the Chinese. Attacks began in the 1850's against Chinese gold miners and continued throughout the century. In 1871, for example, a white mob descended on Los Angeles' Chinatown. Fighting erupted and when it was over, 15 Chinese were found hanged. Six years later, arsonists attempted to burn down the entire Chinatown in Chico, California. Another example of violence against the Chinese is the Rock Spring (Wyoming) Massacre in 1885. Mine owner Union Pacific brought the Chinese into Rock Springs as strike breakers in 1875. When the Chinese declined to join the other workers in their proposed strike for higher wages however, they became targets of white hostility. On September 2nd a mob of white mine workers gathered, marched toward the Chinese workers, guarded all escape routes, and fired at the unarmed and defenseless. These same men also searched Chinese for valuables before shooting them, while others set fire to their shacks. By nightfall the houses owned by the coal company and all 79 huts belonging to the Chinese had been destroyed by fire. Meanwhile, the mob threw the bodies of some dead Chinese, as well as those of live but wounded ones, into the flames. In all, 28 Chinese were killed and 15 wounded. Some of the wounded eventually died from the wounds inflicted upon them at the massacre. President Grover Cleveland called out Federal troops to restore peace, and Congress later paid reparations to the Chinese from the town (although Congress complied, they also declared that this action should not be constructed as precedent for future compensation).

There were, in my opinion, three pivotal events that cemented anti-Chinese forces in their resolve: (1) People vs. Hall; (2) the publication of *The Last Days Of The Republic*, by P.W. Dooner; (3) the economic depression of the 1870's.

(1) People vs. Hall: This case came about when George Hall (a white man) was accused of killing Lem Sing (Chinese male). This California Supreme Court case in 1854 said that the testimony of a Chinese man who witnessed a murder by a white man was inadmissible. The basis for the Court's conclusion was given in the opinion of the Court delivered by Chief Justice Hugh Murray.

All of the following is the opinion of the court in its entirety: "The 394th section of the Act Concerning Civil Cases provides that no Indian or Negro shall be allowed to testify as a witness in any action or proceeding in which a white person is a party.

The 14th section of the Act of April 16th, 1850, regulating Criminal Proceedings, provides that 'No black or mulatto person, or Indian, shall be allowed to give evidence in favor of, or against a white man.'

The true point at which we are anxious to arrive is, the legal signification of the words, 'black, mulatto, Indian, and white person,' and whether the Legislature adopted them as generic terms, or intended to limit their application to specific types of the human species. . . .

The Act of Congress, in defining that description of aliens may become naturalized citizens, provides that every 'free white citizen,' etc.

If the term 'white,' as used in the Constitution, was not understood in its generic sense as including the Caucasian race, and necessarily excluding all others, where was the necessary of providing for the admission of Indians to the privilege of voting, by special legislation?

We are of the opinion that the words 'white,' 'Negro,' 'mulatto,' 'Indian,' and 'black person,' wherever they occur in our Constitution and laws, must be taken in their generic sense, and that, even admitting the Indian of this continent is not of the Mongolian type, that the words 'black person,' in the 14th section, must be taken as contradistinguished from white, and necessarily excludes all races other than the Caucasian.

We have carefully considered all the consequences resulting from a different rule of construction, and are satisfied that even in a doubtful case; we would be impelled to this decision on ground of public policy

The same rule which would admit them to testify, would admit them to all the equal rights of citizenship, and we might soon see them at the polls, in the jury box, upon the bench, and in our legislative halls.

This is not a speculation which exists in the excited and overheated imagination of the patriot and statesman, but it is an actual and present danger.

The anomalous spectacle of a distinct people, living in our community, recognizing no laws of this State, except through necessity, bringing with them their prejudices and national feuds, in which they indulge in open violation of law; whose mendacity is proverbial; a race of people whom nature has marked as inferior, and who are incapable of progress or intellectual development beyond a certain point, as their history has shown; differing in language, opinions, color, and physical conformation; between whom and ourselves nature has placed an impassable difference, is now presented, and for them is claims, not only the right to swear away the life of a citizen, but the further privilege of participating with us in administering the affairs of our Government.

These facts were before the Legislature that framed this Act, and have been known as matters of public history to every subsequent Legislature.

There can be no doubt as to the intention of Legislature, and that if it had ever been anticipated that this class of people were not embraced in the prohibition, then such specific words would have been employed as would have put the matter beyond any possible controversy.

For these reasons, we are of opinion that the testimony was inadmissible."

These inflammatory, as well as racist, statements emboldened the prejudicial and violent attacks against the Chinese in California. This legal sanction of racism did much to provide the setting for the laws and policies that were to follow.

(2) The Publication of P.W. Dooner's <u>**Last Days of the Republic**</u> **(1880):** Though a work of fiction, this novel set the tone (as well as played on existing attitudes) for anti-Chinese sentiment in California. According to Dooner, the destruction of American legal culture was a priority for Chinese immigrants. In this novel, the "Yellow Peril" shows its ugly head. This novel is a tale of California being invaded by Chinese "hordes" and finally winning with a Chinese leader ruling over a new Chinese colony. This book further fueled the prejudices against the Chinese. The cover of the novel shows a building of obvious Chinese architecture on one side and the U.S. Capitol on the other with a caption that reads: "The Ruler Of All Lands." Early editions included illustrations such as Chinese in positions of power in Washington. The already racist suspicions of many Americans against the Chinese were given credence upon this book's publication and circulation.

(3) The economic depression of the 1870's: The economy had been expanding since the end of the Civil War, so that investors became convinced that business profits would continue to increase indefinitely. Eager to take advantage of new business opportunities in the South, Northern and Southern investors borrowed enormous amounts of money and built new facilities as quickly as possible.

Unfortunately many of these new businesses took on more debt than they could afford. A Philadelphia banker named Jay Cooke invested heavily in railroads. Not enough investors bought shares in Cooke's railroad lines to cover his ballooning construction costs, and he could not pay his debts. In September 1873, Cooke's banking firm, the nation's largest, went bankrupt, setting off a series of financial failures known as the Panic of 1873. Smaller banks closed, and the stock market temporarily collapsed. Within a year, 89 railroads went broke. By 1875, more than 18,000 companies had folded. In the five-year depression triggered by the panic, 3 million workers lost their jobs. During this period there were also mounting labor troubles, and the Chinese were repeatedly used as replacement labor, creating further resentment. Chinese labor was specifically useful to business owners because it combined two qualities: the Chinese were disciplined but subordinated, and they were racially unacceptable to white labor unions, with whom they therefore would never be joined. Furthermore, they were also legally rendered "perpetual foreigners," without any political power to protest or contest the terms or conditions of their employment. The employers of various large industries were incredibly canny and thoughtful about dividing the labor force. And so, they very consciously, intentionally used Chinese people as strikebreakers, knowing that it would infuriate and mortify white workers, and could drive them into outraged and self-destructive behavior.

Thus during the financially unstable 1870's, the Chinese became an ideal scapegoat: they were strangers, wore queues (long braids), kept to their own kind, and were very productive (inspiring jealousy and animosity among the American white labor class). Legislation, including immigration taxes, and laundry-operation fees, passed in order to limit the success of the Chinese workers.

Americans attempted to justify their actions with two main claims. First Americans claimed that jobs were scarce, and the Chinese were stealing the only jobs there were because of their willingness to work cheap. Americans also claimed that America's wealth should remain in America and the Chinese sent the majority of their income back to their families in China, thereby taking revenue made in the U.S. out of America.

The Chinese actively challenged the discrimination against them. They sought greater civil rights in the courts and even petitioned President Ulysses S. Grant for relief. "Are the railroads built by the Chinese no benefit to the country?" read part of a letter sent to the

93

President in 1876 by members of the Chinese Six Companies. "Are the manufacturing establishments largely worked by the Chinese, no benefit to this country? Do not the results of the daily toil of a hundred thousand men increase the riches of this country?" Despite their protests, the Chinese could do little to turn back the growing tide against them.

AFTERMATH OF LAW/POLICY

It is important to note that the Chinese Exclusion Act of 1882 lasted for ten years, the Geary Act of 1892 extended it for another 10 years and the Extended Act of 1904 made it permanent (until future legislation rescinded it—this will be treated briefly further in this section).

All Chinese immigrants entering the country were now scrutinized under the severe restrictions of the Chinese Exclusion Act. The Port of San Francisco received the greatest number of Chinese. In the beginning, the Chinese were detained in a two-story, wooden warehouse operated by the Pacific Mail Steamship Company (an overseas transportation firm). Located on the San Francisco waterfront, this makeshift detention center was considered unsafe and unsanitary. Reports of lax security, and improper ventilation and sanitation led to the construction of new detention facilities on Angel Island.

Angel Island consisted of filthy ramshackle buildings in which Chinese immigrants were confined like prisoners. Entering Europeans, Japanese "picture brides" (destined to marry their prospective husbands by proxy in America), and other immigrants not subject to Chinese Exclusion were allowed to either land immediately in San Francisco, or experience short stays on Angel Island to confirm their status. On the other hand, U.S. immigration officials detained Chinese for extensive interrogations for weeks, even months, and occasionally a year or more. U.S. officials hoped to deport as many as possible. The interrogation process was a frightening event for the detainees. The questions were detailed and irrelevant. The questions were designed to confuse and entrap the detainees. As a result, poignant reminders of the detainees' stay on

94

Angel Island were written on the wooden barracks walls. Poems were penciled, carved or brush painted on the walls to express the detainees' anger and frustrations over their treatment and detainment. New arrivals also underwent a medical examination shortly after reaching the island. Unfamiliar with the language, customs and Western medical procedures, the examination was often characterized by newcomers as humiliating and barbaric.

Such treatment quickly squelched the hopes of these unfortunate thousands. Some chose to escape their humiliation by suicide. Life for the detainees was strange, stressful, demoralizing, and humiliating. Separated from family members, they were placed in crowded communal living quarters.

One hundred persons would sleep in bunk beds, three high in columns, in a room about 1,000 square feet. Men and women were separated at all times, and Chinese, Japanese, Korean and European immigrants were segregated from each other. Isolated as it was, immigration officials regarded the island as ideal. Communication was limited, quarantine was possible, and escape was unlikely. Station personnel included immigration inspectors, interpreters, administrative and medical personnel, maintenance men, kitchen workers and missionaries. Although some staff quarters existed, most workers commuted daily to the island on the government ferry. Shortly after opening in 1910, the station was criticized for its physical and sanitary deficiencies. In the 1920s, it was deemed a fire trap that was too expensive to operate. Still, another 20 years passed before the operation was shut down.

The population of Chinese may have reached as many as 135,000 persons on the eve of the passage of the first federal law specifically excluding Chinese immigrants in 1882. However, with the new body of federal immigration law, supplemented by a continuing stream of personal violence and discriminatory state and local laws, the population of the Chinese community in America dwindled to fewer than ninety thousand persons by 1900 and to almost sixty thousand by 1920. The period from the last quarter of the nineteenth century until well into the twentieth century was one of great suffering for Chinese immigrants in America.

The Chinese considered American Exclusion grossly unjust and discriminatory. Boycotts of American goods were organized in large Chinese communities as far away as the Philippines. Chinese diplomats in Hong Kong and community organizations in America would submit letters complaining about the degrading practices and mistreatment by immigration officials. Many Chinese laborers and their family members resorted to methods of circumventing the Act. They would smuggle themselves across the border or purchase identity documents falsely claiming to be an individual of an exempt classification (e.g., a merchant, or child of a merchant, or a U.S. citizen or a child of a U.S. citizen). The creation of "border patrols" and undeniably, the evolution of some of America's largest bureaucracies (the U.S. Customs Department, and Immigration and Naturalization, i.e. the I.N.S.) directly stems from much of the enforcement practices required by Chinese Exclusion.

Something that I believe to be noteworthy is the tenacity in which the Chinese addressed the discrimination and racism that constantly besieged them. It is hard to think of a single law perceived by the Chinese as discriminatory, that they did not challenge in court.

From the soil of these accumulated injustices, grew a Chinese community that became extremely proficient in American jurisprudence. They relentlessly pursued their rights in America's courts. They turned to the justice system precisely because they understood and believed in the American promise of equality and freedom. It was natural for them to ante up a portion of their earnings to fight these discriminatory laws. They hired seasoned lawyers and challenged almost every law or court case enacted against them, sometimes with great success. The hundreds of cases they brought in the 19th and early 20th centuries helped establish legal precedents that ran the gamut, from livelihood and education to immigrant rights and citizenship. Much of the legal advocacy of Chinese immigrants was based upon a new body of civil rights laws passed during the decade following the Civil War. Though their specific goal may have been to liberate the Freedmen, some of the new laws seemed clearly to protect all minorities, including the Chinese. Notable was section 16 of the Civil Rights Act of 1870. It assured a number of rights to "all persons." But the most important basis for the Chinese legal advocacy would be the Fourteenth Amendment. Chinese immigrants scored some major victories under this amendment, the most important being the *Yick Wo v. Hopkins* decision in 1886. In it, the Supreme Court struck down San Francisco ordinances mandating that new laundries be built of brick or stone and that existing wooden ones obtain a permit to continue operation. It found them in violation of Yick Wo's equal protection rights under this amendment.

It is a bittersweet irony that the Chinese, who were accused of not being able to assimilate into "American" life, very much assimilated when it came to resisting discrimination against them. From the early 1850's, they started making use of the American judicial system when such a system did not exist in China.

Desperate attempts to enter America under Exclusion often involved the cooperation and assistance of different members of the Chinese community, as well as those of the white community. Chinese community organizations and import/export companies provided transportation, housing, exchange of important correspondence and other means of support. Progressive members of the white community would sometimes bear both true and sometimes false "witness" to a person's residency or status as a merchant. Corrupt immigration officers could be involved in bribery schemes whereby false birth certificates would be issued or testimony documents changed. There were cases where such officials would be discovered and ousted from government service, only to find employment with some of the most prominent immigration attorneys in town.

Immigrants entering under false identities were often the physically-fit, male members of a family who were considered best suited to find employment in the United States. These male immigrants with false identity documents were commonly referred to as "paper sons." The Chinatowns of America have often been described as "Bachelor Societies," devoid of women and children. However, in reality, many Chinese men in America (during the Exclusion era) actually had wives and children residing in China.

Left behind in China, the wives of Chinese immigrants in the United States were referred to as "grass widows" or "living widows." Though they were married and assumed all the obligations of a wife, these women often led solitary lives separated from the husbands for years and even decades at a time. As a result, the normal formation of family life and community development both in rural villages of China and the early Chinatowns of America suffered.

The Chinese Exclusion Act was a crucial point in U.S. immigration history. Its impact most definitely reverberated throughout the Asian Pacific region as the United States subsequently restricted and/or excluded immigrants of Japanese, Korean, Filipino and Asian Indian descent. By executive agreement, statute, and eventually, by a key clause in the National Origins Act of 1924 (which barred all "aliens ineligible to citizenship"), America closed its doors to more and more immigrants for reasons of race, ethnicity, and country of origin.

As a result of the strict quotas instituted under the National Origin Act of 1924, immigration was still severely restricted for the Chinese. Though primarily passed to limit immigration from Eastern and Southern Europe, and Russia, immigration quotas were now tied to a very small percentage based on U.S. Census figures of how many people from a certain country were living in the United States in 1890 (eight years after the passage of the Chinese Exclusion Act). This translated to only 105 Chinese a year being permitted to enter the United States. A later amendment to the law defined this restriction further by applying it to those who were by blood 50% or more Chinese from anywhere in the world (versus just immigrants from one country-China).

It was not until 1943, when President Franklin D. Roosevelt was motivated by China's war effort against Japan in World War II, that the Chinese Exclusion Act was finally repealed. In statements made at that time, the repeal was in recognition of those who fought valiantly in China, and clearly an attempt to diminish propaganda efforts on the part of Japan that painted America as racist.

Later provisions permitted alien Chinese wives and minor children of domiciled alien merchants to enter outside of these harsh quotas. There was also the War Brides Act, which permitted Chinese (among others) serving in the U.S. armed forces to bring their wives to America. However, the real key to reversing immigration restrictions and allowing meaningful family reunification did not occur until the Kennedy and Johnson administrations finally abolished ethnic quotas with the 1965 Immigration Act.

PLESSY V. FERGUSON 1896

Note: In 1892, a group of Louisiana citizens decided to challenge a state law that required railroads to provide separate railway cars for African Americans. Homer Plessy (classified as black because he was one-eighth African American) boarded a train in New Orleans and sat in a railway car reserved for whites. When he refused to move he was arrested and convicted of breaking the law. Four years later in 1896, his case was tried in the U.S. Supreme Court.

The Supreme Court's decision in the Plessy v. Ferguson case represents the nadir of the post Civil War attack on the rights of African Americans. In this decision we see that state and local governments were given the ability to *legally* discriminate & segregate on the basis of race.

HISTORICAL OVERVIEW

Because much of the history that is involved in and impacts Plessy v. Ferguson is outlined in previous sections (Overview of Colonial Laws and The Fugitive Slave Act of 1850), the period just subsequent to the Civil War will be the focus here.

The Emancipation Proclamation, which Lincoln had issued under his war powers, freed only those slaves living in rebelling states. The government had to decide what to do about the border states, where slavery still existed. The president believed that the only solution was a constitutional amendment abolishing slavery.

The Republican-controlled Senate approved an amendment in the summer of 1864, but the house with its large Democratic membership did not. After Lincoln's reelection, the amendment was reintroduced in the House in January of 1865. This time the administration had convinced a few Democrats to vote in favor of the amendment with promises of government jobs after they left office. The amendment passed with two votes to spare. Spectators, many of them African Americans who were now allowed to sit in the congressional galleries, burst into cheers, while Republicans on the floor shouted in victory. By year's end 27 states, including eight from the South, had ratified the Thirteenth Amendment. The U.S. Constitution now stated that: *"Neither slavery nor involuntary servitude, except as punishment for crime whereof the party shall be convicted, shall exist within the United States."*

In the wake and atmosphere of these sweeping changes, African Americans began to demand broader equality. In Philadelphia, Pennsylvania, where streetcars were segregated before the war, African Americans secured a desegregation law from the state legislature. In Illinois, statutes preventing blacks from testifying in state courts were overturned. Because slaves had been punished if they tried to learn how to read or write, more than 90 percent of the freed African Americans over the age of 20 were illiterate in 1870. During Reconstruction, however, freed people of all ages— grandparents, parents, and children—sought an education. Following protests by African Americans, segregated schools in Detroit, Michigan and in Rhode Island were desegregated. In several states, laws requiring blacks to own property before they could vote were seriously challenged for the first time. Many such practices would continue during Reconstruction.

After the Confederacy was defeated, Southern blacks were confronted with freedom and the challenge of securing food and shelter. Some continued, out of necessity or choice, to work the land they had worked as slaves. Occasionally, African Americans worked out agreements with their former masters regarding wages or other forms of compensation such as food and shelter; however, only in a few cases were their conditions much improved over slavery. Other former slaves migrated to towns and cities, hoping for work, education or relief distributed by Northern freedpeople's aid societies and union troops. Still others traveled more broadly, testing their freedom and seeking relatives from whom they had been separated by war and slavery.

By 1866 former slaves were playing an increasing role in political organizations and were winning a greater number of offices. Many of these black officeholders were ministers or teachers who had been educated in the North. Nevertheless, even thought here were more black voters than white voters in the South, African-American officeholders remained in the minority. Only South Carolina had a black majority in the state legislature. No Southern state elected an African-American governor. Moreover, out of 125 Southerners elected to the U.S. Congress during congressional reconstruction, only 16 were African Americans. Among these was Hiram Revels, the first African-American senator.

By the end of 1866, most of the Republican Southern state governments had repealed the black codes. African-American lawmakers took social equity a step further by proposing bills to desegregate public transportation. However, even when desegregation laws were passed, they were not strictly enforced. State orphanages, for example, usually had separate facilities for white and black children.

In the postwar Reconstruction years, the United States would be forced to confront these issues (as well as many others) arising from the legacy of slavery.

THE CASE & DECISION

(The majority opinion of the Court and the dissenting opinion)

PLESSY v. FERGUSON, 163 U.S. 537 (1896)
163 U.S. 537

PLESSY
v.
FERGUSON.
No. 210.

Mr. Justice BROWN, after stating the facts in the foregoing language, delivered the opinion of the court (*Here is the majority and dissenting opinion verbatim*).

This case turns upon the constitutionality of an act of the general assembly of the state of Louisiana, passed in 1890, providing for separate railway carriages for the white and colored races. Acts 1890, No. 111, p. 152.

The first section of the statute enacts "that all railway companies carrying passengers in their coaches in this state, shall provide equal but separate accommodations for the white, and colored races, by providing two or more passenger coaches for each passenger train, or by dividing the passenger coaches by a partition so as to secure separate accommodations: provided, that this section shall not be construed to apply to street railroads. No person or persons shall be permitted to occupy seats in coaches, other than the ones assigned to them, on account of the race they belong to."

By the second section it was enacted "that the officers of such passenger trains shall have power and are hereby required to assign each passenger to the coach or compartment used for the race to which such passenger belongs; any passenger insisting on going into a coach or compartment to which by race he does not belong, shall be liable to a fine of twenty-five dollars, or in lieu thereof to imprisonment for a period of not more than twenty days in the parish prison, and any officer of any railroad insisting on assigning a passenger to a coach or compartment other than the one set aside for the race to which said passenger belongs, shall be liable to a fine of twenty-five dollars, or in lieu thereof to imprisonment for a period of not more than twenty days in the parish prison; and should any passenger refuse to occupy the coach or compartment to which he or she is assigned by the officer of such railway, said officer shall have power to refuse to carry such passenger on his train, and for such refusal neither he nor the railway company which he represents shall be liable for damages in any of the courts of this state."

The third section provides penalties for the refusal or neglect of the officers, directors, conductors, and employees of railway companies to comply with the act, with a proviso that "nothing in this act shall be construed as applying to nurses attending children of the other race." The fourth section is immaterial.

The information filed in the criminal district court charged, in substance, that Plessy, being a passenger between two stations within the state of Louisiana, was assigned by officers of the company to the coach used for the race to which he belonged, but he insisted upon going into a coach used by the race to which he did not belong. Neither in the information nor plea was his particular race or color averred.

The petition for the writ of prohibition averred that petitioner was seven-eights Caucasian and one-eighth African blood; that the mixture of colored blood was not discernible in him; and that he was entitled to every right, privilege, and immunity secured to citizens of the United States of the white race; and that, upon such theory, he took possession of a vacant seat in a coach where passengers of the white race were accommodated, and was ordered by the conductor to vacate said coach, and take a seat in another, assigned to persons of the colored race, and, having refused to comply with such demand, he was forcibly ejected, with the aid of a police officer, and imprisoned in the parish jail to answer a charge of having violated the above act.

The constitutionality of this act is attacked upon the ground that it conflicts both with the thirteenth amendment of the constitution, abolishing slavery, and the fourteenth amendment, which prohibits certain restrictive legislation on the part of the states.

1. That it does not conflict with the thirteenth amendment, which abolished slavery and involuntary servitude, except a punishment for crime, is too clear for argument. Slavery implies involuntary servitude,-a state of bondage; the ownership of mankind as a chattel, or, at least, the control of the labor and services of one man for the benefit of another, and the absence of a legal right to the disposal of his own person, property, and services. This amendment was said in the Slaughter-House Cases, 16 Wall. 36, to have been intended primarily to abolish slavery, as it had been previously known in this country, and that it equally forbade Mexican peonage or the Chinese coolie trade, when they amounted to slavery or involuntary servitude, and that the use of the word "servitude" was intended to prohibit the use of all

104

forms of involuntary slavery, of whatever class or name. It was intimated, however, in that case, that this amendment was regarded by the statesmen of that day as insufficient to protect the colored race from certain laws which had been enacted in the Southern states, imposing upon the colored race onerous disabilities and burdens, and curtailing their rights in the pursuit of life, liberty, and property to such an extent that their freedom was of little value; and that the fourteenth amendment was devised to meet this exigency.

So, too, in the Civil Rights Cases, 109 U.S. 3 , 3 Sup. Ct. 18, it was said that the act of a mere individual, the owner of an inn, a public conveyance or place of amusement, refusing accommodations to colored people, cannot be justly regarded as imposing any badge of slavery or servitude upon the applicant, but only as involving an ordinary civil injury, properly cognizable by the laws of the state, and presumably subject to redress by those laws until the contrary appears. "It would be running the slavery question into the ground," said Mr. Justice Bradley, "to make it apply to every act of discrimination which a person may see fit to make as to the guests he will entertain, or as to the people he will take into his coach or cab or car, or admit to his concert or theater, or deal with in other matters of intercourse or business."

A statute which implies merely a legal distinction between the white and colored races-a distinction which is founded in the color of the two races, and which must always exist so long as white men are distinguished from the other race by color-has no tendency to destroy the legal equality of the two races, or re-establish a state of involuntary servitude. Indeed, we do not understand that the thirteenth amendment is strenuously relied upon by the plaintiff in error in this connection.

2. By the fourteenth amendment, all persons born or naturalized in the United States, and subject to the jurisdiction thereof, are made citizens of the United States and of the state wherein they reside; and the states are forbidden from making or enforcing any law which shall abridge the privileges or immunities of citizens of the United States, or shall deprive any person of life,

liberty, or property without due process of law, or deny to any person within their jurisdiction the equal protection of the laws.

The proper construction of this amendment was first called to the attention of this court in the Slaughter-House Cases, 16 Wall. 36, which involved, however, not a question of race, but one of exclusive privileges. The case did not call for any expression of opinion as to the exact rights it was intended to secure to the colored race, but it was said generally that its main purpose was to establish the citizenship of the negro, to give definitions of citizenship of the United States and of the states, and to protect from the hostile legislation of the states the privileges and immunities of citizens of the United States, as distinguished from those of citizens of the states. The object of the amendment was undoubtedly to enforce the absolute equality of the two races before the law, but, in the nature of things, it could not have been intended to abolish distinctions based upon color, or to enforce social, as distinguished from political, equality, or a commingling of the two races upon terms unsatisfactory to either. Laws permitting, and even requiring, their separation, in places where they are liable to be brought into contact, do not necessarily imply the inferiority of either race to the other, and have been generally, if not universally, recognized as within the competency of the state legislatures in the exercise of their police power. The most common instance of this is connected with the establishment of separate schools for white and colored children, which have been held to be a valid exercise of the legislative power even by courts of states where the political rights of the colored race have been longest and most earnestly enforced.

One of the earliest of these cases is that of Roberts v. City of Boston, 5 Cush. 198, in which the supreme judicial court of Massachusetts held that the general school committee of Boston had power to make provision for the instruction of colored children in separate schools established exclusively for them, and to prohibit their attendance upon the other schools. "The great principle," said Chief Justice Shaw, "advanced by the learned and eloquent advocate for the plaintiff [Mr. Charles Sumner], is that, by the constitution and laws of Massachusetts, all persons, without distinction of age or sex, birth or color, origin or condition, are equal before the law. ... But, when this great principle comes to be applied to the actual and various conditions of persons in society, it will not warrant the assertion that men and women are legally clothed with the same civil and political powers, and that children and adults are legally to have the same functions and be subject to the same treatment; but only that the rights of all, as they are settled and regulated by law, are equally entitled to the paternal consideration and protection of the law for their maintenance and security." It was held that the powers of the committee extended to the establishment of separate schools for children of different ages, sexes and colors, and that they might also establish special schools for poor and neglected children, who have become too old to attend the primary school, and yet have not acquired the rudiments of learning, to enable them to enter the ordinary schools. Similar laws have been enacted by congress under its general power of legislation over the District of Columbia (sections 281- 283, 310, 319, Rev. St. D. C.), as well as by the legislatures of many of the states, and have been generally, if not uniformly, sustained by the courts. State v. McCann, 21 Ohio St. 210; Lehew v. Brummell (Mo. Sup.) 15 S. W. 765; Ward v. Flood, 48 Cal. 36; Bertonneau v. Directors of City Schools, 3 Woods, 177, Fed. Cas. No. 1,361; People v. Gallagher, 93 N. Y. 438; Cory v. Carter, 48 Ind. 337; Dawson v. Lee, 83 Ky. 49.

Laws forbidding the intermarriage of the two races may be said in a technical sense to interfere with the freedom of contract, and yet have been universally recognized as within the police power of the state. State v. Gibson, 36 Ind. 389.

The distinction between laws interfering with the political equality of the negro and those requiring the separation of the two races in schools, theaters, and railway carriages has been frequently drawn by this court. Thus, in Strauder v. West Virginia, 100 U.S. 303 , it was held that a law of West Virginia limiting to white male persons 21 years of age, and citizens of the state, the right to sit upon juries, was a discrimination which implied a legal inferiority in civil society, which lessened the security of the right of the colored race, and was a step towards reducing them to a condition of servility. Indeed, the right of a colored man that, in the selection of jurors to pass upon his life, liberty, and property, there shall be no exclusion of his race, and no discrimination against them because of color, has been asserted in a number of cases. Virginia v. Rivers, 100 U.S. 313 ; Neal v. Delaware, 103 U.S. 370 ; ush v. Com., 107 U.S. 110 , 1 Sup. Ct. 625; Gibson v. Mississippi, 162 U.S. 565 , 16 Sup. Ct. 904. So, where the laws of a particular locality or the charter of a particular railway corporation has provided that no person shall be excluded from the cars on account of color, we have held that this meant that persons of color should travel in the same car as white ones, and that the enactment was not satisfied by the company providing cars assigned exclusively to people of color, though they were as good as those which they assigned exclusively to white persons. Railroad Co. v. Brown, 17 Wall. 445.

Upon the other hand, where a statute of Louisiana required those engaged in the transportation of passengers among the states to give to all persons traveling within that state, upon vessels employed in that business, equal rights and privileges in all parts of the vessel, without distinction on account of race or color, and subjected to an action for damages the owner of such a vessel who excluded colored passengers on account of their color from the cabin set aside by him for the use of whites, it was held to be, so far as it applied to interstate commerce, unconstitutional and void. Hall v. De Cuir, 95 U.S. 485 . The court in this case, however, expressly disclaimed that it had anything whatever to do with the statute as a regulation of internal commerce, or affecting anything else than commerce among the states.

In the Civil Rights Cases, 109 U.S. 3 , 3 Sup. Ct. 18, it was held that an act of congress entitling all persons within the jurisdiction of the United States to the full and equal enjoyment of the accommodations, advantages, facilities, and privileges of inns, public conveyances, on land or water, theaters, and other places of public amusement, and made applicable to citizens of every race and color, regardless of any previous condition of servitude, was unconstitutional and void, upon the ground that the fourteenth amendment was prohibitory upon the states only, and the legislation authorized to be adopted by congress for enforcing it was not direct legislation on matters respecting which the states were prohibited from making or enforcing certain laws, or doing certain acts, but was corrective legislation, such as might be necessary or proper for counter-acting and redressing the effect of such laws or acts. In delivering the opinion of the court, Mr. Justice Bradley observed that the fourteenth amendment "does not invest congress with power to legislate upon subjects that are within the domain of state legislation, but to provide modes of relief against state legislation or state action of the kind referred to. It does not authorize congress to create a code of municipal law for the regulation of private rights, but to provide modes of redress against the operation of state laws, and the action of state officers, executive or judicial, when these are subversive of the fundamental rights specified in the amendment. Positive rights and privileges are undoubtedly secured by the fourteenth amendment; but they are secured by way of prohibition against state laws and state proceedings affecting those rights and privileges, and by power given to congress to legislate for the purpose of carrying such prohibition into effect; and such legislation must necessarily be predicated upon such supposed state laws or state proceedings, and be directed to the correction of their operation and effect."

Much nearer, and, indeed, almost directly in point, is the case of the Louisville, N. O. & T. Ry. Co. v. State, 133 U.S. 587 , 10 Sup. Ct. 348, wherein the railway company was indicted for a violation of a statute of Mississippi, enacting that all railroads carrying passengers should provide equal, but separate, accommodations for the white and colored races, by providing two or more passenger cars for each passenger train, or by dividing the passenger cars by a partition, so as to secure separate accommodations. The case was presented in a different aspect from the one under consideration, inasmuch as it was an indictment against the railway company for failing to provide the separate accommodations, but the question considered was the constitutionality of the law. In that case, the supreme court of Mississippi (66 Miss. 662, 6 South. 203) had held that the statute applied solely to commerce within the state, and, that being the construction of the state statute by its highest court, was accepted as conclusive. "If it be a matter," said the court (page 591, 133 U. S., and page 348, 10 Sup. Ct.), "respecting commerce wholly within a state, and not interfering with commerce between the states, then, obviously, there is no violation of the commerce clause of the federal constitution. ... No question arises under this section as to the power of the state to separate in different compartments interstate passengers, or affect, in any manner, the privileges and rights of such passengers. All that we can consider is whether the state has the power to require that railroad trains within her limits shall have separate accommodations for the two races. That affecting only commerce within the state is no invasion of the power given to congress by the commerce clause."

A like course of reasoning applies to the case under consideration, since the supreme court of Louisiana, in the case of State v. Judge, 44 La. Ann. 770, 11 South. 74, held that the statute in question did not apply to interstate passengers, but was confined in its application to passengers traveling exclusively within the borders of the state. The case was decided largely upon the authority of Louisville, N. O. & T. Ry. Co. v. State, 66 Miss. 662, 6 South, 203, and affirmed by this court in 133 U.S. 587 , 10 Sup. Ct. 348. In the present case no question of interference with interstate commerce can possibly arise, since the East Louisiana Railway appears to have been purely a local line, with both its termini within the state of Louisiana. Similar statutes for the separation of the two races upon public conveyances were held to be constitutional in Railroad v. Miles, 55 Pa. St. 209; Day v. Owen 5 Mich. 520; Railway Co. v. Williams, 55 Ill. 185; Railroad Co. v. Wells, 85 Tenn. 613; 4 S. W. 5; Railroad Co. v. Benson, 85 Tenn. 627, 4 S. W. 5; The Sue, 22 Fed. 843; Logwood v. Railroad Co., 23 Fed. 318; McGuinn v. Forbes, 37 Fed. 639; People v. King (N. Y. App.) 18 N. E. 245; Houck v. Railway Co., 38 Fed. 226; Heard v. Railroad Co., 3 Inter St. Commerce Com. R. 111, 1 Inter St. Commerce Com. R. 428.

While we think the enforced separation of the races, as applied to the internal commerce of the state, neither abridges the privileges or immunities of the colored man, deprives him of his property

110

without due process of law, nor denies him the equal protection of the laws, within the meaning of the fourteenth amendment, we are not prepared to say that the conductor, in assigning passengers to the coaches according to their race, does not act at his peril, or that the provision of the second section of the act that denies to the passenger compensation in damages for a refusal to receive him into the coach in which he properly belongs is a valid exercise of the legislative power. Indeed, we understand it to be conceded by the state's attorney that such part of the act as exempts from liability the railway company and its officers is unconstitutional. The power to assign to a particular coach obviously implies the power to determine to which race the passenger belongs, as well as the power to determine who, under the laws of the particular state, is to be deemed a white, and who a colored, person. This question, though indicated in the brief of the plaintiff in error, does not properly arise upon the record in this case, since the only issue made is as to the unconstitutionality of the act, so far as it requires the railway to provide separate accommodations, and the conductor to assign passengers according to their race.

It is claimed by the plaintiff in error that, in an mixed community, the reputation of belonging to the dominant race, in this instance the white race, is "property," in the same sense that a right of action or of inheritance is property. Conceding this to be so, for the purposes of this case, we are unable to see how this statute deprives him of, or in any way affects his right to, such property. If he be a white man, and assigned to a colored coach, he may have his action for damages against the company for being deprived of his so-called "property." Upon the other hand, if he be a colored man, and be so assigned, he has been deprived of no property, since he is not lawfully entitled to the reputation of being a white man.

In this connection, it is also suggested by the learned counsel for the plaintiff in error that the same argument that will justify the state legislature in requiring railways to provide separate accommodations for the two races will also authorize them to require separate cars to be provided for people whose hair is of a certain color, or who are aliens, or who belong to certain nationalities, or to enact laws requiring colored people to walk upon one side of the street, and white people upon the other, or requiring white men's houses to be painted white, and colored men's black, or their vehicles or business signs to be of different colors, upon the theory that one side of the street is as good as the other, or that a house or vehicle of one color is as good as one of another color. The reply to all this is that every exercise of the police power must be reasonable, and extend only to such laws as are enacted in good faith for the promotion of the public good, and not for the annoyance or oppression of a particular class. Thus, in Yick Wo v. Hopkins, 118 U.S. 356 , 6 Sup. Ct. 1064, it was held by this court that a municipal ordinance of the city of San Francisco, to regulate the carrying on of public laundries within the limits of the municipality, violated the provisions of the constitution of the United States, if it conferred upon the municipal authorities arbitrary power, at their own will, and without regard to discretion, in the legal sense of the term, to give or withhold consent as to persons or places, without regard to the competency of the persons applying or the propriety of the places selected for the carrying on of the business. It was held to be a covert attempt on the part of the municipality to make an arbitrary and unjust discrimination against the Chinese race. While this was the case of a municipal ordinance, a like principle has been held to apply to acts of a state legislature passed in the exercise of the police power. Railroad Co. v. Husen, 95 U.S. 465 ; Louisville & N. R. Co. v. Kentucky, 161 U.S. 677 , 16 Sup. Ct. 714, and cases cited on page 700, 161 U. S., and page 714, 16 Sup. Ct.; Daggett v. Hudson, 43 Ohio St. 548, 3 N. E. 538; Capen v. Foster, 12 Pick. 485; State v. Baker, 38 Wis. 71; Monroe v. Collins, 17 Ohio St. 665; Hulseman v. Rems, 41 Pa. St. 396; Osman v. Riley, 15 Cal. 48.

So far, then, as a conflict with the fourteenth amendment is concerned, the case reduces itself to the question whether the statute of Louisiana is a reasonable regulation, and with respect to this there must necessarily be a large discretion on the part of the legislature. In determining the question of reasonableness, it is at liberty to act with reference to the established usages, customs, and traditions of the people, and with a view to the promotion of their comfort, and the preservation of the public peace and good order. Gauged by this standard, we cannot say that a law which authorizes or even requires the separation of the two races in public conveyances is unreasonable, or more obnoxious to the fourteenth amendment than the acts of congress requiring separate schools for colored children in the District of Columbia, the constitutionality of which does not seem to have been questioned, or the corresponding acts of state legislatures.

We consider the underlying fallacy of the plaintiff's argument to consist in the assumption that the enforced separation of the two races stamps the colored race with a badge of inferiority. If this be so, it is not by reason of anything found in the act, but solely because the colored race chooses to put that construction upon it. The argument necessarily assumes that if, as has been more than once the case, and is not unlikely to be so again, the colored race should become the dominant power in the state legislature, and should enact a law in precisely similar terms, it would thereby relegate the white race to an inferior position. We imagine that the white race, at least, would not acquiesce in this assumption. The argument also assumes that social prejudices may be overcome by legislation, and that equal rights cannot be secured to the negro except by an enforced commingling of the two races. We cannot accept this proposition. If the two races are to meet upon terms of social equality, it must be the result of natural affinities, a mutual appreciation of each other's merits, and a voluntary consent of individuals. As was said by the court of appeals of New York in People v. Gallagher, 93 N. Y. 438, 448: "This end can neither be accomplished nor promoted by laws which conflict with the general sentiment of the community upon whom they are designed to operate. When the government, therefore, has secured to each of its citizens equal rights before the law, and equal opportunities for improvement and progress, it has accomplished the end for which it was organized, and performed all of the functions respecting social advantages with which it is endowed." Legislation is powerless to eradicate racial instincts, or to abolish distinctions based upon physical differences, and the attempt to do so can only result in accentuating the difficulties of the present situation. If the civil and political rights of both races be equal, one cannot be inferior to the other civilly or politically. If one race be inferior to the other socially, the constitution of the United States cannot put them upon the same plane.

It is true that the question of the proportion of colored blood necessary to constitute a colored person, as distinguished from a white person, is one upon which there is a difference of opinion in the different states; some holding that any visible admixture of black blood stamps the person as belonging to the colored race (State v. Chavers, 5 Jones [N. C.] 1); others, that it depends upon the preponderance of blood (Gray v. State, 4 Ohio, 354; Monroe v. Collins, 17 Ohio St. 665); and still others, that the predominance of white blood must only be in the proportion of three-fourths (People v. Dean, 14 Mich. 406; Jones v. Com., 80 Va. 544). But these are questions to be determined under the laws of each state, and are not properly put in issue in this case. Under the allegations of his petition, it may undoubtedly become a question of importance whether, under the laws of Louisiana, the petitioner belongs to the white or colored race.

The judgment of the court below is therefore affirmed.

Mr. Justice BREWER did not hear the argument or participate in the decision of this case.

Mr. Justice HARLAN dissenting.

By the Louisiana statute the validity of which is here involved, all railway companies (other than street-railroad companies) carry passengers in that state are required to have separate but equal accommodations for white and colored persons, "by providing two or more passenger coaches for each passenger train, or by dividing the passenger coaches by a partition so as to secure separate accommodations." Under this statute, no colored person is permitted to occupy a seat in a coach assigned to white persons; nor any white person to occupy a seat in a coach assigned to colored persons. The managers of the railroad are not allowed to exercise any discretion in the premises, but are required to assign each passenger to some coach or compartment set apart for the exclusive use of is race. If a passenger insists upon going into a coach or compartment not set apart for persons of his race, he is subject to be fined, or to be imprisoned in the parish jail. Penalties are prescribed for the refusal or neglect of the officers, directors, conductors, and employees of railroad companies to comply with the provisions of the act.

Only "nurses attending children of the other race" are excepted from the operation of the statute. No exception is made of colored attendants traveling with adults. A white man is not permitted to have his colored servant with him in the same coach, even if his condition of health requires the constant personal assistance of such servant. If a colored maid insists upon riding in the same coach with a white woman whom she has been employed to serve, and who may need her personal attention while traveling, she is subject to be fined or imprisoned for such an exhibition of zeal in the discharge of duty.

While there may be in Louisiana persons of different races who are not citizens of the United States, the words in the act "white and colored races" necessarily include all citizens of the United States of both races residing in that state. So that we have before us a state enactment that compels, under penalties, the separation of the two races in railroad passenger coaches, and makes it a crime for a citizen of either race to enter a coach that has been assigned to citizens of the other race.

Thus, the state regulates the use of a public highway by citizens of the United States solely upon the basis of race.

However apparent the injustice of such legislation may be, we have only to consider whether it is consistent with the constitution of the United States.

That a railroad is a public highway, and that the corporation which owns or operates it is in the exercise of public functions, is not, at this day, to be disputed. Mr. Justice Nelson, speaking for this court in New Jersey Steam Nav. Co. v. Merchants" Bank, 6 How. 344, 382, said that a common carrier was in the exercise "of a sort of public office, and has public duties to perform, from which he should not be permitted to exonerate himself without the assent of the parties concerned." Mr. Justice

Strong, delivering the judgment of this court in Olcott v. Supervisors, 16 Wall. 678, 694, said: "Those railroads, though constructed by private corporations, and owned by them, are public highways, has been the doctrine of nearly all the courts ever since such conveniences for passage and transportation have had any existence. Very early the question arose whether a state"s right of eminent domain could be exercised by a private corporation created for the purpose of constructing a railroad. Clearly, it could not, unless taking land for such a purpose by such an agency is taking land for public use. The right of eminent domain nowhere justifies taking property for a private use. Yet it is a doctrine universally accepted that a state legislature may authorize a private corporation to take land for the construction of such a road, making compensation to the owner. What else does this doctrine mean if not that building a railroad, though it be built by a private corporation, is an act done for a public use?" So, in Township of Pine Grove v. Talcott, 19 Wall. 666, 676: "Though the corporation [a railroad company] was private, its work was public, as much so as if it were to be constructed by the state." So, in Inhabitants of Worcester v. Western R. Corp., 4 Metc. (Mass.) 564: "The establishment of that great thoroughfare is regarded as a public work, established by public authority, intended for the public use and benefit, the use of which is secured to the whole community, and constitutes, therefore, like a canal, turnpike, or highway, a public easement." "It is true that the real and personal property, necessary to the establishment and management of the railroad, is vested in the corporation; but it is in trust for the public."

In respect of civil rights, common to all citizens, the constitution of the United States does not, I think, permit any public authority to know the race of those entitled to be protected in the enjoyment of such rights. Every true man has pride of race, and under appropriate circumstances, when the rights of others, his equals before the law, are not to be affected, it is his privilege to express such pride and to take such action based upon it as to him seems proper. But I deny that any legislative body or judicial tribunal may have regard to the race of citizens when the civil rights of those citizens are involved. Indeed, such

116

legislation as that here in question is inconsistent not only with that equality of rights which pertains to citizenship, national and state, but with the personal liberty enjoyed by every one within the United States.

The thirteenth amendment does not permit the withholding or the deprivation of any right necessarily inhering in freedom. It not only struck down the institution of slavery as previously existing in the United States, but it prevents the imposition of any burdens or disabilities that constitute badges of slavery or servitude. It decreed universal civil freedom in this country. This court has so adjudged. But, that amendment having been found inadequate to the protection of the rights of those who had been in slavery, it was followed by the fourteenth amendment, which added greatly to the dignity and glory of American citizenship, and to the security of personal liberty, by declaring that "all persons born or naturalized in the United States, and subject to the jurisdiction thereof, are citizens of the United States and of the state wherein they reside," and that "no state shall make or enforce any law which shall abridge the privileges or immunities of citizens of the United States; nor shall any state deprive any person of life, liberty or property without due process of law, nor deny to any person within its jurisdiction the equal protection of the laws." These two amendments, if enforced according to their true intent and meaning, will protect all the civil rights that pertain to freedom and citizenship. Finally, and to the end that no citizen should be denied, on account of his race, the privilege of participating in the political control of his country, it was declared by the fifteenth amendment that "the right of citizens of the United States to vote shall not be denied or abridged by the United States or by any state on account of race, color or previous condition of servitude."

These notable additions to the fundamental law were welcomed by the friends of liberty throughout the world. They removed the race line from our governmental systems. They had, as this court has said, a common purpose, namely, to secure "to a race recently emancipated, a race that through many generations have been held in slavery, all the civil rights that the superior race enjoy." They declared, in legal effect, this court has further said, "that the law in the states shall be the same for the black as for the white; that all persons, whether colored or white, shall stand equal before the laws of the states; and in regard to the colored race, for whose protection the amendment was primarily designed, that no discrimination shall be made against them by law because of their color." We also said: "The words of the amendment, it is true, are prohibitory, but they contain a necessary implication of a positive immunity or right, most valuable to the colored race,-the right to exemption from unfriendly legislation against them distinctively as colored; exemption from legal discriminations, implying inferiority in civil society, lessening the security of their enjoyment of the rights which others enjoy; and discriminations which are steps towards reducing them to the condition of a subject race." It was, consequently, adjudged that a state law that excluded citizens of the colored race from juries, because of their race, however well qualified in other respects to discharge the duties of jurymen, was repugnant to the fourteenth amendment. Strauder v. West Virginia, 100 U.S. 303, 306 , 307 S.; Virginia v. Rives, Id. 313; Ex parte Virginia, Id. 339; Neal v. Delaware, 103 U.S. 370 , 386; Bush v. Com., 107 U.S. 110, 116 , 1 S. Sup. Ct. 625. At the present term, referring to the previous adjudications, this court declared that "underlying all of those decisions is the principle that the constitution of the United States, in its present form, forbids, so far as civil and political rights are concerned, discrimination by the general government or the states against any citizen because of his race. All citizens are equal before the law." Gibson v. State, 162 U.S. 565 , 16 Sup. Ct. 904.

The decisions referred to show the scope of the recent amendments of the constitution. They also show that it is not within the power of a state to prohibit colored citizens, because of their race, from participating as jurors in the administration of justice.

It was said in argument that the statute of Louisiana does not discriminate against either race, but prescribes a rule applicable alike to white and colored citizens. But this argument does not meet the difficulty. Every one knows that the statute in question had its origin in the purpose, not so much to exclude white persons from railroad cars occupied by blacks, as to exclude colored people from coaches occupied by or assigned to white persons. Railroad corporations of Louisiana did not make discrimination among whites in the matter of commodation for travelers. The thing to accomplish was, under the guise of giving equal accommodation for whites and blacks, to compel the latter to keep to themselves while traveling in railroad passenger coaches. No one would be so wanting in candor as to assert the contrary. The fundamental objection, therefore, to the statute, is that it interferes with the personal freedom of citizens. "Personal liberty," it has been well said, "consists in the power of locomotion, of changing situation, or removing one's person to whatsoever places one's own inclination may direct, without imprisonment or restraint, unless by due course of law." 1 Bl. Comm. *134. If a white man and a black man choose to occupy the same public conveyance on a public highway, it is their right to do so; and no government, proceeding alone on grounds of race, can prevent it without infringing the personal liberty of each.

It is one thing for railroad carriers to furnish, or to be required by law to furnish, equal accommodations for all whom they are under a legal duty to carry. It is quite another thing for government to forbid citizens of the white and black races from traveling in the same public conveyance, and to punish officers of railroad companies for permitting persons of the two races to occupy the same passenger coach. If a state can prescribe, as a rule of civil conduct, that whites and blacks shall not travel as passengers in the same railroad coach, why may it not so regulate the use of the streets of its cities and towns as to compel white citizens to keep on one side of a street, and black citizens to keep on the other? Why may it not, upon like grounds, punish whites and blacks who ride together in street cars or in open vehicles on a public road or street? Why may it not require sheriffs to assign whites to one side of a court room, and blacks to the other? And why may it not also prohibit the commingling of the two races in the galleries of legislative halls or in public assemblages convened for the consideration of the political questions of the day? Further, if this statute of Louisiana is consistent with the personal liberty of citizens, why may not the state require the separation in railroad coaches of native and naturalized citizens of the United States, or of Protestants and Roman Catholics?

The answer given at the argument to these questions was that regulations of the kind they suggest would be unreasonable, and could not, therefore, stand before the law. Is it meant that the determination of questions of legislative power depends upon the inquiry whether the statute whose validity is questioned is, in the judgment of the courts, a reasonable one, taking all the circumstances into consideration? A statute may be unreasonable merely because a sound public policy forbade its enactment. But I do not understand that the courts have anything to do with the policy or expediency of legislation. A statute may be valid, and yet, upon grounds of public policy, may well be characterized as unreasonable. Mr. Sedgwick correctly states the rule when he says that, the legislative intention being clearly ascertained, "the courts have no other duty to perform than to execute the legislative will, without any regard to their views as to the wisdom or justice of the particular enactment." Sedg. St. & Const. Law, 324. There is a dangerous tendency in these latter days to enlarge the functions of the courts, by means of judicial interference with the will of the people as expressed by the legislature. Our institutions have the distinguishing characteristic that the three departments of government are co-ordinate and separate. Each must keep within the limits defined by the constitution. And the courts best discharge their duty by executing the will of the law-making power, constitutionally expressed, leaving the results of legislation to be dealt with by the people through their representatives. Statutes must always have a reasonable construction. Sometimes they are to be construed strictly, sometimes literally, in order to carry out the legislative will. But, however construed, the intent of the legislature is to be respected if the particular statute in question is valid, although the courts, looking at the public interests, may conceive the statute to be both unreasonable and impolitic. If the power exists to enact a statute, that ends the matter so far as the courts are concerned. The adjudged cases in which statutes have been held to be void, because unreasonable, are those in which the means employed by the legislature were not at all germane to the end to which the legislature was competent.

The white race deems itself to be the dominant race in this country. And so it is, in prestige, in achievements, in education, in wealth, and in power. So, I doubt not, it will continue to be for all time, if it remains true to its great heritage, and holds fast to the principles of constitutional liberty. But in view of the constitution, in the eye of the law, there is in this country no superior, dominant, ruling class of citizens. There is no caste here. Our constitution is color-blind, and neither knows nor tolerates classes among citizens. In respect of civil rights, all citizens are equal before the law. The humblest is the peer of the most powerful. The law regards man as man, and takes no account of his surroundings or of his color when his civil rights as guarantied by the supreme law of the land are involved. It is therefore to be regretted that this high tribunal, the final expositor of the fundamental law of the land, has reached the conclusion that it is competent for a state to regulate the enjoyment by citizens of their civil rights solely upon the basis of race.

In my opinion, the judgment this day rendered will, in time, prove to be quite as pernicious as the decision made by this tribunal in the Dred Scott Case.

It was adjudged in that case that the descendants of Africans who were imported into this country, and sold as slaves, were not included nor intended to be included under the word "citizens" in the constitution, and could not claim any of the rights and privileges which that instrument provided for and secured to citizens of the United States; that, at time of the adoption of the constitution, they were "considered as a subordinate and inferior class of beings, who had been subjugated by the dominant race, and, whether emancipated or not, yet remained subject to their authority, and had no rights or privileges but such as those who held the power and the government might choose to grant them." 17 How. 393, 404. The recent amendments of the constitution, it was supposed, had eradicated these principles from our institutions. But it seems that we have yet, in some of the states, a dominant race, a superior class of citizens, which assumes to regulate the enjoyment of civil rights, common to all citizens, upon the basis of race. The present decision, it may well be apprehended, will not only stimulate aggressions, more or less brutal and irritating, upon the admitted rights of colored citizens, but will encourage the belief that it is possible, by means of state enactments, to defeat the beneficent purposes which the people of the United States had in view when they adopted the recent amendments of the constitution, by one of which the blacks of this country were made citizens of the United States and of the states in which they respectively reside, and whose privileges and immunities, as citizens, the states are forbidden to abridge. Sixty millions of whites are in no danger from the presence here of eight millions of blacks. The destinies of the two races, in this country, are indissolubly linked together, and the interests of both require that the common government of all shall not permit the seeds of race hate to be planted under the sanction of law. What can more certainly arouse race hate, what more certainly create and perpetuate a feeling of distrust between these races, than state enactments which, in fact, proceed on the ground that colored citizens are so inferior and degraded that they cannot be allowed to sit in public coaches occupied by white citizens? That, as all will admit, is the real meaning of such legislation as was enacted in Louisiana.

The sure guaranty of the peace and security of each race is the clear, distinct, unconditional recognition by our governments, national and state, of every right that inheres in civil freedom, and of the equality before the law of all citizens of the United States, without regard to race. State enactments regulating the enjoyment of civil rights upon the basis of race, and cunningly devised to defeat legitimate results of the war, under the pretense of recognizing equality of rights, can have no other result than to render permanent peace impossible, and to keep alive a conflict of races, the continuance of which must do harm to all concerned. This question is not met by the suggestion that social equality cannot exist between the white and black races in this country. That argument, if it can be properly regarded as one, is scarcely worthy of consideration; for social equality no more exists between two races when traveling in a passenger coach or a public highway than when members of the same races sit by each other in a street car or in the jury box, or stand or sit with each other in a political assembly, or when they use in common the streets of a city or town, or when they are in the same room for the purpose of having their names placed on the registry of voters, or when they approach the ballot box in order to exercise the high privilege of voting.

There is a race so different from our own that we do not permit those belonging to it to become citizens of the United States. Persons belonging to it are, with few exceptions, absolutely excluded from our country. I allude to the Chinese race. But, by the statute in question, a Chinaman can ride in the same passenger coach with white citizens of the United States, while citizens of the black race in Louisiana, many of whom, perhaps, risked their lives for the preservation of the Union, who are entitled, by law, to participate in the political control of the state and nation, who are not excluded, by law or by reason of their race, from public stations of any kind, and who have all the legal rights that belong to white citizens, are yet declared to be criminals, liable to imprisonment, if they ride in a public coach occupied by citizens of the white race. It is scarcely just to say that a colored citizen should not object to occupying a public coach assigned to his own race. He does not object, nor, perhaps, would he object to separate coaches for his race if his rights under the law were recognized. But he does object, and he ought never to cease objecting, that citizens of the white and black races can be adjudged criminals because they sit, or claim the right to sit, in the same public coach on a public highway. The arbitrary separation of citizens, on the basis of race, while they are on a public highway, is a badge of servitude wholly inconsistent with the civil freedom and the equality before the law established by the constitution. It cannot be justified upon any legal grounds.

If evils will result from the commingling of the two races upon public highways established for the benefit of all, they will be infinitely less than those that will surely come from state legislation regulating the enjoyment of civil rights upon the basis of race. We boast of the freedom enjoyed by our people above all other peoples. But it is difficult to reconcile that boast with a state of the law which, practically, puts the brand of servitude and degradation upon a large class of our fellow citizens, our equals before the law. The thin disguise of "equal" accommodations for passengers in railroad coaches will not mislead anyone, nor atone for the wrong this day done.

The result of the whole matter is that while this court has frequently adjudged, and at the present term has recognized the doctrine, that a state cannot, consistently with the constitution of the United States, prevent white and black citizens, having the required qualifications for jury service, from sitting in the same jury box, it is now solemnly held that a state may prohibit white and black citizens from sitting in the same passenger coach on a public highway, or may require that they be separated by a "partition" when in the same passenger coach. May it not now be reasonably expected that astute men of the dominant race, who affect to be disturbed at the possibility that the integrity of the white race may be corrupted, or that its supremacy will be imperiled, by contact on public highways with black people, will endeavor to procure statutes requiring white and black jurors to be separated in the jury box by a "partition," and that, upon retiring from the court room to consult as to their verdict, such partition, if it be a movable one, shall be taken to their consultation room, and set up in such way as to prevent black jurors from coming too close to their brother jurors of the white race. If the "partition" used in the court room happens to be stationary, provision could be made for screens with openings through which jurors of the two races could confer as to their verdict without coming into personal contact with each other. I cannot see but that, according to the principles this day announced, such state legislation, although conceived in hostility to, and enacted for the purpose of humiliating, citizens of the United States of a particular race, would be held to be consistent with the constitution.

I do not deem it necessary to review the decisions of state courts to which reference was made in argument. Some, and the most important, of them, are wholly inapplicable, because they were rendered prior to the adoption of the last amendments of the constitution, when colored people had very few rights which the dominant race felt obliged to respect. Others were made at a time when public opinion, in many localities, was dominated by the institution of slavery; when it would not have been safe to do justice to the black man; and when, so far as the rights of blacks were concerned, race prejudice was, practically, the supreme law of the land. Those decisions cannot be guides in the era introduced by the recent amendments of the supreme law, which established universal civil freedom, gave citizenship to all born or naturalized in the United States, and residing ere, obliterated the race line from our systems of governments, national and state, and placed our free institutions upon the broad and sure foundation of the equality of all men before the law.

I am of the opinion that the state of Louisiana is inconsistent with the personal liberty of citizens, white and black, in that state, and hostile to both the spirit and letter of the constitution of the United States. If laws of like character should be enacted in the several states of the Union, the effect would be in the highest degree mischievous. Slavery, as an institution tolerated by law, would, it is true, have disappeared from our country; but there would remain a power in the states, by sinister legislation, to interfere with the full enjoyment of the blessings of freedom, to regulate civil rights, common to all citizens, upon the basis of race, and to place in a condition of legal inferiority a large body of American citizens, now constituting a part of the political community, called the "People of the United States," for whom, and by whom through representatives, our government is administered. Such a system is inconsistent with the guarantee given by the constitution to each state of a republican form of government, and may be stricken down by congressional action, or by the courts in the discharge of their solemn duty to maintain the supreme law of the land, anything in the constitution or laws of any state to the contrary notwithstanding.

For the reason stated, I am constrained to withhold my assent from the opinion and judgment of the majority.

IN LAYMEN'S TERMS

Plessy v. Ferguson came down to one question: How was the 14th amendment to be construed? The fourteenth amendment itself was both an opportunity and a quandary. Adopted in 1868, it *seemed* to guarantee equal rights for all: "No state shall make or enforce any law which shall abridge the privileges or immunities of citizens of the United States; nor shall any state deprive any person of life, liberty, or property without due process of law; nor deny to any person within its jurisdiction the equal protection of the laws."

The key phrase was "equal protection of the laws." Read broadly, it might mean that hereafter the Constitution would be color-blind: no state law could have the effect of treating whites and blacks differently. Thus a law segregating blacks and whites into separate schools or neighborhoods would be unconstitutional. Read narrowly, "equal protection" might mean only that blacks and whites had certain fundamental legal rights in common, such as the right to sign contracts, serve on juries, or buy and sell property, but otherwise be treated differently.

It has long been debated by historians which view Congress held when it proposed the Fourteenth Amendment. What forms of racial segregation, if any, were still permissible? Segregated trains? Hotels? Schools? Neighborhoods?

The Supreme Court took the narrow view. Though in 1880 it declared unconstitutional a West Virginia law requiring juries to be composed only of white males, it decided in 1883 that it was unconstitutional for Congress to prohibit racial discrimination in public accommodations such as hotels. The difference between the two cases seemed, in the eyes of the Court, to be this: serving on a jury was an essential right of citizenship that the state could not deny to any person on racial grounds without violating the Fourteenth Amendment, but registering at a hotel was a convenience controlled by a private person (the hotel owner), who could treat blacks and whites differently if he or she wished.

In Plessy v. Ferguson the Court held that the Louisiana law treated both races equally even though it required them to be separate. The equal-protection clause guaranteed political, legal but not social equality. "Separate-but-equal" facilities were constitutional because (as stated in the decision of the court): "if one race be inferior to the other socially, the Constitution of the United States cannot put them on the same plane."

SOCIAL & POLITICAL CLIMATE LEADING TO LAW/POLICY

The Supreme Court's decision in Plessy v. Ferguson was but another link (arguably the strongest link) in the ever-growing chain of oppression of African Americans following the Civil War. The shortcomings and failures of Reconstruction give some insight into the attitudes that were present in the U.S. before 1896.

Reconstruction, the time period following the Civil War, lasted from 1865 to 1877. In its broadest sense, this was the period during which the United States began to rebuild after the Civil War. The term also refers to the process the federal government used to readmit the defeated Confederate states to the Union.

Although earlier on African Americans had enjoyed unprecedented freedoms and victories, they began to feel betrayed and unprotected (and with good reason) in the waning years of Reconstruction. This breakdown in securing the rights of former slaves and blacks was total—the executive, judicial and legislative branches of the federal government—all played a role.

The Presidency

Although Lincoln did not live to carry out his plan, before his death he made it clear that he favored a lenient Reconstruction Policy. In December 1863, Lincoln announced his Proclamation of Amnesty and Reconstruction, also known as the Ten-Percent Plan. Under this plan, the government would pardon all Confederates—except high-ranking Confederate officials and those accused of crimes against prisoners of war—who would swear allegiance to the Union and promise to obey its laws. As soon as ten percent of those on the 1860 voting lists took this oath allegiance, a Confederate state could form a new state government. Lincoln intended his Ten-Percent Plan to make the South's return as quick and easy as possible.

Lincoln's moderate Reconstruction plan angered the Radical Republicans in Congress. The Radicals (although a minority in the Republican Party) had been at the forefront in supporting abolition and the war, and they now proposed laws to ensure African-American rights (such as full citizenship and the right to vote). The Radicals wanted to destroy the political power of former slaveholders. In response to Lincoln's Ten-Percent Plan, the Radicals passed the Wade-Davis Bill, which proposed that Congress and not the president, be responsible for Reconstruction. The bill also declared that for a state government to be formed, a majority (not just ten percent) of those eligible to vote in 1860 would have to take a solemn oath to support the Constitution.

Lincoln used a pocket veto to kill the bill after Congress adjourned. The Radicals responded (rather heatedly) calling Lincoln's pocket veto a travesty of justice and asserting that Congress had supreme authority.

John Wilkes Booth's assassination of Lincoln in April 1865 left Lincoln's successor, the former Democrat Andrew Johnson, to deal with the reconstruction controversy. Prior to his assuming the Presidency, Johnson had often expressed his intent to deal harshly with Confederate leaders. Most white Southerners therefore considered Johnson unsympathetic to their region, while Radicals believed that his views were in line with theirs. Both parties would have to greatly modify their perceptions of President Johnson.

In May 1865, with Congress in recess Johnson announced his own plan to reconstruct the seven remaining Confederate states. This plan was called Presidential Reconstruction. He declared that each of these states—Alabama, Florida, Georgia, Mississippi, North Carolina, South Carolina, and Texas—could be readmitted to the Union if it would meet several conditions. Each state would have to declare its secession illegal, swear allegiance to the Union, and ratify the Thirteenth Amendment, which abolished slavery.

The Radicals were especially upset that Johnson's plan, like Lincoln's, failed to address the needs of former slaves in three areas: land, voting rights, and protection under the law. Contrarily, Johnson's polices relieved most white Southerners. Johnson's support of states' rights instead of a strong central government reassured Southern states that they could do as they wished about African-American civil liberties and voting rights. In addition even though Johnson had promised to punish traitors, he pardoned more than 13,000 former Confederates because he believed that "white men alone must manage the South" and thought that former slaves should not gain the right to vote.

The remaining Ex-Confederate States quickly agreed to Johnson's terms. Within a few months, these states—except Texas—held conventions to draw up new state constitutions, set up new state governments, and elect representatives to Congress. However, some Southern states did not fully comply with the conditions for returning to the Union. For example, Mississippi did not ratify the Thirteenth Amendment.

Despite such examples of noncompliance, in December 1865, the newly elected Southern legislators arrived in Washington to take their seats. Fifty-eight of them had previously sat in the Congress of the Confederacy, six had served in the Confederate cabinet and four had fought against the United States as a Confederate general. Johnson pardoned them all—a gesture that incensed the Radicals. So liberal was Johnson in granting pardons that the Radical Republicans accused him of giving the Northern victory away.

Supreme Court Decisions

Although Congress had passed important laws to protect the political and civil rights of African Americans, the Supreme Court began to take away some of those protections. During the 1870's, the Supreme Court issued a series of decisions that undercut the strength of both the Fourteenth and Fifteenth Amendments.

In the **Slaughterhouse** cases of 1873, the Court decided that the Fourteenth Amendment protected only the rights people had by virtue of their citizenship in the **United States**, such as the right to federal protection when traveling on the high seas and abroad. The Court contended that most of American's basic civil rights were obtained through their citizenship in a state and that the amendment did not protect those rights.

In 1883, The United States Supreme Court ruled that the Civil Rights act of 1875, forbidding discrimination in hotels, trains, and other public spaces, was unconstitutional and not authorized by the 13th or 14th Amendments of the Constitution. The ruling read in part:

"The 14th Amendment is prohibitory upon the States only, and the legislation authorized to be adopted by Congress for enforcing it is not direct legislation on the matters respecting which the States are prohibited from making or enforcing certain laws, or doing certain acts, but it is corrective legislation, such as may be necessary or proper for counteracting and redressing the effect of such laws or acts."

"The 13th Amendment relates to slavery and involuntary servitude (which it abolishes); ... yet such legislative power extends only to the subject of slavery and its incidents; and the denial of equal accommodations in inns, public conveyances and places of public amusement (which is forbidden by the sections in question), imposes no badge of slavery or involuntary servitude upon the party, but at most, infringes rights which are protected from State aggression by the 14th Amendment."

The decision outraged the black community and many whites as well, for they felt it opened the door to legalized segregation. Bishop Henry McNeil Turner raged at the court for its decision: "The world has never witnessed such barbarous laws entailed upon a free people as have grown out of the decision of the United States Supreme Court, issued October 15, 1883. For that decision alone authorized and now sustains all the unjust discriminations, proscriptions and robberies perpetrated by public carriers upon millions of the nation's most loyal defenders. It fathers all the 'Jim-Crow cars' into which colored people are huddled and compelled to pay as much as the whites, who are given the finest accommodations. It has made the ballot of the black man a parody, his citizenship a nullity and his freedom a burlesque. It has engendered the bitterest feeling between the whites and blacks, and resulted in the deaths of thousands, who would have been living and enjoying life today." One of the justices on the court, John Harlan, gave a now-famous dissent, writing, "Whereas it is essential to just government we recognize the equality of all men before the law, and hold that it is the duty of government in its dealings with the people to mete out equal and exact justice to all, of whatever nativity, race, color, or persuasion, religious or political; and it being the appropriate object of legislation to enact great fundamental principles into law; I am of opinion that such discrimination is a badge of servitude, the imposition of which congress may prevent under its power, through appropriate legislation, to enforce the thirteenth Amendment; and consequently, without reference to its enlarged power under the fourteenth Amendment, the act of March 1, 1875, is not, in my judgment, repugnant to the constitution." African Americans would have to wait until 1964 before Congress would again pass a civil-rights law, this time constitutionally acceptable, which would forbid discrimination in public accommodations, employment, and unions.

Another blow to African-American civil liberties was delivered by the Supreme Court in **U.S. v. Cruikshank** in 1876. The Court ruled that the Fourteenth Amendment did not give the federal government the right to punish individual whites who oppressed blacks. The same year, in **U.S. v. Reese**, the Court ruled in favor of officials who had barred African Americans from voting, stating that the Fifteenth Amendment did not "confer the right of suffrage on anyone" but merely listed grounds on which states *could not deny* suffrage. By the late 1870's, the Supreme Court's restrictive rulings had narrowed the scope of these amendments that it effectively rendered the federal government powerless to protect the rights of African Americans.

Congressional Duplicity

Although the U.S. Congress was responsible for the passing of the: 13th, 14th and 15th Amendments; The Freedman Bureau Acts (1865-66), Civil Rights Act (1866), Reconstruction Act (1867), Enforcement Act (1870), Civil Rights Act (1875), it would buckle under the pressure of the social, economic and political realities of the 1870's.

As the Supreme Court rejected Reconstruction policies in the 1870's, Northern voters grew indifferent to events in the South. Tired of the "Negro question" many Northern voters shifted their attention to such national concerns as the Panic of 1873 and the corruption of President Ulysses S. Grant's administration. In addition, a desire for reconciliation between the regions spread through the North. Although political violence continued in the South and African Americans were denied civil and political rights, anti-Reconstruction sentiment steadily increased in the North.

As both judicial and public support decreased, Republicans began to back away from their commitment to Reconstruction. The fervent Radicals who piloted the fight for congressional Reconstruction, Charles Sumner and Thaddeus Stevens, were dead. Business interests deflected the attention of both moderates and Radicals, and scalawags (white Southerners, who for the purpose of political advantage joined the Republican Party after the Civil War) and carpetbaggers (northerners who moved to the South after the Civil War) deserted the Republican Party. In time, Republicans began to slowly retreat from the policies of Reconstruction.

Between 1869 and 1875, Democrats recaptured the state governments of Alabama, Arkansas, Georgia, Mississippi, North Carolina, Tennessee, Texas and Virginia. The Southern Democrats called their return to power redemption. However, the virtual abandonment by Congress of Reconstruction policies and the cause of equality for African Americans occurred in 1876.

Both major political parties were influenced by the Grant era corruption and sought to nominate candidates who could win the public trust.

The Democrats turned to Samuel J. Tilden, who had established an enviable record as the reform-minded governor of New York. Tilden was on record as favoring the removal of the remaining federal occupation soldiers from the South, a position regarded favorably by his supporters in that region.

The Republicans passed over the front-runner, James G. Blaine, because of his participation in some questionable dealings. The nomination was eventually given to the respected governor of Ohio, Rutherford B. Hayes. While the platform called for taking steps to assure black equality, Hayes was skeptical at best. Attacks were made on Tilden's questionable health and his ties to the railroads.

Peter Cooper, 85 years of age, received the nomination from the National Greenback Party.

The election results left the nation in suspense. All agreed that Tilden had won the majority of the popular vote, but there was little agreement on what the electoral results should be. In order to win, a candidate needed 185 electoral votes. Tilden controlled 184 votes and Hayes 165; 20 votes, however, were in dispute in South Carolina, Louisiana, and Florida where Reconstruction Republican governments were still in control. (A single elector was challenged in Oregon.)

Each of the states with disputed votes submitted two sets of electoral ballots, one favoring Tilden, the other Hayes. The Constitution had not foreseen this event and offered no remedy. Loose talk was heard in some quarters about the possibility of war breaking out. In the end, Congress opted to appoint an Electoral Commission to find a solution.

An informal agreement between the two parties, sometimes called the "Compromise of 1877," convinced the Democrats that they should accept the Commission's 8-7 vote, which made Hayes the new President.

In the months following the Election of 1876, but prior to the inauguration in March 1877, Republican and Democratic leaders secretly hammered out a compromise to resolve the election impasse and address other outstanding issues.

Under the terms of this agreement, the Democrats agreed to accept the Republican presidential electors (thus assuring that Rutherford B. Hayes would become the next President), provided the Republicans would agree to the following:

- To withdraw federal soldiers from their remaining positions in the South;
- To enact federal legislation that would spur industrialization in the South;
- To appoint Democrats to patronage positions in the South;
- To appoint a Democrat to the president's cabinet.

Once the parties had agreed to these terms, the Electoral Commission performed its duty. The Hayes' electors were selected and Hayes was named President two days before the inauguration.

Why did the Democrats so easily give up the presidency that they had probably legitimately won? In the end it was a matter of practicality. Despite months of inflammatory talk, few responsible people could contemplate going to war. A compromise was mandatory and the one achieved in 1877, if it had been honored, would have given the Democrats what they wanted. There was no guarantee that with Samuel J. Tilden as president the Democrats would have fared as well.

To the four million former slaves in the South (and African Americans as a whole), the Compromise of 1877 was the "Great Betrayal." Republican efforts to assure civil rights for the blacks were totally abandoned. The white population of the country was anxious to get on with making money. No serious move to restore the rights of black citizens would surface again until the 1950's.

AFTERMATH OF LAW/POLICY

Plessy v. Ferguson plunged this nation in general and African Americans in particular, into over 50 years of legally sanctioned discrimination. This intricate system of laws, customs and etiquette was called Jim Crow.

Examples of Jim Crow Laws

Nurses: No person or corporation shall require any white female nurse to nurse in wards or rooms in hospitals, either public or private, in which negro men are placed. *Alabama*

Buses: All passenger stations in this state operated by any motor transportation company shall have separate waiting rooms or space and separate ticket windows for the white and colored races. *Alabama*

Railroads: The conductor of each passenger train is authorized and required to assign each passenger to the car or the division of the car, when it is divided by a partition, designated for the race to which such passenger belongs. *Alabama*

Restaurants: It shall be unlawful to conduct a restaurant or other place for the serving of food in the city, at which white and colored people are served in the same room, unless such white and colored persons are effectually separated by a solid partition extending from the floor upward to a distance of seven feet or higher, and unless a separate entrance from the street is provided for each compartment. *Alabama*

Pool and Billiard Rooms: It shall be unlawful for a Negro and white person to play together or in company with each other at any game of pool or billiards. *Alabama*

Toilet Facilities, Male: Every employer of white or Negro males shall provide for such white or Negro males reasonably accessible and separate toilet facilities. *Alabama*

135

Intermarriage: The marriage of a person of Caucasian blood with a Negro, Mongolian, Malay, or Hindu shall be null and void. *Arizona*

Intermarriage: All marriages between a white person and a Negro, or between a white person and a person of Negro descent to the fourth generation inclusive, are hereby forever prohibited. *Florida*

Cohabitation: Any negro man and white woman, or any white man and negro woman, who are not married to each other, who shall habitually live in and occupy in the nighttime the same room shall each be punished by imprisonment not exceeding twelve (12) months, or by fine not exceeding five hundred ($500.00) dollars. *Florida*

Education: The schools for white children and the schools for Negro children shall be conducted separately. *Florida*

Juvenile Delinquents: There shall be separate buildings, not nearer than one fourth mile to each other, one for white boys and one for Negro boys. White boys and Negro boys shall not, in any manner, be associated together or worked together. *Florida*

Mental Hospitals: The Board of Control shall see that proper and distinct apartments are arranged for said patients, so that in no case shall Negroes and white persons be together. *Georgia*

Intermarriage: It shall be unlawful for a white person to marry anyone except a white person. Any marriage in violation of this section shall be void. *Georgia*

Barbers: No colored barber shall serve as a barber [to] white women or girls. *Georgia*

Burial: The officer in charge shall not bury, or allow to be buried, any colored persons upon ground set apart or used for the burial of white persons. *Georgia*

Restaurants: All persons licensed to conduct a restaurant, shall serve either white people exclusively or colored people exclusively and shall not sell to the two races within the same room or serve the two races anywhere under the same license. *Georgia*

Amateur Baseball: It shall be unlawful for any amateur white baseball team to play baseball on any vacant lot or baseball diamond within two blocks of a playground devoted to the Negro race, and it shall be unlawful for any amateur colored baseball team to play baseball in any vacant lot or baseball diamond within two blocks of any playground devoted to the white race. *Georgia*

Parks: It shall be unlawful for colored people to frequent any park owned or maintained by the city for the benefit, use and enjoyment of white persons...and unlawful for any white person to frequent any park owned or maintained by the city for the use and benefit of colored persons. *Georgia*

Wine and Beer: All persons licensed to conduct the business of selling beer or wine...shall serve either white people exclusively or colored people exclusively and shall not sell to the two races within the same room at any time. *Georgia*

Reform Schools: The children of white and colored races committed to the houses of reform shall be kept entirely separate from each other. *Kentucky*

Circus Tickets: All circuses, shows, and tent exhibitions, to which the attendance of...more than one race is invited or expected to attend shall provide for the convenience of its patrons not less than two ticket offices with individual ticket sellers, and not less than two entrances to the said performance, with individual ticket takers and receivers, and in the case of outside or tent performances, the said ticket offices shall not be less than twenty-five (25) feet apart. *Louisiana*

Housing: Any person...who shall rent any part of any such building to a Negro person or a Negro family when such building is already in whole or in part in occupancy by a white person or white family, or vice versa when the building is in occupancy by a Negro person or Negro family, shall be guilty of a misdemeanor and on conviction thereof shall be punished by a fine of not less than twenty-five ($25.00) nor more than one hundred ($100.00) dollars or be imprisoned not less than 10, or more than 60 days, or both such fine and imprisonment in the discretion of the court. *Louisiana*

The Blind: The board of trustees shall...maintain a separate building...on separate ground for the admission, care, instruction, and support of all blind persons of the colored or black race. *Louisiana*

Intermarriage: All marriages between a white person and a Negro, or between a white person and a person of Negro descent, to the third generation, inclusive, or between a white person and a member of the Malay race; or between the negro and a member of the Malay race; or between a person of Negro descent, to the third generation, inclusive, and a member of the Malay race, are forever prohibited, and shall be void. *Maryland*

Railroads: All railroad companies and corporations, and all persons running or operating cars or coaches by steam on any railroad line or track in the State of Maryland, for the transportation of passengers, are hereby required to provide separate cars or coaches for the travel and transportation of the white and colored passengers. *Maryland*

Education: Separate schools shall be maintained for the children of the white and colored races. *Mississippi*

Promotion of Equality: Any person...who shall be guilty of printing, publishing or circulating printed, typewritten or written matter urging or presenting for public acceptance or general information, arguments or suggestions in favor of social equality or of intermarriage between whites and Negroes, shall be guilty of a misdemeanor and subject to fine or not exceeding five hundred (500.00) dollars or imprisonment not exceeding six (6) months or both. *Mississippi*

Intermarriage: The marriage of a white person with a Negro or mulatto or person who shall have one-eighth or more of negro blood, shall be unlawful and void. *Mississippi*

Hospital Entrances: There shall be maintained by the governing authorities of every hospital maintained by the state for treatment of white and colored patients separate entrances for white and colored patients and visitors, and such entrances shall be used by the race only for which they are prepared. *Mississippi*

Prisons: The warden shall see that the white convicts shall have separate apartments for both eating and sleeping from the Negro convicts. *Mississippi*

Education: Separate free schools shall be established for the education of children of African descent; and it shall be unlawful for any colored child to attend any white school, or any white child to attend a colored school. *Missouri*

Intermarriage: All marriages between...white persons and Negroes or white persons and Mongolians...are prohibited and declared absolutely void...No person having one-eighth part or more of Negro blood shall be permitted to marry any white person, nor shall any white person be permitted to marry any negro or person having one-eighth part or more of negro blood. *Missouri*

Education: Separate rooms [shall] be provided for the teaching of pupils of African descent, and [when] said rooms are so provided; such pupils may not be admitted to the school rooms occupied and used by pupils of Caucasian or other descent. *New Mexico*

Textbooks: Books shall not be interchangeable between the white and colored schools, but shall continue to be used by the race first using them. *North Carolina*

Libraries: The state librarian is directed to fit up and maintain a separate place for the use of the colored people who may come to the library for the purpose of reading books or periodicals. *North Carolina*

Militia: The white and colored militia shall be separately enrolled, and shall never be compelled to serve in the same organization. No organization of colored troops shall be permitted where white troops are available, and where colored and white are permitted to be organized, colored troops shall be under the command of white officers. *North Carolina*

Transportation: The...Utilities Commission...is empowered and directed to require the establishment of separate waiting rooms at all stations for the white and colored races. *North Carolina*

Teaching: Any instructor who shall teach in any school, college or institution where members of the white and colored race are received and enrolled as pupils for instruction shall be deemed guilty of a misdemeanor, and upon conviction thereof, shall be fined in any sum not less than ten dollars ($10.00) nor more than fifty dollars ($50.00) for each offense. *Oklahoma*

Fishing, Boating, and Bathing: The [Conservation] Commission shall have the right to make segregation of the white and colored races as to the exercise of rights of fishing, boating and bathing. *Oklahoma*

Mining: The baths and lockers for the Negroes shall be separate from the white race, but may be in the same building. *Oklahoma*

Telephone Booths: The Corporation Commission is hereby vested with power and authority to require telephone companies...to maintain separate booths for white and colored patrons when there is a demand for such separate booths. That the Corporation Commission shall determine the necessity for said separate booths only upon complaint of the people in the town and vicinity to be served after due hearing as now provided by law in other complaints filed with the Corporation Commission. *Oklahoma*

Lunch Counters: No persons, firms, or corporations, who or which furnish meals to passengers at station restaurants or station eating houses, in times limited by common carriers of said passengers, shall furnish said meals to white and colored passengers in the same room, or at the same table, or at the same counter. *South Carolina*

Child Custody: It shall be unlawful for any parent, relative, or other white person in this State, having the control or custody of any white child, by right of guardianship, natural or acquired, or otherwise, to dispose of, give or surrender such white child permanently into the custody, control, maintenance, or support, of a Negro. *South Carolina*

Libraries: Any white person of such county may use the county free library under the rules and regulations prescribed by the commissioners' court and may be entitled to all the privileges thereof. Said court shall make proper provision for the Negroes of said county to be served through a separate branch or branches of the county free library, which shall be administered by [a] custodian of the negro race under the supervision of the county librarian. *Texas*

Education: [The County Board of Education] shall provide schools of two kinds; those for white children and those for colored children. *Texas*

Theaters: Every person...operating...any public hall, theatre, opera house, motion picture show or any place of public entertainment or public assemblage which is attended by both white and colored persons, shall separate the white race and the colored race and shall set apart and designate...certain seats therein to be occupied by white persons and a portion thereof, or certain seats therein, to be occupied by colored persons. *Virginia*

Railroads: The conductors or managers on all such railroads shall have power, and are hereby required, to assign to each white or colored passenger his or her respective car, coach or compartment. If the passenger fails to disclose his race, the conductor and managers, acting in good faith, shall be the sole judges of his race. *Virginia*

Intermarriage: All marriages of White persons with Negroes, Mulattos, Mongolians, or Malaya hereafter contracted in the State of Wyoming are and shall be illegal and void. *Wyoming*

Jim Crow: Etiquette & Customs

Jim Crow was the name of the racial class system which operated primarily, but not exclusively in southern and border states, between 1877 and the mid-1960's. Jim Crow was more than a series of rigid anti-black laws. It was a way of life. Under Jim Crow, African Americans were relegated to the status of second class citizens. Jim Crow represented the legitimization of anti-black racism. Many Christian ministers and theologians taught that whites were the Chosen people, Blacks were cursed to be servants, and God supported racial segregation. Craniologists, eugenicists, phrenologists, and Social Darwinists, at every educational level, strengthened the belief that Blacks were innately intellectually and culturally inferior to Whites. Pro-segregation politicians gave speeches on the great danger of integration: the mongrelization of the white race. Newspaper and magazine writers routinely referred to blacks as niggers, coons, and darkies; and worse, their articles reinforced anti-black stereotypes. Even children's games portrayed blacks as inferior beings. All major societal institutions reflected and supported the oppression of blacks.

The Jim Crow system was undergirded by the following beliefs or rationalizations: whites were superior to blacks in all important ways, including but not limited to intelligence, morality, and civilized behavior; sexual relations between blacks and whites would produce a mongrel race which would destroy America; treating blacks as equals would encourage interracial sexual unions; any activity which suggested social equality encouraged interracial sexual relations; if necessary, violence must be used to keep blacks at the bottom of the racial hierarchy. The following Jim Crow etiquette norms show how inclusive and pervasive these norms were:

a. A Black male could not offer his hand (to shake hands) with a White male because it implied being socially equal. Obviously, a Black male could not offer his hand or any other part of his body to a White woman, because he risked being accused of rape.
b. Blacks and Whites were not supposed to eat together. If they did eat together, Whites were to be served first, and some sort of partition was to be placed between them.
c. Under no circumstance was a Black male to offer to light the cigarette of a White female—that gesture implied intimacy.

d. Blacks were not allowed to show public affection toward one another in public, especially kissing, because it offended Whites.

e. Jim Crow etiquette prescribed that Blacks were introduced to Whites, never Whites to Blacks. For example: "Mr. Smith (the White person), this is Eddie (the Black person), that I spoke to you about."

f. Whites did not use courtesy titles of respect when referring to Blacks, for example, Mr., Mrs., Miss., Sir, or Ma'am. Instead, Blacks were called by their first names. Blacks had to use courtesy titles when referring to Whites, and were not allowed to call them by their first names.

g. If a Black person rode in a car driven by a White person, the Black person sat in the back seat, or the back of a truck.

h. White motorists had the right-of-way at all intersections.

Stetson Kennedy, the author of *Jim Crow Guide,* offered these simple rules that Blacks were supposed to observe in conversing with Whites:

1. Never assert or even intimate that a White person is lying.
2. Never impute dishonorable intentions to a White person.
3. Never suggest that a White person is from an inferior class.
4. Never lay claim to, or overly demonstrate, superior knowledge or intelligence.
5. Never curse a White person.
6. Never laugh derisively at a White person.
7. Never comment upon the appearance of a White female.

Jim Crow etiquette operated in conjunction with Jim Crow laws (black codes). When most people think of Jim Crow they think of laws (not the Jim Crow etiquette) which excluded Blacks from public transport and facilities, juries, jobs, and neighborhoods. The passage of the 13th, 14th, and 15th Amendments to the Constitution had granted Blacks the same legal protections as Whites, but Plessy v. Ferguson effectively negated these freedoms.

Blacks were denied the right to vote by grandfather clauses (laws that restricted the right to vote to people whose ancestors had voted before the Civil War), poll taxes (fees charged to poor Blacks), white primaries (only Democrats could vote, only Whites could be Democrats), and literacy tests ("Name all the Vice Presidents and Supreme Court Justices throughout America's history"). Plessy sent this message to Southern and border states: Discrimination against blacks is acceptable.

Jim Crow states passed statutes severely regulating social interactions between the races. Jim Crow signs were placed above water fountains, door entrances and exits, and in front of public facilities. There were separate hospitals for Blacks and Whites, separate prisons, separate public and private schools, separate churches, separate cemeteries, separate public restrooms, and separate public accommodations. In most instances, the Black facilities were grossly inferior—generally, older, less-well-kept. In other cases, there were no Black facilities—no Colored public restroom, no public beach, no place to sit or eat. Plessy gave Jim Crow states a legal way to ignore their constitutional obligations to their Black citizens.

The Jim Crow laws and system of etiquette were undergirded by violence, real and threatened. Blacks who violated Jim Crow norms (for example, drinking from the White water fountain or trying to vote) risked their homes, their jobs, even their lives. Whites could physically beat Blacks with impunity. Blacks had little legal recourse against these assaults because the Jim Crow criminal justice system was all-White: police, prosecutors, judges, juries, and prison officials. Violence was instrumental for Jim Crow. It was a method of social control. The most extreme forms of Jim Crow violence were lynchings.

Lynchings were public, often sadistic, murders carried out by mobs. Between 1882, when the first reliable data was collected, and 1968, when lynchings had become rare, there were 4,730 known lynchings, including 3,440 Black men and women. Most of the victims of Lynch-Law were hung or shot, but some were burned at the stake, castrated, beaten with clubs, or dismembered. In the mid-1800's, Whites constituted the majority of victims (and perpetrators); however, by the period of Radical Reconstruction,

Blacks became the most frequent lynching victims. This is an early indication that lynching was used as an intimidation tool to keep Blacks, in this case the newly-freedmen, "in their places." The great majority of lynchings occurred in Southern and border states, where the resentment against Blacks ran deepest. According to the social economist Gunnar Myrdal: "The Southern states account for nine-tenths of the lynchings. More than two thirds of the remaining one-tenth occurred in the six states which immediately border the South."

Under Jim Crow any and all sexual interactions between black men and white women was illegal, illicit, socially repugnant, and within the Jim Crow definition of rape. Although only 19.2 percent of the lynching victims between 1882 and 1951 were even accused of rape, Lynch Law was often supported on the popular belief that lynchings were necessary to protect white women from black rapists. Myrdal refutes this belief in this way: "There is much reason to believe that this figure (19.2) has been inflated by the fact that a mob which makes the accusation of rape is secure from any further investigation; by the broad Southern definition of rape to include all sexual relations between Negro men and white women; and by the psychopathic fears of white women in their contacts with Negro men." Most blacks were lynched for demanding civil rights, violating Jim Crow etiquette or laws, or in the aftermath of race riots.

Lynchings were most common in small and middle-sized towns where blacks often were economic competitors to the local whites. These whites resented any economic and political gains made by blacks. Lynchers were seldom arrested, and if arrested, rarely convicted. It has been estimated that "at least one-half of the lynchings are carried out with police officers participating, and that in nine-tenths of the others the officers either condone or wink at the mob action." Lynching served many purposes: it was cheap entertainment; it served as a rallying, uniting point for whites; it functioned as an ego-massage for low-income, low-status whites; it was a method of defending White domination and helped stop or retard the fledgling social equality movement.

Lynch mobs directed their hatred against one (sometimes several) victims. The victim was an example of what happened to a black man, who tried to vote, or who looked at a white woman, or who tried to get a white man's job. Unfortunately for blacks, sometimes the mob was not satisfied to murder a single or several victims. Instead, in the spirit of pogroms, the mobs went into black communities and destroyed additional lives and property. Their immediate goal was to drive out—through death or expulsion—all blacks; the larger goal was to maintain, at all costs, White supremacy. These pogrom-like actions are often referred to as riots; however, Gunnar Myrdal was right when he described these "riots" as "a terrorization or massacre...a mass lynching." Interestingly, these mass lynchings were primarily urban phenomena, whereas the lynching of single victims was primarily a rural occurrence.

James Weldon Johnson, the famous Black writer, labeled 1919 as "The Red Summer." It was red from racial tension; it was red from bloodletting. During the summer of 1919, there were race riots in Chicago, Illinois; Knoxville and Nashville, Tennessee; Charleston, South Carolina; Omaha, Nebraska; and two dozen other citizens. A compelling characteristic of the riots of 1919 was the extent of black retaliation. W.E.B. DuBois, the Black social scientist and civil rights activist, wrote: "During that year seventy-seven Negroes were lynched, of whom one was a woman and eleven were soldiers; of these, fourteen were publicly burned, eleven of them being burned alive. That year there were race riots large and small in twenty-six American cities including thirty-eight killed in a Chicago riot of August; from twenty-five to fifty in Phillips County, Arkansas; and six killed in Washington."

The riots of 1919 were not the first or last "mass lynchings" of Blacks, as evidenced by the race riots in Wilmington, North Carolina (1898); Atlanta, Georgia (1906); Springfield, Illinois (1908); East St. Louis, Illinois (1917); Tulsa, Oklahoma (1921); and Detroit, Michigan (1943). The riots of the 1900's had the following traits:

1. In each of the race riots, with few exceptions, it was White people that sparked the incident by attacking Black people.

2. In the majority of the riots, some extraordinary social condition prevailed at the time of the riot: pre-war social changes, wartime mobility, post-war adjustment, or economic depression.

3. The majority of the riots occurred during the hot summer months.

4. Rumor played an extremely important role in causing many riots. Rumors of some criminal activity by Blacks against Whites perpetuated the actions of the White mobs.

5. The police force, more than any other institution, was invariably involved as a precipitating cause or perpetuating factor in the riots. In almost every one of the riots, the police sided with the attackers, either by actually participating in, or by failing to quell the attack.

6. In almost every instance, the fighting occurred within the Black community.

The following was also a factor: The mass media. Newspapers often published inflammatory articles about "Black criminals" immediately before the riots; blacks were not only killed, but their homes and businesses were looted, and many who did not flee were left homeless; and, the goal of the white rioters, as was true of white lynchers of single victims, was to instill fear and terror into blacks, thereby strengthening White domination. The Jim Crow hierarchy could not work without violence being used against those on the bottom rung. George Fredrickson, a historian, stated it this way: "Lynching represented...a way of using fear and terror to check 'dangerous' tendencies in a black community considered to be ineffectively regimented or supervised. As such it constituted a confession that the regular institutions of a segregated society provided an inadequate measure of day-to-day control."

The Ku Klux Klan

The Ku Klux Klan was originally organized in the winter of 1865-66 in Pulaski, Tennessee as a social club by six Confederate veterans. In the beginning, the Klan was a secret fraternity club rather than a terrorist organization. (Ku Klux was derived from the Greek "kuklos," meaning circle, and the English word clan.) The costume adopted by its members (disguises were quite common) was a mask and white robe and high conical pointed hat.

The Klan spread beyond Tennessee to every state in the South and included mayors, judges, and sheriffs as well as common criminals. The Klan systematically murdered black politicians and political leaders. It beat, whipped, and murdered thousands, and intimidated tens of thousands of others from voting. Blacks often tried to fight back, but they were outnumbered and out gunned. While the main targets of Klan wrath were the political and social leaders of the black community, blacks could be murdered for almost any reason. Men, women, children, aged and crippled, were victims. A 103-year-old woman was whipped, as was a completely paralyzed man. In Georgia, Abraham Colby, an organizer and leader in the black community, was whipped for hours in front of his wife and children. His little daughter begged the Klansman, "Don't take my daddy away." She never recovered from the sight and died soon after. In Mississippi, Jack Dupree's throat was cut and he was disemboweled in front of his wife, who had just given birth to twins. Klansman burned churches and schools, lynching teachers and educated blacks.

Black landowners were driven off their property and murdered if they refused to leave. Blacks were whipped for refusing to work for whites, for having intimate relations with whites, for arguing with whites, for having jobs whites wanted, for reading a newspaper or having a book in their homes... or simply for being black. Klan violence led one black man to write: "We have very dark days here. The colored people are in despair. The rebels boast that the Negroes shall not have as much liberty now as they had under slavery. If things go on thus, our doom is sealed. God knows it is worse than slavery."

A few state governments fought back. In Tennessee and Arkansas, Republicans organized a police force that arrested Klansmen and carried out executions. In Texas, Governor Edmund Davis organized a crack state police unit, 40 percent of whose officers were black. The police made over 6,000 arrests and stopped the Klan. Armed groups of blacks and whites fought or threatened Klansman in North and South Carolina. The federal government also exerted its influence, empowering federal authorities with the Enforcement Acts of 1870 and 1871. Klan activity ended by 1872 and disappeared until it was revived again in 1915.

Woodrow Wilson and Governmental Segregation

In 1912 Woodrow Wilson, the Democratic candidate for president, promised fairness and justice for blacks if elected. In a letter to a black church official, Wilson wrote, "Should I become President of the United States they may count upon me for absolute fair dealing for everything by which I could assist in advancing their interests of the race." But after the election, Wilson changed his tune. He dismissed 15 out of 17 black supervisors who had been previously appointed to federal jobs and replaced them with whites. He also refused to appoint black ambassadors to Haiti and Santa Domingo, posts traditionally awarded to African Americans. Two of Wilson's cabinet ministers, Postmaster General Albert Burelson and Treasury Secretary William McAdoo, both Southerners, issued orders segregating their departments. Throughout the country, blacks were segregated or dismissed from federal positions. In Georgia, the head of the Internal Revenue division fired all black employees: "There are no government positions for Negroes in the South. A Negro's place is in the corn field." The President's wife, Ellen Wilson, was said to have had a hand in segregating employees in Washington, encouraging department chiefs to assign blacks separate working, eating, and toilet facilities. To justify segregation, officials publicized complaints by white women, who were thought to be threatened by black men's sexuality and disease.

Some African Americans were fearless in fighting back. Mary Church Terrell, a federal employee and leading African-American clubwoman, embarrassed officials by publicly threatening to publicize the fact that restrooms had been segregated in her area. In return for her not publicizing the situation, her department agreed to cancel the order.

Also, W.E.B. Dubois sharply criticized President Wilson in *THE CRISIS*: "The federal government has set the colored apart as if mere contact with them were contamination. Behind screens and closed doors they now sit as though leprous. How long will it be before the hateful epithets of 'Nigger' and 'Jim Crow' are openly applied?" The NAACP's active campaign forced Wilson to back off from segregating the federal government. Jim Crow was checked but not rooted out. It would remain in place until the New Deal of Franklin Roosevelt.

The legacy of Jim Crow is a powerful one. Despite decades of progress towards equality in the eyes of the law, few would argue that ours is a truly prejudice-free society. The various differences between now and the Jim Crow era are conspicuous; but in far too many cases, so are the parallels.

EXECUTIVE ORDER NO. 9066

HISTORICAL OVERVIEW

The Japanese have been a presence in the continental United States for more than a century, but some Japanese, slaves held by several Indian tribes, were in the Northwest even before the arrival of the first Whites. From 1636 to around 1860, Japanese were forbidden to emigrate. The Tokugawa shogunate imposed an embargo on emigration in the 17th century, and because of fear of the corrupting influence of the West, had effectively sealed off the borders. But the arrival of Admiral Perry in 1853, and the signing of a peace treaty between the United States and Japan, reversed for a short time Japan's emigration policy. Laws forbidding emigration were reinstated when Japan feared that the export of labor would lower their prestige among nations of the world. Emigration laws were later relaxed again only because of severe economic conditions and crop failures in southern Japan. From 1886 until 1924 there was considerable Japanese emigration to Hawaii (238,758) and the United States (196,543).

Japanese in Hawaii

Sugar is believed to have been first milled in Hawaii as early as 1802; however, it was not until the 1840's that it became a major crop. Native Hawaiians were hired first to do the growing, harvesting, and milling of sugar, but there eventually became an acute shortage of Hawaiian laborers. Compounding the problem was the Hawaiian emigration to California during the gold rush and thousands of Hawaiians dying from diseases brought to the Islands by foreigners. Recognizing the need for cheap labor for sugar plantations, the Hawaiian ambassador to Japan persuaded the government to allow 180 contract laborers to sign up for work.

The Japanese found conditions on the sugar plantation harsh. They worked from dawn to dusk, unaccustomed to the scorching hot Hawaiian sun. Because they did not understand orders given in

English, workers were often bullwhipped. After the Japanese government learned of these conditions, Special Commissioner Katsunosuke Inouye was sent to Hawaii to investigate charges of cruelty to Japanese workers. Japan threatened to stop sending workers unless something was done to stop this abuse. Frightened by the possibility of termination of the labor source and hoping to satisfy Japan's concern for Japanese workers in Hawaii, the Hawaiian government entered into an agreement with Japan making Japanese immigrants wards of the Hawaiian government, and the planters its agents. Waiting to see if the agreement with Hawaii stopped Japanese worker abuse, Japan did not allow further emigration until 1886. Between 1886 and 1894, 26 sailings brought 29,069 Japanese immigrants. Another 30,000 Japanese immigrants were brought in during the two years after Hawaii's annexation in 1898.

After the Organic Act was passed in 1900, giving Japanese laborers more freedom, there were many small strikes for increased wages and better working conditions. Dissatisfied and unhappy, over 40,000 left Hawaii for employment in the United States. This, and an outbreak of bubonic plague among the immigrants of Honolulu, caused a critical labor shortage. Sugar planters then turned to the Filipinos as a source of cheap labor.

Japanese in the United States

In 1880, two years before the passage of the Chinese Exclusion Act, fewer than 200 Japanese lived in the United States. A decade later, Japanese immigrated at an annual rate of 1,000. From 1899 to 1903, another 60,000 entered the United States, largely because of the acute labor shortage in California. The exclusion of the Chinese had left many menial and unskilled jobs without takers. The Japanese population at this time was concentrated largely on the Pacific Coast, with the center at San Francisco. They were rural farmers from southern Honshu and Kyushu, and unlike the Chinese who migrated to urban living, the Japanese preferred rural farming. The early Japanese farmers and farm organizations laid the groundwork for future Japanese immigrants by providing capital and agriculture expertise. Like the Chinese, the Japanese received few loans from banks, so a Japanese rotating credit association, one of many variations, would accept subscriber deposits and give loans to the neediest Japanese workers who wanted to purchase land. The cooperation between the association and the workers was built on trust and honor, and the rate of default was rare.

As with the Chinese, the Japanese welcome began to fade as their numbers began to rise. Unlike the Chinese, however, the Japanese did not disperse. America began to stereotype Asians into two categories: the Chinese, humble and "inferior," who could be tolerated; and the Japanese, who were cunning and aggressive and required domination to keep them in place.

In 1907, President Theodore Roosevelt negotiated a "Gentlemen's Agreement" that called for Japan to issue passports to Japanese coming to the continental United States only if they were coming to join a parent, husband, child, or to return to a former home or farm. This agreement greatly diminished Japanese emigration to America. Between 1930 and 1940 the number returning to Japan exceeded new immigrants to the United States. This trend continued up to the Japanese attack on Pearl Harbor. Many Japanese parents sent their children to Japan to be educated, and by 1942 it was estimated that more than 25,000 Asian Americans had been educated in Japan.

The Japanese American Citizens League

The Japanese American Citizens League, the nation's oldest and largest Asian American civil rights organization, was founded in 1929 to address issues of discrimination targeted specifically at persons of Japanese ancestry residing in the United States. In California, where the majority of Japanese Americans resided, there were over one hundred statutes in California that proscribed the limits of rights of anyone of Japanese ancestry. Organizations like the Grange Association and Sons of the Golden West exerted powerful influence on the state legislature and on Congress to limit participation and rights of Japanese Americans, and groups like the Japanese Exclusion League were established with the sole purpose of ridding the state of its Japanese population, even those who were American citizens by birth.

Amidst this hostile environment, the JACL was established to fight for the civil rights primarily of Japanese Americans but also for the benefit of Chinese Americans and other peoples of color. Although still a small California-based organization, the JACL was one of only a few organizations in the 1920's and 1930's willing to challenge the racist policies of the state and federal governments. With limited resources and virtually no experience in state or federal politics, the JACL nevertheless took it upon itself to set the course for civil rights for persons of Asian ancestry in the West Coast region of the United States as well as at the federal level by combating congressional legislation aimed at excluding the rights of Japanese Americans and Asian Americans.

THE LAW/POLICY

Author's Note: While Congress has the power to declare war and support and maintain an army and navy (Article 1 Section 8:11-16 of the Constitution), only the President (as Commander-In-Chief) has the power to give orders to American military forces (Article 2 Section 2:1).

EXECUTIVE ORDER AUTHORIZING THE SECRETARY OF WAR TO PRESCRIBE MILITARY AREAS

WHEREAS the successful prosecution of the war requires every possible protection against espionage and against sabotage to national defense material, national defense premises, and national defense utilities as defined in Section 4, Act of April 20, 1918, 40 Stat. 533, as amended by the Act of November 30, 1940, 54 Stat. 1220, and the Act of August 21, 1941, 55 Stat. 655 (U.S.C., Title 50, Sec. 104);

NOW, I THEREFORE, by virtue of the authority vested in me as President of the United States, and Commander in Chief of the Army and Navy, I hereby authorize and direct the Secretary of War, and the Military Commanders whom he may from time to time designate, whenever he or any designated Commander deems such action necessary or desirable, to prescribe military areas in such places and of such extent as he or the appropriate Military

Commander may determine from which any or all persons may be excluded, and with respect to which the right of any person to enter, remain in, or leave shall be subject to whatever restrictions the Secretary of War or the appropriate Commander may impose in his discretion. The Secretary of War is hereby authorized to provide for residents of any such area who are excluded therefrom, such transportation, food, shelter, and other accommoclations as may be necessary, in the judgment of the Secretary of War or the said Military Commander, and until other arrangements are made, to accomplish the purpose of this order. The designation of military areas in any region or locality shall supersede designations of prohibited and restricted areas by the Attorney General under the Proclamations of December 7 and 8, 1941, and shall supersede the responsibility and authority of the Attorney General under the said Proclamations in respect of such prohibited and restricted areas.

I hereby further authorize and direct the Secretary of War and the said Military Commanders to take such other steps as he or the appropriate Military Commander may deem advisable to enforce compliance with the restrictions applicable to each Military area hereinabove authorized to be designated, including the use of Federal troops and other Federal Agencies, with authority to accept assistance of state and local agencies.

I hereby further authorize and direct all Executive Departments, independent establishments and other Federal Agencies, to assist the Secretary of War or the said Military Commanders in carrying out this Executive Order, including the furnishing of medical aid, hospitalization, food, clothing, transportation, use of land, shelter, and other supplies, equipment, utilities, facilities, and services.

This order shall not be construed as modifying or limiting in any way the authority heretofore granted under Executive Order No. 8972 dated December 12, 1941, nor shall it be construed as limiting or modifying the duty and responsibility of the Federal Bureau of Investigation, with respect to the investigation of alleged acts of sabotage or the duty and responsibility of the Attorney General and the Department of Justice under the Proclamations of December 7 and 8, 1941, prescribing regulations for the conduct and control of alien enemies, except as such duty and responsibility is superseded by the designation of military areas hereunder.

FRANKLIN D. ROOSEVELT
THE WHITE HOUSE, February 19, 1942

IN LAYMEN'S TERMS

Executive Order 9066, dated February 19, 1942, gave the military broad powers to ban any citizen from a fifty- to sixty-mile-wide coastal area stretching from Washington state to California and extending inland into southern Arizona. The order also authorized transporting these citizens to assembly centers hastily set up and governed by the military in California, Arizona, Washington state, and Oregon. Although it is not well known, the same executive order (and other war-time orders and restrictions) were also applied to smaller numbers of residents of the United States who were of Italian or German descent. For example, 3,200 resident aliens of Italian background were arrested and more than 300 of them were interned. About 11,000 German residents—including some naturalized citizens—were arrested and more than 5000 were interned (most of the these interned Germans and Italians were considered criminals, dissidents or radicals before their internment). Yet while these individuals suffered grievous violations of their civil liberties, the war-time measures applied to Japanese Americans were worse and more sweeping, uprooting entire communities and targeting citizens as well as resident aliens.

Western Defense Command was an army command consisting of eight Western states. Wartime Civil Control Administration (WCCA) was responsible for the "assembly centers" evacuation. War Relocation Authority ran the internment camps.

The Executive Order No. 8972 ("This order shall not be construed as modifying or limiting in any way the authority heretofore granted under Executive Order No. 8972") was an order signed by the President after the bombing of Pearl Harbor. The President gave authority to the Secretary of War and the Secretary of the Navy to establish and maintain military guards and patrols (or other appropriate means) to prevent any further sabotage of national defense utilities, materials or premises.

SOCIAL AND POLITICAL CLIMATE LEADING TO LAW/POLICY

Japanese immigrants and their American children were frequent targets of prejudice and political attacks for 50 years before World War II. In May 1905, delegates from 67 organizations convened in San Francisco, California, to form the Asiatic Exclusion League, later known as the Japanese Exclusion League. After the transcontinental railroad was completed in 1869, competition for jobs increased. Many organized labor groups first blamed Chinese, then Japanese immigrants for unemployment and low wages.

Led primarily by labor groups, the League's goal was complete job exclusion of those of Japanese ancestry. They lobbied for anti-Japanese legislation, conducted boycotts, promoted segregation and produced propaganda. The League pressured Congress to keep Japanese people out of agriculture and other industries, and to stop all immigration of Japanese to the U.S. They held anti-Japanese rallies and worked to restrict employment of Japanese Americans. The League acted to ensure that children of Japanese ancestry remained in segregated schools, as reflected in the San Francisco School Board statement, "children should not be placed in any position where their youthful impressions may be affected by association with pupils of the Mongolian race."

Protests from Japan led President Theodore Roosevelt to intervene. The president persuaded the city to drop its segregation order in exchange for a promised limit on Japanese immigration. The promise was fulfilled in the Gentlemen's Agreement of 1907 in which Japan agreed not to allow any more of its workers to come to the United States.

As Japanese immigrants became successful farmers in California, white farmers sought ways to eliminate the competition. The Whites succeeded in 1913 when the state legislature passed a law prohibiting aliens ineligible for American citizenship from owning land in the state. Under federal law, all Asians were ineligible for naturalization.

One of the greatest conquests by the anti-Japanese forces came in 1924 when Congress passed the National Origins Quota Act barring all further immigration from Japan. The Grizzly Bear, a publication of the Native Sons of the Golden West, wrote: "And so, after a strenuous campaign, another advance has been made in the battle with the Japs to keep California White."

The Commission on Wartime Relocation and Internment of Civilians (CWRIC) reported that within three years, the Japanese Exclusion League had more than 100,000 members and 238 affiliated groups, mostly from labor unions. Other groups along the West Coast also acted against people of Japanese ancestry: the Native Sons (and Native Daughters) of the Golden West; the American Legion; the California State Federation of Labor; the California State Grange; and the Anti-Jap Laundry League.

Greed was also a powerful motivator. The potential for economic gain was a major factor leading to the incarceration of people of Japanese ancestry.

Groups that had competed with Japanese immigrant farmers and laborers for more than half a century, lobbied for the incarceration. As with other minorities before them, people from Japan found that the United States' principles of equality were not applied to all, and rewards for hard work in the "land of opportunity" were often denied. Their hard work was often resented and successes on the West Coast were envied. In Hawaii, though, more than one-third of the population was of Japanese ancestry. They formed a major part of the labor force. Hawaii was the site of Japan's military attack on Pearl Harbor, and thus one might have expected an outcry there for the mass removal of people of Japanese ancestry. Different economic motivations were a factor in the prevention of such action.

Farming was the main occupation for early immigrant Japanese. Many did farm labor that paid by the piece, where they could earn more by working faster, harder, longer. They accepted lower wages than those paid to white workers, because low pay in the United States was still higher than the wages many could earn in Japan.

By 1920, Japanese Americans farmed more than 458,000 acres in California, either as owners, lessees, or contractors. These farms produced $67 million worth of crops, or more than 10 percent of the California total value. In 1940, Japanese Americans in Oregon raised $2.7 million worth of produce, while those in Washington raised more than $4 million.

Japanese farmers were pioneers in West Coast agriculture, clearing land unwanted by whites and introducing labor-intensive techniques that yielded abundant harvests from small plots of land. Their success fueled the growth of anti-Japanese organizations. These organizations—created solely to incite anti-Japanese sentiment—held propaganda rallies, spread racist rhetoric through the newspapers, and successfully lobbied Congress to stop immigration from Japan. All this was done in hopes of keeping people of Japanese ancestry out of agriculture and other industries, as well as restricting their employment as laborers.

Japanese immigrants to the continental U.S. performed manual labor in industries including railroads, lumber, canneries, mining and fishing. Around the early 1900's, railroad workers earned between $1.00 and $1.25 per day, and Alaskan cannery workers earned between $100 and $200 for a six-month season. These workers toiled under poor, unsanitary and often dangerous conditions.

Initially they tried to improve their wages and living conditions through labor unions and strikes. After 1910 they were less involved in labor organizing, largely due to the blatant racism of the American Federation of Labor (AFL). When the Sugar Beet and Farm Laborers Union of Oxnard, CA applied for membership in the AFL, farmer Samuel Gompers replied, "Your union must guarantee that it will under no circumstances accept membership of any Chinese or Japanese."

Governmental & Media Bias

During the crisis of war, many influential news and media sources failed to investigate claims that Japanese Americans were spying and committing sabotage against the United States. They did not check questionable "evidence" of these claims, but rushed to print sensational headlines and stories that were later proved false. Retractions and corrections were rarely printed, so the public believed what they had read.

Attention-getting headlines and the competition to sell papers may have compromised the media's role of providing objective information. Instead of presenting evidence and well-informed commentary, many news sources supported and, at times, led a public opinion campaign against Japanese Americans. Some journalists claimed there was no difference between U.S. citizens of Japanese ancestry and the Japanese citizens who attacked Pearl Harbor. "A viper is nonetheless a viper wherever the egg is hatched. So a Japanese-American... grows up to be Japanese, not an American," wrote a journalist in the *Los Angeles Times*.

Other reporters expressed hatred and encouraged that loyal and innocent Japanese Americans be forced out of their homes on the West Coast. "Herd 'em up, pack 'em off and give 'em the inside room in the badlands. Let 'em be pinched, hurt, hungry and dead up against it ... Let us have no patience with the enemy or anyone whose veins carry his blood ... Personally, I hate the Japanese. And that goes for all of them," wrote United Press correspondent Henry McLemore in January of 1942.

President Roosevelt ignored reports from Naval Intelligence, the FBI and other official sources that there was no need for either mass removal or incarceration of people of Japanese ancestry. According to then FBI Director J. Edgar Hoover, "... the decision to evacuate was ... based primarily on public and political pressures rather than factual data." Perhaps Roosevelt was influenced by anti-Japanese sentiments or misled by key advisors. Perhaps it was because there was no strong opposition to the incarceration on the West Coast. In any case, President Roosevelt encountered little resistance when he chose to violate the civil rights of a small, easily identifiable and politically powerless minority group rather than go against the rising tide of hostility. The U.S. Supreme Court upheld Roosevelt's decision. In sharp contrast to the mainland, the military leadership in Hawaii discouraged public hysteria and there was no mass incarceration on the islands.

By official accounts there never was any evidence of actual spying, sabotage or "fifth column activity" by Japanese Americans, including both U.S. citizens and legal residents of Japanese ancestry. The FBI, the Office of Naval Intelligence, and the Federal Communications Commission, along with the President's own intelligence sources all reported very consistently: There was no need for a mass exclusion or detention of people of Japanese ancestry.

In Roosevelt's cabinet, Attorney General Francis Biddle opposed the incarceration as unnecessary and unconstitutional. Biddle, however, was younger and less experienced than those who were encouraging the incarceration, primarily Henry L. Stimson, Secretary of War. Stimson was one of the most distinguished public servants of his time, having served as Secretary of War under President Taft and Secretary of State under President Hoover. Biddle later recounted, "The decisions were not made on the logic of events or on the weight of evidence, but on the racial prejudice that seemed to be influencing everyone."

AFTERMATH OF LAW/POLICY

In December of 1941, World War II was already raging in Europe, but the Japanese attack on the naval base at Pearl Harbor still stunned the American public and drew the nation into the war. The attack cast unfounded suspicion on all persons of Japanese ancestry in the U.S., and came on top of a century of anti-Asian prejudice and discriminatory legislation. Despite being warned there was no military necessity and having no evidence of planned sabotage or imminent invasion, President Franklin D. Roosevelt's Executive Order 9066 made possible the mass removal of 110,000 persons of Japanese ancestry from the West Coast to 10 American concentration camps in seven states: California, Wyoming, Idaho, Utah, Arizona, Colorado and Arkansas. They held both the Issei, first-generation immigrants who were barred from U.S. citizenship, and their children, the Nisei, born in this country as U. S. citizens. Two-thirds of those incarcerated were U.S. citizens. Those persons of Japanese ancestry in Hawaii were not removed.

Federal & Military Measures

After the Japanese bombing of Pearl Harbor, Japanese Americans encountered strong hostility, prejudice, and discrimination. As stated in the previous chapter, the Japanese and Japanese Americans had already been targets of racism and discrimination in the U.S. The Japanese attack on Pearl Harbor made many Americans feel justified in their intolerance.

Local authorities and the F.B.I. began to round-up the Issei leadership of the Japanese-American communities in Hawaii and on the mainland. By 6:30 a.m. (the morning following the bombing of Pearl Harbor) 736 Issei were in custody; within 48 hours the number had risen to 1,291. Caught by surprise for the most part, these men were held under no formal charges and family members were forbidden from seeing them. Most spent the war years in enemy alien internment camps.

It is worth mentioning and taking note, that Executive Order 9066 did not explicitly, in and of itself, order the evacuation and internment of people of Japanese ancestry. In fact, the Order did not specifically mention Japanese Americans at all. However, since the authority that the President gave the Secretary of War (and the Military Commanders that he chose to designate) was rather broad, it led to measures and actions directly aimed at Japanese and Japanese-Americans. The Commanding General of the Western Defense Command, Lt. General John L. DeWitt, quickly (on March 2, 1942) designated California, Oregon, Washington and Arizona to be "military areas." This Public Proclamation by General DeWitt was quickly followed by Executive Order 9102 (March 18, 1942). This Order established the War Relocation Authority to formulate and effectuate a program (including all necessary regulations) for the removal, relocation, maintenance and supervision of all persons excluded pursuant to Executive Order 9066. Then General DeWitt issued another Public Proclamation, which established an 8 p.m. to 6 a.m. curfew for "all persons of Japanese ancestry" as well as "alien Japanese, Germans and Italians," living within the "military areas." The proclamation also "encouraged" Japanese Americans to leave voluntarily. For various reasons, voluntary resettlement failed and was effectively called off on March 27 after fewer than five thousand people- out of over 110,000- had left the area.

The first of 108 "Civilian Exclusion Orders" was issued, informing Japanese Americans of Bainbridge Island, Washington that they had to leave. For the rest of the spring, through the summer and into the fall, Japanese Americans up and down the West Coast were removed neighborhood by neighborhood through these "exclusion orders." Most Japanese Americans were taken to a local assembly center, or temporary detention camp, upon arrival.

Government, political and military leaders on the U.S. mainland did not stand up for the rights of Japanese Americans. This contrasted with leadership in Hawaii, the site of the attack on Pearl Harbor. While General DeWitt responded to and increased anti-Japanese sentiment, his counterpart in control of Hawaii, General Delos Emmons discouraged public hysteria and exposed false rumors. He consistently treated people of Japanese ancestry as loyal to the United States, and presumed that they were innocent. In his first radio address to the public as Military Governor and Commander of the Hawaiian Department, Emmons clearly set a different tone than DeWitt by stating, "While we have been subjected to a serious attack by a ruthless and treacherous enemy, we must remember that this is America and we must do things the American Way."

It may be said, however, that the absence of exclusion and internment of Japanese Americans in Hawaii was more a result of economics, than benevolence. The Japanese American community's size and influence in Hawaii were key. In 1940, more than 35 percent of the population in Hawaii was of Japanese ancestry. Immigration to the Hawaiian islands had begun earlier than immigration to the mainland, and Hawaii had a more tolerant racial climate. As a result, the Japanese American population was better integrated into Hawaii's economy. According to Angus Macbeth, Special Counsel, CWRIC, they were "earning places in the municipal and territorial government, becoming schoolteachers and administrators, practicing law and medicine, and working in businesses owned by old line "haole" (white) families." In other words, people of Japanese ancestry had more influence economically, socially and politically in Hawaii than on the U.S. mainland. They were a large part of Hawaii's labor force, and some leaders were concerned that Hawaii's economy would collapse if all Japanese Americans were removed.

The "Big Five" families of Hawaii's politically dominant white plantation aristocracy formed an influential barrier to evacuation. Indeed, Roosevelt was convinced that Emmons took his information from the "Big Five," and he remarked scornfully to the Cabinet after evacuation was defeated that the plan was stymied by the pineapple and sugar growers, who wished to retain their Japanese laborers.

Continued Governmental & Media Bias

Many public officials made statements and called for actions that were not based on hard evidence, and which contradicted democratic principles. For example, then California Attorney General Earl Warren (who would later become Chief Justice of the U.S. Supreme Court) falsely claimed that Japanese Americans had "infiltrated themselves into every strategic spot in our coastal and valley counties" for spying and sabotage, and therefore they should all be removed from the West Coast. Warren had no real evidence, but offered as "proof" lists such as the following:

Alameda County -
Japs adjacent to new Livermore Military Airport
Japs adjacent to Southern Pacific and Western Pacific Railroads
Japs in vicinity of Oakland Airport
Japs in vicinity to Hold Caterpillar Tractor Co., San Leandro

A simple list of locations where some Japanese Americans lived and worked was not proof they were spies, but in the atmosphere of crisis and anger, many U.S. leaders and citizens felt Japanese Americans were guilty. In reality, the FBI, U.S. Naval Intelligence and other government sources reported no incidents of sabotage by Japanese Americans. Despite these reports, irrational arguments were made. "The very fact that no sabotage has taken place to date is a disturbing and confirming indication that such action will be taken," according to General DeWitt.

U.S. Secretary of the Navy, Frank Knox, falsely stated that spies in Honolulu aided Japan in the attack on Pearl Harbor. He had no evidence, and his claim was contrary to the findings of U.S. intelligence sources. In fact, many Japanese Americans, including members of the U.S. National Guard, acted to defend the islands at the time of the attack. Knox made his claim after spending only 36 hours in Hawaii. Were the false charges a simple error in judgment, a misstatement or the result of prejudice and unjust motives? Knox may have been anxious to find another target for blame—to prevent criticism of the Navy for being unprepared at Pearl Harbor. Yet, as early as 1933, Knox had warned of the danger of war with Japan and had publicly advocated the internment of every Japanese resident of the Hawaiian Islands. Knox's false charges played a major role in escalating the hysteria and anti-Japanese sentiments among many U.S. citizens and key government leaders.

Soon after the attack on Pearl Harbor, the U.S. government knew that Japanese Americans and Japanese resident aliens in Hawaii had not assisted Japan. U.S. Navy intelligence, the FBI and military intelligence investigations all reported that no such sabotage had been conducted. Credible leaders in positions of responsibility knew these people of Japanese ancestry were innocent. In spite of this knowledge, military and government officials did not announce that Secretary Knox's statement was false. They allowed the American public to wrongly believe that Japanese Americans and their immigrant elders were guilty of acting against the United States.

The report of the Commission on Wartime Relocation and Internment of Civilians (CWRIC) found the government's intelligence sources argued three major points: First, all intelligence indicated that Japanese Americans were overwhelmingly loyal to the

United States. Second, the FBI had people under surveillance long before the U.S. entered the war. The FBI was confident that they had enough evidence to identify individuals who might pose a threat, including Italian and German aliens. Third, the physical appearance of people of Japanese ancestry made them most noticeable among the majority white population. Spies and saboteurs would be less noticeable if they were white; thus, the Japanese would be more likely to use non-Japanese for espionage in the U.S. As stated by a British Intelligence officer at the time, "... the Japanese in all probability employed many more 'Whites' than 'Japanese' for carrying out their work and this 'White' danger is not eliminated by the evacuation of the Japanese."

Many individuals and groups tried to influence President Roosevelt's decision. The majority of Congress and powerful political groups on the West Coast were demanding that all people of Japanese ancestry be forced out. The Commanding General of the Western Defense Command, John L. DeWitt conceded that there was no evidence of sabotage or spying, but supported the mass removal as a precautionary measure. He argued that ancestry determined loyalty and U.S. citizenship was meaningless: "A Jap is a Jap," according to DeWitt.

People of Japanese ancestry were a small minority with no political influence. Japanese immigrants were not allowed to become naturalized U.S. citizens, and could not vote. Most of their children were U.S. citizens but under voting age. They were victims of decades of legalized discrimination and negative stereotypes. During a time of war hysteria, anti-Japanese propaganda and false rumors of sabotage; many leaders chose to take a better-safe-than-sorry position, rather than uphold Constitutional principles.

U.S. intelligence staff and others who tried to prevent the removal and incarceration gave information reports to the President denying that Japanese Americans posed any serious threat, but their assessments were ignored. The majority of the American public did not see or hear this information. Leaders in Congress and those advising the President failed to question the lobbying by anti-Japanese American groups and biased, false anti-Japanese news and media reports that alarmed the public. The American Civil Liberties Union (ACLU) and the Quakers (Society of Friends) were among the few who spoke out against the government decisions and publicly supported the rights of people of Japanese ancestry.

The Internment/Concentration Camps

Locations:

Central Utah (Topaz, UT, 9/42 - 10/45)
Colorado River (Poston, AZ, 5/42 - 11/45)
Gila River (Rivers, AZ, 7/42 - 11/45)
Granada (Amache, CO, 8/42 - 10/45)
Heart Mountain, WY, (8/42 - 11/45)
Jerome (Denson, AK, 10/42 - 6/44)
Manzanar, CA (6/42 - 11/45)
Minidoka, CA (Hunt, ID, 8/42 - 10/45)
Rohwer, AK (9/42 - 11/45)
Tule Lake (Newell, CA, 5/42 - 3/46)

The exclusion and incarceration of Japanese Americans began in March 1942. The War Relocation Authority, or WRA, was established to administer the camps. During the first phase, internees were transported on trains and busses under military guard to the hastily prepared temporary detention centers.

Twelve temporary detention centers were in California and one was in Oregon. They were set up on race tracks, fairgrounds, or livestock pavilions. Detainees were housed in livestock stalls or windowless shacks that were crowded and lacked sufficient ventilation, electricity, and sanitation facilities. Food was often spoiled. There was a shortage of food and medicine.

The second phase began midsummer and involved moving approximately 500 deportees daily from the temporary detention centers to permanent concentration camps. These camps were located in remote, uninhabitable areas. In the desert camps, daytime temperatures often reached 100 degrees or more. Sub-zero winters were common in the northern camps.

The internment camps were surrounded by barbed wire and guard towers. Armed guards patrolled the perimeter and were instructed to shoot anyone attempting to leave. The barracks consisted of tar paper over two-by-sixes and no insulation. Many families were assigned to one barrack and lived together with no privacy. Meals were taken communally in mess halls and required a long wait in line. A demonstration in Manzanar over the theft of food by personnel led to violence in which two died and many were injured. The attempt at screening for loyalty and registering inmates for military induction with the U.S. Army's questionnaire, "Application for Leave Clearance," was conducted in a manner fraught with such confusion and distrust that violence broke out at both California camps.

The camps were overcrowded and provided poor living conditions. According to a 1943 report published by the War Relocation Authority (the administering agency), Japanese Americans were housed in "tarpaper-covered barracks of simple frame construction without plumbing or cooking facilities of any kind." Coal was hard to come by, and internees slept under as many blankets as they were allotted. Food was rationed out at an expense of 48 cents a day per internee, and served by fellow internees in a mess hall of 250-300 people. Most of the 110,000 persons removed for reasons of "national security" were school-age children, infants and young adults not yet of voting age.

Leadership positions within the camps were only offered to the *Nisei*, or American-born, Japanese. The older generation, or the *Issei*, were forced to watch as the government promoted their children and ignored them.

Through the relocation program the Japanese Americans suffered greatly. They first endured the shock of realizing they were not being sent to resettlement communities, as many had been led to believe, but to prison. They lost their homes and businesses. Their educations and careers were interrupted and their possessions lost. Many lost sons who fought for the country that imprisoned their parents. They suffered the loss of faith in the government and the humiliation of being confined as traitors in their own country.

Something I believe to be worthy of comment is that in Canada, similar evacuation orders were established. Nearly 23,000 *Nikkei*, or Canadians of Japanese descent, were sent to camps in British Columbia. It was the greatest mass movement in the history of Canada.

Though families were generally kept together in the United States, Canada sent male evacuees to work in road camps or on sugar beet projects. Women and children *Nikkei* were forced to move to six inner British Columbia towns.

Various Responses

It is ironic that the Japanese Americans were basically being accused and targeted, because of the belief that they had some uniform loyalty to the government of Japan, when the responses from the Japanese-American people during this time was anything but uniform. Some quietly acquiesced to the measures being taken against them. Others were actively involved with the United States government in uprooting potential "dissenters" and those whose loyalty to America was deemed "uncertain." Some refused to be drafted, because they felt their rights as American citizens had been violated (such as the members of the Fair Play Committee), while others who were anxious to prove their loyalty to the U.S. enlisted in the Armed Services (i.e. The Nisei Soldiers, the 442nd Regimental Combat Team). Historically these differences in the Japanese-American community have not been addressed, in my opinion, in any significant way. This, I believe, is due in part to the common American error of painting portraits of communities of color with an extremely broad brush. For this reason I want to outline some of these distinctions that were present in the Japanese-American community during this time.

Cooperation of the Japanese-American Citizens League

The Japanese American Citizens League was the only national organization of its kind, forged at a national convention in 1930 from groups of educated doctors and lawyers with such names as the American Loyalty League and the Progressive Citizens League.

Only the Nisei, born in America as citizens, could belong. In 1940 a 25-year-old college speech teacher from Utah, Mike Masaoka, was appointed to lead the organization through the coming war.

Mike Masaoka was 26 years old when the JACL bid for power and influence with the wartime government, and got it. Under Masaoka's leadership, JACL leaders advised the War Relocation Authority on how to modify Japanese American behavior inside the camps to create "Better Americans," and offered guidance on how to identify and segregate so-called "agitators and troublemakers." In a 1988 interview, Masaoka implied, but would not directly say, that he was compelled to write memos like these under pressure from the government.

JACL's response to the expulsion order was to pledge "cheerful cooperation" with the government, in exchange for humane treatment. Some JACL officers bragged of leading raids with the FBI to arrest Issei leaders they suspected of harboring sympathies for Japan. Under Masaoka's leadership JACL also opposed all constitutional challenges to which the JACL itself was not a party.

The Fair Play Committee

When the government in 1944 announced it would draft the Nisei in the internment camps, many answered the call and even welcomed it -but for others it presented one last chance to protest their continued incarceration and loss of rights. Within a week, a Fair Play Committee was organized at the camp at Heart Mountain, Wyoming. It received editorial support from a journalist in Denver, James Omura. In early March, at a packed mess hall meeting attended by 400, the Fair Play Committee crossed the line from protest to resistance with the key phrase quoted above and young men soon failed to appear for their pre-induction physicals.

For some in the camps, reinstitution of the draft was the last straw. At Heart Mountain, they organized, and Frank Emi would lead them. An engineer named Kiyoshi Okamoto had been writing manifestoes, calling himself the Fair Play Committee of One. He taught others about the Constitution and the Bill of Rights. With Okamoto as chair, the Fair Play Committee rallied support through the only means they had: writing letters, mimeographing bulletins, and posting them throughout camp.

The government and the JACL cracked down, but despite that, one of every nine young men drafted at Heart Mountain refused induction. On June 12, 1944, 63 resisters from Heart Mountain stood trial at the Federal Courthouse in Cheyenne, Wyoming, for draft evasion. The men were found guilty and sentenced to three years in a federal penitentiary. Twenty-two more later resisted, bringing the total from Heart Mountain to 85.

The government then tried the seven leaders of the Fair Play Committee and journalist James Omura for conspiracy to counsel draft evasion. The jury convicted the resistance leaders but acquitted Omura on the First Amendment-freedom of the press. On Christmas, 1945, the Tenth Circuit Court of Appeals in Denver threw out the convictions of the FPC leaders, ruling their jury improperly ignored civil disobedience as a defense. The U.S. Supreme Court refused to hear the appeal from the resisters in the mass trial; and they served more than two years and were released in 1946. On Christmas 1947, President Truman pardoned all wartime draft resisters, including Nisei resisters from all the camps.

The Nisei Soldiers

In February, 1943, teams of U.S. Army officers and enlisted men visited the relocation centers to register draft age men for military service and others for non-military duty such as the Army Nurse Corps and WAC's. Over 33,000 Nisei soldiers served in the American army during the war. Nisei soldiers were used in the Pacific Theater as interpreters as well as in combat in North Africa, Italy and France. The principle units in which the Nisei served were the 100th Infantry Battalion, which was formed in Hawaii, the 442nd Regimental Combat Team, formed from volunteers from the internment camps, and the secret Nisei Military Intelligence Service whose members served with army and navy units from the Aleutians to the far reaches of the South Pacific. The Nisei soldiers became famous for their heroism and the high number of casualties they sustained in combat.

The 442nd/100th sustained 9,486 wounded and over 600 killed- the highest casualty rate of any American unit during the war. For their heroism, the men of the 442nd/100th won fifty-two Distinguished Service Crosses and 560 Silver Stars (the Congressional Medal of Honor was awarded posthumously to Pfc. Sadao Munemori). The 442nd Regimental Combat Team also won seven coveted Presidential Unit Citations for its performance. The men in the 100th Battalion alone had earned 900 Purple Hearts, thirty-six Silver Stars, twenty-one Bronze Stars, and three Distinguished Service Crosses.

It is from this background that 14 extraordinary brave young men serving in the "Nisei Military Intelligence Service" volunteered for a "Dangerous and Hazardous Mission" and became members of the 5307th Composite Unit Provisional, better known as Merrill's Marauders. Assigned 2 to each of the six combat teams and 2 to the Headquarters, these men continuously performed acts of heroism while fighting against the Japanese army in the jungle and mountains of Northern Burma.

It is ironic however, in justifying the evacuation of the Japanese, that General DeWitt would point to the Nisei as being untrustworthy because of their knowledge of the Japanese language and culture (and the Kibei in particular because they were educated in Japan), when the recruiters who went to the detention centers were recruiting them for the very expertise that led to their internment. In MIS (Military Intelligence Service) the real linguists were guys educated in Japan. They were Kibei.

Points Of Law

Japanese Americans filed lawsuits to stop the mass incarceration, but the wartime courts supported the hysteria. The U.S. Supreme Court ruled in *Hirabayashi v. U.S.*, *Yasui v. U.S.*, and *Korematsu v. U.S.* that the denial of civil liberties based on race and national origin were legal. In a later, contradictory ruling in *Endo v. U.S.*, the

Supreme Court decided that a loyal citizen could not be detained, but this did not stop the internment.

The Korematsu case, filed by Fred Korematsu, addressed the key issue: Can American citizens be summarily relocated to detention camps based solely on their race? Aren't there constitutional protections against such arbitrary actions?

The great Supreme Court jurist Hugo Black wrote the majority opinion of the court in the *Korematsu* case. He held that military necessity justified the relocation.

Compulsory exclusion of large groups of citizens from their homes, except under circumstances of direct emergency and peril, is inconsistent with our basic governmental institutions. But when under conditions of modern warfare our shores are threatened by hostile forces, the power to protect must be commensurate with the threatened danger.

Not all the justices agreed that American citizens of Japanese ancestry posed such a threat. Frank Murphy wrote a searing dissent and was joined in his opinion by two others.

I dissent, therefore, from this legalization of racism. Racial discrimination in any form and in any degree has no justifiable part whatever in our democratic way of life. It is unattractive in any setting but it is utterly revolting among a free people who have embraced the principles set forth in the Constitution of the United States.

In the late 1980's, the *Korematsu* case was reopened, and Mr. Fred Korematsu's conviction (of violating an exclusion order) was vacated (nullified) at the federal district court. This ruling was made on the basis of evidence showing that high-ranking government and military officials knowingly suppressed vital evidence and misrepresented facts in their original presentations to the Supreme Court.

Yet, the Supreme Court's 1944 decision in *Korematsu v. United States* remains as a legal and historical precedent that can still be used to justify denying people's constitutional rights on the basis of their race or ancestry. In her opinion on the *Korematsu coram nobis* case, District Judge Marilyn Patel warned against this:

Korematsu remains on the pages of our legal and political history ... As historical precedent it stands as a constant caution that in times of war or declared military necessity our institutions must be vigilant in protecting constitutional guarantees. It stands as a caution that in times of distress the shield of military necessity and national security must not be used to protect governmental actions from close scrutiny and accountability. It stands as a caution that in times of international hostility and antagonisms our institutions, legislative, executive and judicial, must be prepared to exercise their authority to protect all citizens from the petty fears and prejudices that are so easily aroused.

After the War

On December 17, 1944 (almost 2 years after the Presidential order), President Roosevelt announced the end of the exclusion of Japanese Americans from the West Coast, thus allowing the return home of the internees. Some Japanese Americans died in the camps due to inadequate medical care and the emotional stresses they encountered. Several were killed by military guards posted for allegedly resisting orders. Relocation after incarceration was difficult, especially since prejudice still ran high on the West Coast. Many Issei (first generation Japanese Americans) never regained their losses, living out their lives in poverty and poor health.

The challenges and burdens of resettlement after the internment were shouldered primarily by members of the Nisei generation (second-generation, American-born Japanese Americans). Most Nisei came of age during and after the internment years. Having witnessed the sacrifices and losses of their Issei (first-generation Japanese immigrant) parents, the Nisei persevered as active citizens, determined to claim their rightful place in America.

The vibrant pre-war Japanese-American communities, including Little Tokyo in Los Angeles, Japantown in San Francisco, and many small farming communities on the West Coast were greatly diminished in the post-war period. Although many returned, a significant number of Japanese Americans resettled permanently in East Coast and Midwestern states.

Those who returned to their pre-war homes often found them vandalized and even marred with racial epithets. Many farms and fields were in shambles from neglect or lost to new owners.

Through the 1950's, many Japanese Americans faced housing and employment discrimination and were denied access to many recreational and retail services. Many had to start over with their lives. They often had to share housing with friends or relatives, seek rooms in boarding homes or cluster together in trailer parks. Many had to become migrant workers, taking on any jobs they could find.

Despite losses in property, businesses, homes, and communities, most Japanese Americans, in time, rebuilt their lives. The Nisei raised their families, took care of their aging parents, and became active in schools and community activities.

Beyond rebuilding their lives, some Japanese Americans, particularly in Hawaii and the West Coast sought electoral office and became active in public service on the local, regional and statewide levels.

In 1952, the Walter-McCarran Act was passed, largely through the efforts of Nisei legislators. This Act enabled Issei (first-generation, immigrant Japanese) and other Asian immigrants—previously ineligible for citizenship—to become U.S. citizens. In 1959, Hawaii became the 50th state and Daniel Inouye, a veteran of the celebrated 442nd Regimental Combat Team during World War II, became the first Japanese American senator.

In 1964, Patsy Takemoto Mink became the first Japanese American woman elected to the House of Representatives. In 1974, Norman Mineta of San Jose became the first Japanese American Congressman from the U.S. mainland. Other Japanese Americans pursued public service as well, thus establishing a presence in the various governmental institutions. By 1965, Over 48,000 had become proud naturalized citizens.

Almost 50 years after Executive Order 9066, through the efforts of leaders and advocates of the Japanese-American community, Congress passed the Civil Liberties Act of 1988. Popularly known as the Japanese American Redress Bill, this act acknowledged that "a grave injustice was done" and mandated Congress to pay each victim of internment $20,000 in reparations. The reparations were sent with a signed apology from the President of the United States on behalf of the American people. The period for reparations ended in August of 1998.

Despite this redress, the mental and physical health impacts of the trauma of the internment experience continue to affect tens of thousands of Japanese Americans. Health studies have shown a 2 times greater incidence of heart disease and premature death among former internees, compared to non-interned Japanese Americans.

During WWII the injustices incurred against Japanese Americans, was the product of a blind, unreasoning mob-mentality that is indicative of a society deeply steeped in racism and discrimination. Let us consider the words of Robert Linder: *"In the crowd, herd or gang, it is a mass-mind that operates—which is to say, a mind without subtlety, a mind without compassion, a mind, finally, uncivilized."*

OVERVIEW OF U.S. EUGENICS (STERILZATION) LAWS

HISTORICAL OVERVIEW

"To understand why eugenics gained such a following in the first three decades of the 20th century, one needs to examine the economic, social, and political context in which it flourished. Science, or what is claimed to be science, is a product of culture – like any other human activity."- *Dr. Garland E. Allen* (Professor of Biology-Washington University)

Social Foundations of Eugenics: Garland E. Allen, Washington University

American eugenics developed in the wake of turbulent economic and social problems following the Civil War. The rapid growth of American industry, coupled with the increased mechanization of agriculture, created the first major migration away from farms, and cities expanded faster than adequate housing. Exploitation of labor created militant labor union organizations. Price fluctuations bankrupted many businesses and precipitated a series of depressions, starting in 1873, and reoccurring about every decade through the early 1900s. This further fueled labor unrest. The situation was made worse by an ever-increasing tide of immigrants, mostly from Southern and Eastern Europe, which peaked just before, and again after, World War I.

Social Darwinism had attempted to explain away social and economic inequalities as the "survival of the fittest." However, by the turn of the century, this simplistic idea had been turned on its head. A declining birthrate among the wealthy and powerful indicated that the captains of industry were, in fact, losing the struggle for existence. The working class not only was organizing against them, but they were also out-reproducing them. At the same time, traditional approaches to solving the problems of the urban poor – charity, social work, and religious institutions – were proving of little help.

Solving the new problems of industrialization demanded a change from laissez-faire to managed capitalism – toward the increased role of government and planning in the economic and social sphere. This new philosophy became known as progressivism. Embedded in progressivism was the idea of scientific management – long-range planning by university-trained experts. This new managerial class became increasingly vital to the economic process. In a country that had nurtured a reverence for invention, the use of scientific management had a special appeal. Progressive reformers had a strong faith in science as the cure-all that would herald in a new era of rational control of both nature and human society. Under these conditions, it is not surprising that the revelations of a new science of genetics gave birth to a new science of social engineering – eugenics.

Genetics appeared to explain the underlying cause of human social problems – such as pauperism, feeble-mindedness, alcoholism, rebelliousness, nomadism, criminality, and prostitution – as the inheritance of defective germ plasm. Eugenicists argued that society paid a high price by allowing the birth of defective individuals who would have to be cared for by the state. Sterilization of one defective adult could save future generations thousands of dollars.

Eugenicists and their wealthy supporters also shared a mutual antipathy for political radicalism and class struggle. They were alarmed by the increasing strength of militant labor unions and the rise of the American socialist party, especially after the success of the Bolshevik Revolution in 1917. These movements were, to some extent, correctly judged to be associated with immigrants from southern Europe, especially Italians, eastern Europeans, and Jews. These new immigrants were seen as troublemakers, and the eugenicists purported to have data showing that the problem was in their genes. The solution to the problem was simple – selective immigration restriction.

Eugenics was seen as a way to solve all of these combined problems because it placed the cause in the defective germ plasm of individuals and ethnic groups, and not in the structure of society itself. Eugenics used the cover of science to blame the victims for their own problems. Eugenicists seemed to have the weight of rigorous, quantitative, and thus scientific evidence on their side. To those with economic and social power – and filled with the new spirit of scientific planning – eugenicists appeared to offer a rational and efficient approach of treating social problems.

In an era troubled by rapid and seemingly chaotic change, eugenics offered the prospect of a planned, gradual, and smooth transition to a more harmonious future. With its emphasis on planned breeding, eugenics provided the biological counterpart to new theories of scientific control and rational management in business. Just as a new group of professional managers was making a place for itself in American economic life, eugenicists emerged as scientists with a special expertise in the solution of perennial social problems. Eugenics provided what seemed to offer an objective, scientific approach to problems that previously had been cast almost wholly in subjective, humanitarian terms. Whereas charity and state welfare had treated only symptoms, eugenics promised to attack social problems at their roots.

Scientific Foundations of Eugenics: Elof Carlson, State University of New York at Stony Brook

Eugenics as a framework originated at the end of the 19th century with the British gentleman scientist Sir Francis Galton. Inspired by the ideas in his cousin Charles Darwin's recently published volume, The Origin of Species, Galton reoriented its theory of "survival of the fittest." Instead of enquiring who would survive under evolutionary pressure, Galton asked who should survive. If higher civilization and its protective policies interfered with Nature's control of the fitness of human stock through the death rate, was not it thus appropriate to consider instituting policies to control it through the birth rate? Sir Francis Galton was ever mindful of the fate of the ancient Greeks (in particular, the Athenians), in his judgement the most gifted people in history. In <u>Hereditary Genius</u>

(1869), he attributed their unique qualities to a "system of partly unconscious selection". For the unrivalled opportunities offered by Athens had attracted foreigners of caliber, while slavery (Galton implied) protected the racial purity of the "high Athenian breed". He maintained that the Athenians declined when morality deteriorated and marriage became unfashionable, the balance of the population being kept up by immigrants "of a heterogeneous class". Galton's idiosyncratic reading of ancient history persuaded him that man has the power both to improve and to damage the qualities of his own species.

For Galton feared that his own fine country was threatened with decline brought on by social class differentials in fertility. In Inquiries into Human Faculty (1883), he complained that those who possessed sufficient foresight and self-control to delay marriage, as advised by Malthus, were exactly the people whose reproduction it was vital to encourage. Galton assumed that social distinctions reflect differences in innate endowment and that the middle and upper classes tended to possess more "civic worth". Ability, he believed, is determined by heredity and runs in families, revealing itself by success in competitive careers. The early marriage and reproduction of members of such "thriving families" therefore ought to be encouraged, in his view. Only by raising the average intellectual standard of the nation by one grade could its survival and expansion be assured, since that standard was not keeping pace with the fast-changing requirements of modern civilization. Eugenics, then, was nothing less than a program for national survival.

On May 16th, 1904, Galton read his paper *"Eugenics: Its Definition, Scope and Aims"* to a meeting of the Sociological Society (founded the previous year) held at the London School of Economics. Galton urged its members to disseminate eugenics as a national religion. Some were prepared to, notably George Bernard Shaw, who decried a civilization in which men and women "... select their wives and husbands less carefully than they select their cashiers and cooks".

But the discussion of Galton's essay indicated the disagreements among those whom the chairman, Karl Pearson—who went on to become Galton Professor of Eugenics at University College,

London—described as "... the heterogeneous elements classed together as sociologists". Reservations were expressed by J.M. Robertson and L.T. Hobhouse about Galton's reduction of the laws of history to selection. The Society, "a herd without a leader" in Pearson's view, proved quite unsuited to the role imagined for it by Galton. His reception at this meeting helps explain the founding of the Eugenics Education Society, in 1907.

In 1911, his endowment of the Francis Galton Laboratory for National Eugenics at University College London, and his induction of the prolific statistician and eugenicist Karl Pearson as its chair, established the first institutional body specifically for the study and promotion of eugenics. By then, the newly embraced theory of Mendelian genetics provided a biological justification for the scientific study of heredity and its effects on national vitality. The science of eugenics — defined by Galton as "the study of agencies under social control, that may improve or impair the racial qualities of future generations, either physically or mentally" (1) — promptly ascended to academic legitimacy with the founding of academic institutes, research stations, private foundations and academic journals. (2) While Britain led the world in eugenic "science," eugenic policies were argued but never formally enacted there. The most extensive implementation of such policies occurred in two democratic states: the progressive-era United States and Nazi-era Germany. Practical eugenics took two directions – positive eugenics and negative eugenics. The goal of positive eugenics was to increase birth rates amongst the "fit." Concern by policymakers around the higher birthrates of recent immigrants, and declining birthrates among middle- and upper-class American-born white women, spurred popular discourse around such ideas as "race suicide." In 1911 Theodore Roosevelt, a vocal opponent of "willful sterility" among non-immigrant white Americans; argued that the greatest danger to civilization was that "there will be failure to have enough children of the marriages that ought to take place." (3) Through eugenics, reproduction was recast in terms of its contribution or detriment to the strength of a nation. From this new position of state interest in a previously private concern, it was a logical jump to more extensive state involvement in reproductive policy.

Positive eugenics created distinctions between those who ought and ought not to bear children. More pernicious and ultimately more codified was negative eugenics. Negative eugenics encompassed programs and policies that aimed to decrease the proportion of "unfit" members of a population. This was accomplished through a number of methods: Policies to prevent "undesirable" births included segregation or sterilization of "defectives," and laws denying marriages between first cousins and across races. The "unfit" population was also limited through differential immigration quotas structured to favor those from more "desirable" regions. Programs to eliminate economic poverty were derided as dysgenically fostering a greater biological poverty. Throughout the 1920s and 1930s, negative eugenics replaced positive eugenics as the primary approach for eugenic policy and practice in the United States.

Concerns about environmental influences that might damage heredity – leading to ill health, early death, insanity, and defective offspring – were formalized in the early 1700s as degeneracy theory. Degeneracy theory maintained a strong scientific following until late in the 19th century. Masturbation, then called onanism, was presented in medical schools as the first biological theory of the cause of degeneracy. Fear of degeneracy through masturbation led Harry Clay Sharp, a prison physician in Jeffersonville, Indiana, to carry out vasectomies on prisoners beginning in 1899. The advocacy of Sharp and his medical colleagues, culminated in an Indiana law mandating compulsory sterilization of "degenerates." Enacted in 1907, this was the first eugenic sterilization law in the United States.

By the mid-19th century most scientists believed bad environments caused degenerate heredity. Benedict Morel's work extended the causes of degeneracy to some legitimate agents – including poisoning by mercury, ergot, and other toxic substances in the environment. The sociologist Richard Dugdale believed that good environments could transform degenerates into worthy citizens within three generations. This position was a backdrop to his very influential study on The Jukes (1877), a "degenerate" family of paupers and petty criminals in Ulster County, New York. The inheritance of acquired (environmental) characters was challenged in the 1880s by August Weismann, whose theory of the germ plasm convinced most scientists that changes in body tissue (the soma) had little or no effect on reproductive tissue (the germ plasm). At the beginning of the 20th century, Weismann's views were absorbed by degeneracy theorists who embraced negative eugenics as their favored model.

Adherents of the new field of genetics were ambivalent about eugenics. Most basic scientists – including William Bateson in Great Britain, and Thomas Hunt Morgan in the United States – shunned eugenics as vulgar and an unproductive field for research. However, Bateson's and Morgan's contributions to basic genetics were quickly absorbed by eugenicists, who took interest in Mendelian analysis of pedigrees of humans, plants, and animals. Many eugenicists had some type of agricultural background. Charles Davenport and Harry Laughlin, who together ran the Eugenics Record Office, were introduced through their shared interest in chicken breeding. Both also were active in Eugenics Section of the American Breeder's Association (ABA). Davenport's book, Eugenics: The Science of Human Improvement through Better Breeding, had a distinct agricultural flavor, and his affiliation with the ABA was included under his name on the title page. Agricultural genetics also provided the favored model for negative eugenics: human populations, like agricultural breeds and varieties, had to be culled of their least productive members, with only the healthiest specimens used for breeding.

Evolutionary models of natural selection and dysgenic (bad) hereditary practices in society also contributed to eugenic theory. For example, there was fear that highly intelligent people would have smaller families (about 2 children), while the allegedly degenerate elements of society were having larger families of four to eight children. Public welfare might also play a role in allowing less fit people to survive and reproduce, further upsetting the natural selection of fitter people.

Eugenicists argued that "defectives" should be prevented from breeding, through custody in asylums or compulsory sterilization. Most doctors probably felt that sterilization was a more humane way of dealing with people who could not help themselves. Vasectomy and tubal ligation were favored methods, because they did not alter the physiological and psychological contribution of the reproductive organs. Sterilization allowed the convicted criminal or mental patient to participate in society, rather than being institutionalized at public expense. Sterilization was not viewed as a punishment because these doctors believed, erroneously, that the social failure of "unfit" people was due to an irreversibly degenerate germ plasm.

THE LAW/POLICY

Note: The first twenty states that passed sterilization (eugenics) laws will be listed in chronological order.

1. Indiana- 1907

2. Washington- 1909

3. California- 1909

4. Connecticut- 1910

5. Nevada- 1911

6. Iowa- 1911

7. New Jersey- 1912

8. New York- 1912

9. North Dakota- 1913

10. Kansas- 1913

11. Minnesota- 1913

12. Michigan- 1913

13. Nebraska- 1913

14. Vermont- 1917

15. Oregon- 1917

16. South Dakota- 1917

17. Alabama- 1921

18. Montana- 1923

19. Vermont- 1924

20. Virginia- 1924

Other states that passed eugenics laws: Idaho, Utah, Maine, Mississippi, North & South Carolina, West Virginia, Arizona, Delaware, New Hampshire, Oklahoma & Maine.

THE MANY FACETS OF EUGENICS

In this chapter the social and political attitudes will be divided into three parts: 1. Eugenics & The "Socially Unfit"; 2. Eugenics & Anti-Immigrant Sentiment; 3. Eugenics & Racism/Sexism.

Eugenics & "The Socially Unfit"

Sterilization began in the prison system of Indiana in 1907. A law was passed that allowed for the involuntary sterilization of inmates. The law extended to cover all "wards of the state," and those "maintained wholly or in part by public expense," to include "feebleminded, insane, criminalistic, epileptic, inebriate, diseased, blind, deaf; deformed; and dependent." Also included on the list were "orphans, ne'er-do-wells, tramps, the homeless and paupers" (the statements in quotations were taken from the Indiana Sterilization law of 1907).

Eugenicists claimed that criminal behavior was a result of defective genes. Most eugenicists adhered to the prevailing social theory of the early decades of the twentieth century that "culture does not make the man, but man makes the culture," meaning that poor people gravitate toward and contribute to a poverty-stricken environment, and thus create their own degenerate conditions. Thus, while not denying that poor social and cultural background might contribute to criminality, eugenicists argued that criminality, like many other social traits, was ultimately biological in origin.

Eugenicists were concerned with the noticeable rise in crime rates, especially in the fast-developing urban areas of the United States. They conducted both family pedigree studies and surveys by ethnic and national origin to show that criminality ran high in certain families and groups. Cyril Burt's pedigree analyses in England (on delinquency) supported eugenicists' views that if a trait ran in families it must be genetic. Similarly, Harry H. Laughlin gathered data on incarceration rates by country of origin to show that immigrants to the U.S. from eastern and southern Europe and the Mediterranean countries were disproportionately represented in prisons than "old stock" Americans or recent immigrants from Germany and other Nordic or Anglo-Saxon countries. Laughlin's data had such serious statistical problems that, according to a critique at the time, totally invalidated the conclusions. However, these data formed a cornerstone of the argument Laughlin made to the House Committee on Immigration and Naturalization to curb immigration from Southern and Eastern Europe and the Mediterranean. They were also highly influential in eugenicists' lobbying efforts for sterilization laws that would prevent incarcerated criminals from giving birth to "criminal" offspring. If the number of criminals could be reduced through these biological measures eugenicists argued, it would save the state millions of dollars a year.

Eugenicists were not so naive as to claim that social and economic conditions had no effect in bringing about criminal behavior. In 1928 Charles B. Davenport of the Eugenics Record Office at Cold Spring Harbor, wrote an article titled "Crime, Heredity and Environment," in which he recognized that laws change from time to time, and vary from country to country. What would be technically a criminal act at one place and point in time would not necessarily be a criminal act at another place or point in time. Davenport solved this problem by arguing that criminality was the result of a more general genetic defect known as "feeble-inhibition," that is, criminals were people who could not control (inhibit) their impulses. They could not plan for the future and consequently did whatever came to mind at the moment, regardless of the consequences.

Biological arguments for criminality continued from Laughlin and Davenport's day to the present. In 1939, rather late in the eugenics era, Harvard anthropologist Earnest A. Hooten compiled a massive statistical publication, The American Criminal: An Anthropological Study, in which he argued even more strongly than Laughlin that criminality was a biological trait found more in certain ethnic and national groups than others. In 1965, a group of researchers in Scotland found that a significant percentage of men in prison had an extra Y-chromosome (they were XYY while most males are XY), suggesting a chromosomal cause for criminality. In 1985 Harvard psychologist Richard Herrnstein and political scientist James Q. Wilson published a highly-publicized book, Crime and Human Nature that surveyed vast amounts of literature from the twentieth century, arguing for a biological basis for criminality. In the 1990s, with large grants from the National Institutes of Mental Health, prominent researchers, largely in departments of psychiatry and psychology around the United States, have revived the argument that there is a genetic basis for criminality, pointing especially to the possibility that low levels of a neurotransmitter, dopamine oxidase, may be at the root of uncontrolled ("feebly-inhibited") behavior. At the moment, however, the status of such studies remains unconfirmed by independent research teams.

Eugenicists were particularly interested in mental illnesses, although some were known by different names. Notably, "dementia praecox" we now know as schizophrenia and "Mongolian idiocy" is Down's syndrome. By the turn of the 20th century, people with mental disorders were usually wards of the state, and eugenicists argued that their care was a growing burden on society. Mental patients made good subjects for eugenic study in state institutions, where eugenics case workers could interview them and obtain their family records. Studies at state mental institutions turned up some of the first "evidence" that "social inadequacy" might be in the genes—some institutions housed a number of related inmates. Harry Laughlin used data from state institutions in his first testimony before the House Committee on Immigration, which purported to show that a disproportionate number of immigrants were insane.

"Feeblemindedness," was considered the most important mental disorder by eugenicists. In addition to abnormal behavior and very low scores on IQ tests, "feeblemindedness" was frequently linked to promiscuity, criminality, and social dependency. Eugenicists feared the "feebleminded," because they could potentially "pass for normal" and reproduce with normal people. This was the case of Martin Kallikak, a normal man who fathered an allegedly corrupt line through his union with an attractive, but "feebleminded" girl.

We find another example of this scientific ignorance, as well as arrogance, in the case of Fred Aslin. Fred Aslin was 10 years old in 1936, when he was confined to the Lapeer State School, a closed psychiatric facility in the state of Michigan. His eight siblings were confined there as well. His father had died shortly before, and his mother was unable to care for the children on her own. Aslin, a former farmer in Indiana, had never understood exactly why he and his siblings were thrown into a psychiatric clinic, since neither he nor they were in any way mentally handicapped. "But we were poor, and we were Indians," he notes. At the age of 18, he was sterilized against his will, as were four of his siblings.

Feeblemindedness is no longer used in medical terminology or popular language. It was clearly a catch-all term that had virtually no clinical meaning. Many people who were classified as feebleminded would now be called mildly retarded, learning disabled, or simply underachievers. Many were victims of poverty and abuse. The promiscuity shown by some feebleminded would shock relatively few people today and would be within the scope of "normal" sexual activity portrayed on many prime time television shows.

Although Mendel's laws were first rigorously tested in pea plants and fruit flies, evidence quickly mounted that they applied to all living things. Early in the 20th century, the first examples of recessive, dominant, and sex-linked inheritance were found in humans. Recessive inheritance was first revealed in alkaptonuria (1902), an enzyme deficiency that leads to cartilage degeneration, and albinism (1903). Dominant inheritance was discovered in brachydactyly (short fingers, 1905), congenital cataracts (1906), and Huntington's chorea (1913). And sex-linked inheritance was discovered in Duchenne muscular dystrophy (1913), red-green color blindness (1914), and hemophilia (1916).

Eugenicists made early contributions to our understanding of some of these disorders by constructing pedigrees of affected families. However, these disorders have easily definable symptoms (phenotypes) and are caused by single genes. Eugenicists were wrong to use simple Mendelian schemes to explain complex disorders and traits, whose phenotypes are difficult to define and which are now known to involve multiple genes or are influenced by the environment.

Eugenicists were especially concerned about hereditary blindness, because the institutionalized blind were considered a burden to society. The ophthalmologist Lucien Howe conducted a study on hereditary blindness for the American Medical Association and lobbied for legislation to restrict the marriage of blind persons. Eugenicists considered epilepsy an inherited disorder, and many states sterilized epileptics to prevent its spread. This was another of the eugenicists' misinformed stands—epilepsy's causes are still not fully understood.

Today, we know of more than 5,000 single gene disorders in humans. Modern medicine views each disorder as discretely inherited; the inheritance of one disorder is unrelated to the inheritance of another disorder. Eugenics viewed disabilities as related symptoms of "bad stock." Though eugenicists believed that immorality or poor living habits were inherited, they also thought that "degenerate" traits were inherited together. Eugenicists were generally less concerned about the people affected by genetic disorders than about the threat such people posed to the purity of the national "germ plasm."

Eugenics & Anti-Immigrant Sentiment: Paul Lombardo, University of Virginia

The eugenics movement coincided with one of the greatest eras in U.S. immigration. During the first two decades of the 20th century, 600,000-1,250,000 immigrants per year entered the country through Ellis Island (except during World War I). Unlike earlier waves of immigrants who came primarily from northern Europe, the 20th century brought an influx from southern and eastern Europe. Eugenicists, most of who were of Northern and Western European heritage, worried that the new immigrants weakened America biologically, and lobbied for federal legislation to selectively restrict immigration from "undesirable" countries.

Congress passed America's first naturalization law in 1790. It limited the privilege of US citizenship to "free white persons." About a century later, immigration laws began to restrict who could enter the country. The 1882 Act to Regulate Immigration prohibited entry to "any person unable to take care of him or herself without becoming a public charge". The law was designed to exclude immigrants whose undesirable conditions might prove costly to society – including convicted criminals, the poor, and the mentally ill. In that same year, the Chinese Exclusion Act was the first measure to specifically target immigrants by race or ethnicity.

In the 1890's the federal government assumed sole jurisdiction to monitor immigration, a task that had previously been delegated by contract to states with port cities. The government built a depot on Ellis Island in New York Harbor, through which all immigrants were to be processed. Outbreaks of smallpox, typhus and cholera in New York between 1882 and 1892, heightened concern about the possibility of alien contagion and prompted the adoption of individual health inspections for each arriving immigrant–especially for the contagious eye disease trachoma.

Pressures for further immigration restrictions arose from several quarters of American society. Advocates for American workers wanted to forestall competition from cheap foreign labor. The Boston-based Immigration Restriction League joined this chorus of alarm with calls to require a "literacy test" as a condition of entry into the United States. The League's proposal was given more credence with the publication of Carl Brigham's Study of American Intelligence, which cited the supposed low quality of army recruits of southern and eastern European heritage.

The sheer number of new arrivals troubled many U.S. citizens. In the late 1870's, the annual average number of immigrants fell just short of 150,000. By the turn of the century, that number had increased to almost 800,000, and in 1907 it passed 1,250,000. As the numbers of immigrants increased, eugenicists allied themselves with other interest groups to provide biological arguments to support immigration restriction.

In 1911, Immigration Restriction League President Prescott Hall asked his former Harvard classmate Charles Davenport of the Eugenics Record Office (ERO) for assistance to influence Congressional debate on immigration. Davenport recommended a survey to determine the national origins of "hereditary defectives" in American prisons, mental hospitals and other charitable institutions. Davenport appointed ERO colleague Harry Laughlin to manage the research program.

The Public Health Service (PHS), whose duties included performing medical inspections of disembarking passengers at Ellis Island, also adopted eugenic arguments to help stem the flood of "inferior stock" represented by the new immigrants. Beginning in 1914, the Surgeon General and a number of senior officers in the PHS became publicly aligned with the eugenics movement. They took prominent roles in eugenic organizations and published articles to support the eugenicists' position in the immigration restriction debate. The key role of PHS physicians as medical guardians of U.S. ports – particularly at Ellis Island – gave the PHS additional credibility.

Without specific support from eugenicists, by 1917, Congress had expanded the legal definition of those "likely to become a public charge" to include: "all idiots, imbeciles, feebleminded persons, epileptics, insane persons…;" "persons of constitutional psychopathic inferiority…", and "mentally or physically defective..." Later involvement of eugenicists further broadened that definition by specifying the immigrant groups most likely to represent what Laughlin called the "socially inadequate."

In 1920, Laughlin appeared before the U.S. House of Representatives Committee on Immigration and Naturalization. Using data for the U.S. Census Bureau and a survey of the number of foreign-born persons in jails, prisons and reformatories, he argued that the "American" gene pool was being polluted by a rising tide of intellectually and morally defective immigrants – primarily from eastern and southern Europe. Sympathetic to Laughlin's message, Committee Chairman Albert Johnson of Washington State appointed Laughlin as "expert eugenics agent."

In this capacity, Laughlin conducted research from 1921 to 1931. He took a fact-finding trip to Europe, used free postage to conduct large-scale surveys of charitable institutions and mental hospitals, and had his results published by the Government Printing Office. His research culminated in his 1924 testimony to Congress in support of a eugenically-crafted immigration restriction bill. The Eugenics Research Association displayed a chart beneath the Rotunda of the Capitol building in Washington showing the cost to taxpayers of supporting Laughlin's "social inadequates."

The eugenics movement provided a scientific rationale for growing anti-immigration sentiments in American society. The earlier wave of Irish immigrants joined "established" Americans of northern and western European extraction in their disregard of "new" immigrants from southern and eastern Europe. Labor organizations fed on fears that working class Americans would be displaced from their jobs by an oversupply of cheap immigrant labor, and anti-communist factions stirred up fears of the "red tide" entering the U.S. from Russia and Eastern Europe.

Eugenics Record Office Superintendent Harry Laughlin became the anti-immigration movement's most persuasive lobbyist. Between 1920 and 1924 he testified three times before the House of Representatives Committee on Immigration and Naturalization. He first testified that a disproportionate number of inmates in mental institutions were from Southern and Eastern Europe—even though his own data clearly showed a high proportion was German and Irish.

The Immigration Restriction Act of 1924, sponsored by Johnson, did everything eugenicists had hoped for. First, it limited total immigration to 165,000 -- about 15-20% of peak years. More important, it restricted immigration from Southern and Eastern European countries (designed consciously to halt the immigration of supposedly "dysgenic" Italians and Eastern European Jews, whose numbers had mushroomed during the period from 1900 to 1920) to only 9% of the total. Northern and western European countries got 86% of the quota, even though they made up the minority of immigrants in 1923. This change in the complexion of immigration was accomplished by a cunning use of statistics. The Johnson Act limited immigrants from each country according to their proportion in the U.S. population in 1890 -- a time prior to the major waves of southern and eastern European immigration when the U.S. was decidedly more Anglo-Nordic in composition. This law also had another chilling side effect. It prevented many Jews from entering the U.S. during the time of the Nazi Germany's implementation of their "Final Solution."

Upon signing the Act, President Calvin Coolidge commented, "America must remain American." This statement would become the catch-phrase of anti-immigration sentiment until after World War II. The eugenic intent of the 1924 law and the quota system it established remained in place until they were repealed by the Immigration and Nationality Act of 1965.

U.S. immigration did not reach pre-Johnson Act levels again until the late 1980s. Less than 10% of the 660,477 legal immigrants to the U.S. in 1998 were from northern and western European countries.

Eugenics & Racism

We are all members of one species, *Homo sapiens.* Human beings from any part of the world can mate with each other to produce offspring. Historically, people chose mates who lived within a 15-

193

mile radius, but by the beginning of the 20th century, Americans were marrying people of different races, religions, and ethnicities. Demographic changes—including the exodus from farm to city and the influx of new immigrants—and the increasing use of motor vehicles and telephones encouraged mixing.

In 1908, George Shull at the Station for Experimental Evolution, Cold Spring Harbor, showed that crossing different corn strains produced a more vigorous hybrid. Applying this model to human biology stirred a debate among eugenicists. Shull's advisor, Charles Davenport, could not ignore completely his work, and he even found some evidence for increased vigor among the mixed race people of Jamaica. However, he ultimately concluded that race crossing led to behavioral "disharmony."

However, Shull's work was lost on the vast majority of lay eugenicists who subscribed to the Biblical notion of "like with like" and who believed that miscegenation (race mixing) produced undesirable mongrels. In his influential book, *The Passing of the Great Race*, Madison Grant warned that racial mixing was "a social and racial crime" that would lead to the demise of white civilization. Eugenicists emphasized the supposed hereditary differences among races and ignored the social-economic variables that might account for differences in behavior and customs. Thus, the eugenic concept of degenerate heredity provided a pseudo-scientific gloss to age-old prejudices.

Laws forbidding marriage between people of different races were common in America from the Colonial period through the middle of the 20th century. By 1915, twenty-eight states made marriages between "Negroes and white persons" invalid; six states included this prohibition in their constitutions.

In the early 1900's, the eugenics movement supplied a new set of arguments to support existing restrictions on interracial marriage. These arguments incorporated a "scientific" brand of racism, emphasizing the supposed biological dangers of mixing the races – also known as miscegenation. Writers like Madison Grant warned that racial mixing was "a social and racial crime." He said that acceptance of racial intermarriage would lead America toward "racial suicide" and the eventual disappearance of white civilization.

According to Grant, the mixture of "higher racial types," such as Nordic whites, with other "lower" races would inevitably result in the decline of the higher race. In *The Passing of the Great Race* Grant further asserted: "The cross between a white man and an Indian is an Indian; the cross between a white man and a Negro is a Negro... When it becomes thoroughly understood that the children of mixed marriages between contrasted races belong to the lower type, the importance of transmitting in unimpaired purity the blood inheritance of ages will be appreciated at its full value."

Grant's assertions on the perils of race mixing mirrored warnings by Charles Davenport and Harry Laughlin, leaders of the American eugenic bureaucracy at the Eugenics Record Office. In turn, American political leaders like Vice President Calvin Coolidge repeated similar sentiments as scientific fact. Said Coolidge: "Biological laws tell us that certain divergent people will not mix or blend."

To prevent further pollution of the country's collective "germ-plasm" and a subsequent contamination of the white race, eugenicists argued for even tighter restrictions against racial mixing. Their efforts focused on new legal definitions of who could qualify to receive a marriage license as a "white" person.

Virginia's Racial Integrity Act of 1924 stands out among anti-miscegenation laws that can be traced to eugenic advocacy. To fashion a successful legislative strategy, three local Virginia eugenicists – John Powell, Earnest Cox and Walter Plecker – consulted with Madison Grant and Harry Laughlin. Powell, a celebrated pianist and composer, was the founder of the Anglo-Saxon Clubs of America (an organization dedicated to maintaining "Anglo-Saxon ideals and civilization in America."). Like *The Passing of the Great Race*, Cox's book *White America* emphasized white supremacy and the dangers of racial mixing. Plecker was registrar at the Bureau of Vital Statistics of the Virginia Board of Health. His ideas on racial interbreeding as the source of "public health" problems appeared in state-published pamphlets distributed to all who planned to marry.

When The Racial Integrity Act became law, it included provisions requiring racial registration certificates and strict definitions of who would qualify as members of the white race. It emphasized the "scientific" basis of race assessment, and the "dysgenic" dangers of race mixing. Its major provision declared: "It shall hereafter be unlawful for any white person in this State to marry any save a white person, or a person with no other admixture of blood than white and American Indian. …the term "white person" shall apply only to such person as has no trace whatever of any blood other than Caucasian; but persons who have one-sixteenth or less of the blood of the American Indian and have no other non-Caucasoid blood shall be deemed to be white persons…."

Alabama and Georgia eventually copied the Virginia law. Within a decade, similar laws prohibiting inter-ethnic marriages and attempting to sort citizens by percentage of Jewish "blood" were adopted by the government of Nazi Germany.

Popenoe and Johnson of the Human Betterment Foundation give a laundry list of "defectives," including the blind, deaf, insane, feeble-minded, paupers, criminals, epileptics, tramps, prostitutes and beggars. Popenoe and Johnson provided extensive (erroneous) rationale for the inferiority of black Americans, stating that, "If the number of original contributions which it has made to the world's civilization is any fair criterion of the relative value of a race, then the Negro race must be placed very near zero on the scale." It should be noted here that in the lexicon of the day, "race" had a meaning strongly linked to national identity, at least among the "white races." Thus one could speak of the Germans, the French, and the Italians in terms of specific "racial qualities." Amongst these white races, the most frequent eugenic concern was voiced over those tainted by Catholicism: the Irish and the Italians. In any case, given the social structure of vagrancy, criminality and feeble-mindedness in the early 20th century, there can be no doubt that even when not explicitly voiced, the definition of "defective" would be understood along racial lines.

The 1958 case of Loving v. Commonwealth of Virginia initiated a challenge that would eventually overturn the law. That year, Mildred Jeter (a black woman) and Richard Loving (a white man) were married in the District of Columbia. After moving to Virginia, they were indicted for violating the Racial Integrity Act. They pleaded guilty and were sentenced to one year in jail. The trial judge suspended their sentences on the condition that they accept banishment from the state and not return together for 25 years. The judge's written opinion declared: "Almighty God created the races white, black, yellow, Malay and red, and he placed them on separate continents. And but for the interference with this arrangement there would be no cause for such marriages. The fact that he separated the races shows that he did not intend for the races to mix."

The Virginia Supreme Court upheld the judge's decision, and the Lovings moved back to Washington, D.C. In 1963, another attempt to overturn their convictions in Virginia was unsuccessful. The Lovings finally appealed to the United States Supreme Court. By unanimous decision, in 1967 the Court struck down the Racial Integrity Act and similar laws of fifteen other states, saying: "There can be no doubt that restricting the freedom to marry solely because of racial classifications violates the central meaning of the Equal Protection Clause ... Under our Constitution, the freedom to marry, or not marry, a person of another race resides with the individual and cannot be infringed by the state."

EUGENICS IN MAINSTREAM AMERICA

BETTER BABIES & FITTER FAMILIES

When one considers the strong contribution of agricultural breeding to the eugenics movement, it is not difficult to see why eugenicists used state fairs as a venue for popular education. A majority of Americans were still living in rural areas during the first several decades of the 20th century, and fairs were major cultural events. Farmers brought their products of selective breeding—fat pigs, speedy horses, and large pumpkins—to the fair to be judged. Why not judge "human stock" to select the most eugenically fit family?

197

This was exactly the concept behind Fitter Families for Future Firesides – known simply as Fitter Families Contests. The contests were founded by Mary T. Watts and Florence Brown Sherbon - two pioneers of the Baby Health Examination Movement, which sprang from a "Better Baby" contest at the 1911 Iowa State Fair and spread to 40 states before World War I. The first Fitter Family Contest was held at the Kansas State Free Fair in 1920. With support from the American Eugenics Society, the contests were held at numerous fairs throughout the United States during the 1920's.

At most contests, competitors submitted an Abridged Record of Family Traits, and a team of medical doctors performed psychological and physical exams on family members. Fitter Families were families with little or no incidences of physical or mental disability. Their ethnic heritage also had to be "intact". Racial intermarriages resulted in disqualification. Each family member was given an overall letter grade of eugenic health, and the family with the highest grade average was awarded a silver trophy. Trophies were typically awarded in three family categories: small (1 child), medium (2-4 children), and large (5 or more children). All contestants with a B+ or better received bronze medals bearing the inscription, "Yea, I have a goodly heritage." Childless couples were eligible for prizes in contests held in some states. As expected, the Fitter Families Contest mirrored the eugenics movement itself; winners were invariably white with northern and western European heritage.

INDOCTRINATION, EDUCATION & BIG-NAME CONTRIBUTORS

Financial support for the popularization of eugenics came both from individuals and foundations in America. In 1906, the breakfast cereal magnate J. H. Kellogg created the Race Betterment Foundation in Battle Creek Michigan, which sponsored a series of conferences at its sanatorium in 1914, 1915, and 1928. Beginning in 1910, the Eugenics Record Office propagandized eugenics with financial support from Mrs. E. H. Harriman and the leadership of Charles Davenport and Harry Laughlin.

The First International Congress of Eugenics was held in London in 1912 and was attended by a certain Winston Churchill. On the agenda of the Third International Congress in 1932 was the "problem" of African Americans which, according to the delegates, revealed a need to sterilize and to "cut off bad stock". At this meeting were several Nazis, including Dr Ernst Rudin, who had been enabled to attend by the Hamburg-Amerika Shipping Line, owned by the Harriman and Bush families. On returning to Germany, Rudin, who was funded by the Rockefellers, supervised the policy of sterilizing those who were retarded, deaf, blind or alcoholics. Between 1941 and 1943, at the same time as the "master race" mentality in Hitler's Germany was being condemned by the rest of the world, 42,000 people were sterilized in the US. Five years later the Sterilization League/ Birthright Inc. established a eugenics center in North Carolina.

After the war, John D. Rockefeller III and John Foster Dulles campaigned against the extension of the non-white populations, and in 1952 launched the Population Council. This still exists and is still advocating zero population growth in the US, family planning in the developing sector and the expansion of the Club of Rome's "Malthusianism". (The Club of Rome was launched by Aurelio Peccei in 1968. Its purpose is to issue propaganda about the environmental crisis to justify centralization of power, the suppression of industrial development in the Third World and eugenics.)

By 1918, a group of socially prominent and influential men organized the Galton Society. Reflecting its namesake's interests, the Society was concerned with presumed human racial differences and policies of differential breeding. Under the direction of eugenicists such as Davenport and pro-eugenics authors, Madison Grant and Lothrop Stoddard, the Galton Society brought together scientific and philanthropic leaders to popularize eugenics through a newsletter, the *Eugenical News*. After the second of these meetings, the American Eugenics Society (AES) was formed. The AES organized several committees devoted to popularizing eugenics: Cooperation with Clergymen, Religious Sermon Contests, Crime Prevention, Formal Education, and Selective Immigration.

The AES also organized Fitter Families Contests and eugenics exhibits at state fairs at locations as varied as Topeka, Kansas and Springfield, Massachusetts throughout 1920s. Typical of the tone of these exhibits, the 1926 display in Philadelphia warned that "some Americans are born to be a burden on the rest." The display used flashing lights to emphasize the supposed dire consequences for America's prosperity if the reproduction of inferior persons was not controlled.

Positive eugenics became prevalent in school curricula. College classes instructed undergrads—especially women—to remember their patriotic duty to spawn well. Popular advice books urged young adults to pick mates wisely to ensure the best possible offspring.

After 1914, courses on eugenics were being offered at some of America's leading universities. Harvard, Columbia, Cornell, and Brown were among those listing courses that included eugenics. In the 1920s, the National Education Association's Committee on Racial Well-Being sponsored programs to help college teachers integrate eugenic content in their courses.

By 1928, eugenics was a topic in 376 separate college courses, which enrolled approximately 20,000 students. A content analysis of high school science texts published between 1914 and 1948 indicates that a majority presented eugenics as a legitimate science. These texts embraced Galton's concept of differential birthrates between the biological "fit" and "unfit," training high school students that immigration restriction, segregation, and sterilization were worthy policies to maintain in American culture.

THE U.S.-NAZI GERMANY ASSOCIATION

With regard to eugenic sterilization, the United States served as an example to the rest of the world. As was stated previously, the first sterilization law was passed in Indiana in 1907. Between 1928 and 1936, a number of European countries also passed sterilization (eugenics) laws, including Denmark (1929), Germany (1933), Sweden and Norway (1934), Finland and Danzig (1935), and Estonia (1936). All these laws, according to Dr. Marie Kopp, who toured Germany studying the Nazi Sterilization Laws for the American Eugenics Society in 1935, were modeled and inspired by American efforts.

The Nazi sterilization law was promulgated on July 14, 1933. Within two months, the *Eugenical News* (a publication of the eugenics organization, published by the Galton Society) printed a major evaluation of the law, including its complete text in translation. The Nazi government was praised for being the "first of the world's nations to enact a modern sterilization law." The German law "reads almost like the American model sterilization law" (Harry Laughlin being the architect of the "American" law). The German law along with the American statutes were expected to "constitute a milestone" in the movement to control human reproduction.

"The new law is clean-cut, direct and 'model.' Its standards are social and genetical," the *Eugenical News* article commented. "It's application is entrusted to specialized courts and procedure. *From a legal point of view nothing more could be desired.*"

In 1934 some eighteen months after the Nazis came to power, Falk Ruttke, a member of both Hitler's elite SS and the Committee for Population and Race Policies, spoke at an international meeting of eugenicists in Zurich. Ruttke thoroughly outlined the steps the Nazis had already taken toward rebuilding Germany along racial lines. These included the infamous Law on Preventing Hereditarily Ill Progeny which allowed for the sterilization, and ultimately the gassing, of persons with mental or physical afflictions and the Decree for the Granting of Marriage Loans, which explicitly excluded Jews. The US Journal of Heredity appreciatively reported Ruttke's speech as reflecting the eugenic foundation of the Nazi state. Even more to the point, Clarence G. Campbell senior member of the American contingent at the 1935 eugenics conference in Berlin, praised Hitler's race policies in glowing terms, referring to them as "epochal in racial history", and as setting a pattern "which other nations and racial groups must follow." In Germany, his remarks were widely published as particularly valuable propaganda. Back in the US, Campbell busied himself drumming up support for the Nazi regime.

Throughout the pre-war period, there was considerable influence of American eugenics policy on Nazi racial policy. Specific Nazi legislation on sterilization was based on similar American laws, or on model legislation proposed by Harry Laughlin of the Eugenics Record Office, and that US scientists were proud of their influence on the Hitler regime. German publishing houses eagerly reprinted American racial and eugenics books and articles, while American foundations such as the Pioneer Fund, underwrote the distribution of Nazi race propaganda films in the US. In an almost spherical mutuality, the Nazis used the prestige of the American scientists and legislators to validate their own eugenics and racial policies, while American eugenicists used the new Nazi eugenics laws as evidence that widespread human sterilization policies could be feasibly put into practice with a minimum of social resistance.

Even after World War II had begun, notable American eugenicists continued to visit Nazi Germany; such visits were virtual collaborations. Ellinger, a geneticist, met with Wolfgang Abel, a scientist and SS officer, who was active in sterilization programs involving both blacks and Jews.

Returning to the U.S., Ellinger wrote that the Nazi racial program had nothing to do with religious persecution, characterizing it instead as a "breeding project" designed to eliminate the "hereditary attributes of the Semitic race." At the same time, the anthropologist Lothrop Stoddard was meeting with both Himmler and Hitler. Stoddard himself was a thoroughgoing racist, and author of *The Rising Tide of Color Against White-Supremacy* and other works, which are still today being sold by neo-Nazi publication houses. Not only were his writings cited in Nazi schoolbooks, but also he won the praise of President Hoover during his testimony to the House Immigration Committee. Also, particular attention should be paid to Stoddard's chilling claim as early as 1940 - that the "Jews problem" would "soon be settled in fact by the physical elimination of the Jews themselves from the Third Reich."

Support for Nazi eugenics was not confined to eugenic societies. In the mid-thirties many biology texts commented explicitly and favorably on the German eugenics program.

Nazi Germany also had the support of a man who was considered the leading industrialist of his time, not only in America, but the world—Henry Ford. It is important to note that we do not know a great deal regarding Ford's views of the German sterilization laws. However, I do believe that the atmosphere of prejudice and hatred of Jews that his publications helped to disseminate can't be ignored when speaking of the U.S.-Nazi Germany eugenics collaboration.

Ford's contribution to the rise of anti-Semitism internationally lies primarily with his propaganda campaign of 1920-22, followed by a more cunning patronage of anti-Semitic forces. The industrialist spent a fortune in publishing and disseminating *The Protocols of the Learned Elders of Zion* and conducting a two-year campaign of anti-Semitic agitation in the *Dearborn Independent*, his personal newspaper, beginning May 20, 1920. These tracts, compiled and published as *The International Jew,* were circulated widely and translated into a number of languages.

The impact of this initiative was significant. Henry Ford was at the time one of the most successful businessmen in the world, with a net worth estimated at well over a billion dollars. He was, in 1920, the sole proprietor of the largest industrial empire that had ever been built, controlling about 60 percent of the American car market, while simultaneously enjoying a reputation as a man of the people and the pioneer of the $5-a-day wage. The auto magnate's prestige lent credibility to American anti-Semitism. Ford's publications, has been viewed by some historians, as a major influence on young Nazi adherents in Germany.

Ford's impact on Hitler was evidenced by a framed photograph of the industrialist that hung on Hitler's office wall. Tens of thousands of copies of Ford's anti-Semitic tracts were circulated in Germany in 1921-22, just as Hitler was gaining control of the Nazi Party. *Mein Kampf* contains sections that appear to be lifted from the *Dearborn Independent.*

Hitler refers to the industrialist, the only American mentioned in his biography, stating: "Every year makes them [the Jews] more and more the controlling masters of the producers in a nation of 120 million; only a single great man, Ford, to their fury still maintains full independence."

Another major American contributor to the furtherance of the Nazi regime in Germany was the Union Banking Corporation (whose director was Prescott Bush, grandfather of the current President of the United States). In October 1942, ten months after entering World War II, America was preparing its first assault against Nazi military forces. Prescott Bush was managing partner of Brown Brothers Harriman. His 18-year-old son George, the future U.S. President, had just begun training to become a naval pilot. On Oct. 20, 1942, the U.S. government ordered the seizure of Nazi German banking operations in New York City which were being conducted by Prescott Bush.

Under the Trading with the Enemy Act, the government took over the Union Banking Corporation, in which Bush was a director. The U.S. Alien Property Custodian seized Union Banking Corp.'s stock shares, all of which were owned by Prescott Bush, E. Roland "Bunny" Harriman, three Nazi executives, and two other associates of Bush.

By Oct. 26, 1942, U.S. troops were under way for North Africa. On Oct. 28, the government issued orders seizing two Nazi front organizations run by the Bush-Harriman bank: the Holland-American Trading Corporation and the Seamless Steel Equipment Corporation.

U.S. forces landed under fire near Algiers on Nov. 8, 1942; heavy combat raged throughout November. Nazi interests in the Silesian-American Corporation, long managed by Prescott Bush and his father-in-law George Herbert Walker, were seized under the Trading with the Enemy Act on Nov. 17, 1942. In this action, the government announced that it was seizing only the Nazi interests, leaving the Nazis' U.S. partners to carry on the business.

These and other actions taken by the U.S. government in wartime were, tragically, too little and too late. The Union Banking Corporation had already played a central role in financing and arming Adolf Hitler for his takeover of Germany; in financing and managing the buildup of Nazi war industries for the conquest of Europe and war against the U.S.A.; and in the development of Nazi genocide theories and racial propaganda, with their well-known results.

The American and German eugenics movements were one in their identification of human beings being classified as valuable, worthless, or of inferior value in supposedly hereditary terms. Eugenics was synonymous with "race hygiene," and its primary focus was to purify their respective nations of "low grade" and "degenerate" groups. Thus American and German eugenicists (as well as those from other European countries) created a generic discrimination- the genetically inferior. Not surprisingly, the victims always turned out to be the long-established victims of racism and prejudice: blacks, Jews, women, immigrants and the poor.

In the late 1930s there were last-ditch attempts to waive some of the restrictions in the 1924 Immigration Act in order to grant asylum to a few eventual victims of the Holocaust. These efforts were vigorously opposed by eugenicists, especially by [Harry Hamilton] Laughlin, who submitted a new report, *Immigration and Conquest*, reiterating the biological warnings against the "human dross" that would produce a "breakdown in race purity of the ...superior stocks." While almost one thousand German Jews seeking to immigrate waited hopefully in a ship off the coast of Florida, Laughlin's report singled them out as a group "slow to assimilate to the American pattern of life." In addition Laughlin also recommended a 60 percent reduction in quotas, together with procedures to denationalize and deport some immigrants who had already attained citizenship. For the eugenicists, Nordic purity was as important in the United States as it was in Germany. The ship was sent back to Germany.

By 1945, when the murderous nature of the Nazi government was made perfectly clear, the American eugenicists sought to downplay the close connections between themselves and the German program. But the damage had already been done. The American intellectual and scientific encouragement for first German and then Nazi ideas on eugenics had already left its fingerprints on the most comprehensive attempt to enforce racial purity in the history of the world. The fault, I believe, lies in either a disregard or an indifference towards the reality that inherent in the ideology of forced *sterilization* ("they should not be allowed to reproduce.") is the seed that gives birth to *extermination* ("they should not be allowed to exist").

THE AFTERMATH OF THE LAWS

INVOLUNTARY STERILIZATION: TOP 10 STATES

- **California:** 20,208 men and women sterilized

  - Virginia: 8,250
  - North Carolina: 6,297
  - Michigan: 3,786
  - Georgia: 3,284
  - Kansas: 3,032
  - Indiana: 2,424
  - Minnesota: 2,350
  - Oregon: 2,341
  - **Iowa:** 1,910
  - **Other states:** Wisconsin, North Dakota, Delaware, Nebraska, South Dakota, Utah, Washington, Mississippi, New Hampshire, Connecticut, Oklahoma, Maine, South Carolina, Montana, Vermont, Alabama, West Virginia, New York, Idaho, Arizona
  - Total, all states: 63,966

Buck v. Bell

By 1924, approximately 3,000 people had been involuntarily sterilized in America; the vast majority (2,500) in California. That year Virginia passed a Eugenical Sterilization Act based on Laughlin's Model Law. It was adopted as part of a cost-saving strategy to relieve the tax burden in a state where public facilities for the "insane" and "feebleminded" had experienced rapid growth. The law was also written to protect physicians who performed sterilizing operations from malpractice lawsuits. Virginia's law asserted that "heredity plays an important part in the transmission of insanity, idiocy, imbecility, epilepsy and crime…" It focused on "defective persons" whose reproduction represented "a menace to society."

Carrie Buck, a seventeen-year-old girl from Charlottesville, Virginia, was picked as the first person to be sterilized. Carrie had a child, but was not married. Her mother Emma was already a resident at an asylum, the Virginia Colony for the Epileptic and the Feebleminded. Officials at the Virginia Colony said that Carrie and her mother shared the hereditary traits of "feeblemindedness" and sexual promiscuity. To those who believed that such traits were genetically transmitted, Carrie fit the law's description as a "probable potential parent of socially inadequate offspring." A legal challenge was arranged on Carrie's behalf to test the constitutional validity of the law.

At her trial, several witnesses offered evidence of Carrie's inherited "defects" and those of her mother Emma. Colony Superintendent Dr. Albert Priddy testified that Emma Buck had "a record of immorality, prostitution, untruthfulness and syphilis." His opinion of the Buck family more generally was: "These people belong to the shiftless, ignorant, and worthless class of anti-social whites of the South." Although Harry Laughlin never met Carrie, he sent a written deposition echoing Priddy's conclusions about Carrie's "feeblemindedness" and "moral delinquency."

Sociologist Arthur Estabrook, of the Eugenics Record Office, traveled to Virginia to testify against Carrie. He and a Red Cross nurse examined Carrie's baby Vivian and concluded that she was "below average" and "not quite normal." Relying on these comments, the judge concluded that Carrie should be sterilized to prevent the birth of other "defective" children.

The decision was appealed to United States Supreme Court. Justice Oliver Wendell Holmes Jr., himself a student of eugenics, wrote the formal opinion for the Court in the case of Buck v. Bell (1927). His opinion repeated the "facts" in Carrie's case, concluding that a "deficient" mother, daughter, and granddaughter justified the need for sterilization. The decision includes the now infamous words: "It is better for all the world, if instead of waiting to execute degenerate offspring for crime or to let them starve for their imbecility, society can prevent those who are manifestly unfit from continuing their kind...Three generations of imbeciles are enough."

Recent scholarship has shown that Carrie Buck's sterilization was based on a false "diagnosis" and her defense lawyer conspired with the lawyer for the Virginia Colony to guarantee that the sterilization law would be upheld in court. Carrie's illegitimate child was not the result of promiscuity; she had been raped by a relative of her foster parents. School records also prove that Vivian was not "feebleminded." Her 1st grade report card showed that Vivian was a solid "B" student, received an "A" in deportment, and had been on the honor roll.

Nevertheless, Buck v. Bell supplied a precedent for the eventual sterilization of approximately 8,300 Virginians.

Buck v. Bell also stands out because it was the first time that the American eugenics movement received the "seal of approval," if you will, from the highest court in the land thus giving eugenics an air of validity and credibility. The Buck v. Bell precedent allowing sterilization of the so-called "feebleminded" has never been overruled.

California- The Bloodiest Offender

The first sterilization law in California was enacted on April 26, 1909. It was aimed at the inmates of both state hospitals and institutions for the mentally retarded, and prison inmates who fit certain categories. The categories for this last group included those inmates displaying "sex or moral perversions" while in prison, those twice convicted of sexual offenses, or those convicted three times for other crimes. Interestingly, inmates committed for life were also included in the list – men who would presumably have little opportunity to start families. This is probably because at that time sterilization was thought to have certain therapeutic effects such as to curtail masturbation or violent tendencies. Decisions on who was to be sterilized were made by a "board consisting of the superintendent or resident physician of the institution in consultation with the general superintendent of state hospitals and the secretary of the State Board of Health." The approval of any two of these three individuals would ensure that the operation was carried out. There was no provision made for special funding to pay for sterilizations.

This original sterilization law was superseded by a new one on June 13, 1913. This new law was more specifically worded, broader in scope and more complex than the 1909 law. It enlarged the powers of the state mental health bureaucracy and had a more purely eugenic focus, as eugenics advocates themselves proudly pointed out. These revisions created a law that was to be in force from 1913 through the 1930's - the period when most of the involuntary sterilizations were performed in California. Whereas the 1909 law merely referred to "inmates of State Hospitals and the Home for the Feeble-minded (at Sonoma)," the revised law of 1913 specifically targeted for possible sterilization those "afflicted with hereditary insanity or incurable chronic mania or dementia..." It appears that at least for those formulating the policy, hereditarian and eugenic concerns needed to be addressed to a greater extent than before, perhaps at the expense of the older and more anecdotal approach to sterilization as something therapeutic - something to improve the lives of the patients themselves. In the change of vocabulary one can also see a greater confidence in the ability to diagnose psychiatric conditions with the (false) certainty that they can be passed down from generation to generation.

Along with more precise and specific terminology, the 1913 law also contained references to a "State Lunacy Commission," which was headed by Frederick Winslow Hatch. This commission had existed since 1897, but had not until this time been integrated into a coherent policymaking structure dealing with sterilization. Those suffering from certain mental illnesses could be sterilized on the order of the Lunacy Commission as a condition of release from an institution. In the case of the mentally retarded, or "feeble-minded," who were legally minors, the new law conditioned surgery upon the written consent of parents or guardians. This consent provision may be one reason why the law was not subjected to constitutional attack.

209

And as with the earlier law, there was no special provision for funding. Sterilization costs would come out of the regular institutional budgets.

The legislation of 1917 made some minor alterations. It established an institution called the Pacific Colony which was to be for epileptics and the mentally retarded. Sterilizations performed at this institution had to be authorized by a Board of Trustees and approved by a clinical psychologist holding the degree of Ph.D. The authority of the State Lunacy Commission was enlarged somewhat, and additional "eugenical" language was added. Again, there were no special monetary appropriations for sterilization. This was to be the last legislative action in California to implement eugenic sterilization policy.

The evolution of the sterilization laws, then, shows an expanding bureaucracy as well as a growing concern among policymakers with genetically defective individuals and the threat of their continued reproduction. The expansion of the role of government, the creation of commissions of degree-holding "experts" to deal with various problems, and the willingness to abridge individual freedoms for the good of society are some of the central features of the Progressive Era. The general features of policy development in California followed the pattern of the United States as a whole in many ways, even if the end result was to be more extreme in the case of eugenics.

The term "involuntary," as it is often applied to sterilization in California during this time period, requires clarification. California's eugenic sterilization legislation in 1909, 1913 and 1917 called for the sterilization of various classes of mental defectives and criminals. Sterilization was involuntary in that the consent of the "patient" was not required, and the operation could be made a condition of release from an insane asylum. Considering that the inmates of asylums in this era included recovering alcoholics, people with mild cases of epilepsy, and others who today would not be considered "insane," one can see that many patients were probably very motivated to leave and would have given their consent for sterilization out of impatience or even desperation. It was not necessary to obtain the consent of the (adult) individual's family either, although this was frequently done to avoid legal challenges. Sterilization as a completely voluntary procedure was also carried out during the Progressive Era and even before, but this phenomenon is beyond the scope of this paper. It should also be noted that a case such as that of parents choosing to temporarily commit a mentally retarded or "delinquent" daughter to an institution for the sole purpose of sterilization should also be considered "involuntary."

The sterilizations seem fairly well divided between northern and southern California. Also, it is apparent that most of the patients sterilized were what was then considered mentally ill rather than mentally retarded. Of 291 persons sterilized between June of 1920 and June of 1922 at all California institutions, 149 were listed as manic depressive, 68 were diagnosed schizophrenic, 27 were epileptic, 14 were suffering from "imbecility" (mental retardation), 19 had drug and alcohol-related problems and 14 were classified as "other."

Although a wide variety of intellectuals, scientists, reformers, dreamers and uninformed supporters could be counted among the advocates of eugenics, it is not surprising that those who served and directed state institutions had the greatest impact on the most vulnerable segments of the population: the institutionalized and the poor. Superintendents and state officials were probably the most responsible for the vast number of forced sterilizations performed in California. Two of these officials are Frederick W. Hatch, head of the State Lunacy Commission, and U. S. Webb, attorney general for the state of California during much of the Progressive Era.

Frederick Winslow Hatch, Jr. was evidently instrumental both in the passage of the 1909 sterilization law and in the implementation of that and successive laws. In 1909, Dr. Hatch was secretary of the State Lunacy Commission in California. Shortly after the law was passed (it was introduced by a friend of Hatch, Senator W. F. Price), Hatch became the General Superintendent of State Hospitals, and held the post until his death in 1924. From such a position, Dr. Hatch would have been in a position to both implement policy and hire hospital administrators who favored eugenic sterilization. During his tenure, about three thousand persons were sterilized in California.

Hatch was a California native and the son of a prominent physician in the Sacramento area. Interestingly, the elder Hatch was elected Superintendent of Schools in 1856 as a candidate of the Know-Nothing party. Other than this, there is little available information on F. W. Hatch Jr.'s background and personal life. Much of the information that can be readily obtained, in the form of official correspondence, is courtesy of Harry Laughlin, a eugenics advocate at the national level who wrote extensively on sterilization. According to Laughlin's data, Hatch had a great deal of control over who was to be sterilized until his death in 1924. The assumptions and preconceptions visible in his and his close associates' writings will therefore be of special interest.

Hatch was a firm believer in hereditary mental defect. In a 1914 report by the State Commission in Lunacy, Hatch writes:

"That sterilization in appropriate cases should be done is undoubted. The influence of heredity, the engrafting of the weaknesses of parents upon children, perhaps in modified form, is so well established that there is no room for argument. An answer might be made that those where sterilization seemed urgent should never be discharged from the hospital but would be kept there through life; but it is easy to realize what the result would be. We would be over-crowded with the class of cases who are unfit to bring children into the world. A majority of the public would be maintaining a minority of the unfit by reason of their possession of procreative powers. Sterilization prevents the transmission of their weaknesses to children, the public is protected, and the sterilized individual can be a breadwinner but not a producer of his kind."

Obviously Hatch would not be disposed to listen to arguments in favor of environmental factors. Perhaps we can also see in the above passage a public administrator concerned with cutting costs or at least slowing their rise in the face of an increasing public need for services. Hatch states that "those who keep in touch with insane work must have become convinced of the increasing number of defectives and departures from normal among the fairly young people." But Hatch's motives for sterilizing those under his control are more complex than this. He actually believes that sterilization often reduces the severity of mental illness, even though a vasectomy or salpingectomy has little effect on the body's biochemistry. He goes on to state in his report that

"There is on the part of some writers a tendency to take it for granted that vasectomy is negligible in its affects. Such a conclusion is contrary to our experience, for we find that many of our cases show a marked clearing up a few weeks after operation."

It is difficult to tell how valid this observation is. "Clearing up" might be due to a placebo affect: since hospital staff always tried to get some form of consent from the patient if they could, we can assume that a candidate for sterilization would have been told of the many benefits of the surgery.

By examining letters written by F. W. Hatch in the years immediately before the beginning of the sterilization policy, one can detect a kind of traditional, negative attitude toward the mentally ill based perhaps more on fear than anything else. This was especially true for epileptics. People with this affliction had been unfairly linked to crime and degeneracy since the work of the Italian criminologist Cesare Lombroso in the late 19th century, and probably much earlier. In a letter dated May 13th, 1904, Hatch writes to California governor George C. Pardee in regard to an epileptic mental patient named V. A. Strader, who had presumably written to the governor complaining of unfair treatment. At this time Hatch was the General Superintendent of State Hospitals. Hatch writes that "Strader has been an epileptic since childhood, has undoubtedly been insane and I have no doubt like most epileptics is given to great exaggeration in his accounts of cruel treatment. His description however of the kneeing process was to some extent confirmed by the investigation of last year." It is unclear what the "kneeing process" was, since Strader's letter is not available. Hatch's letter goes on to describe Strader's uncooperative attitude and behavioral problems. It is tempting to speculate that preconceptions brought about by

Lombroso and others often created a self-fulfilling prophecy with institutionalized epileptics, but at the very least letters such as the above are illustrative of a lack of sensitivity, at least by today's standards. As shown earlier, epileptics figured prominently among those groups of inmates subject to sterilization.

Many of those working under Hatch shared his enthusiasm for sterilization. Some worked as Eugenics Field Workers. These were individuals that traveled around the state studying families to determine instances of hereditary degeneracy. Field work such as this was carried out extensively in the eastern United States under the direction of the Eugenics Records Office in Cold Spring Harbor, and there was clearly at least some such activity in California as well. In a letter dated March 12, 1915, a Eugenics Field Worker named Miss Ethel H. Thayer wrote:

"I spoke to Dr. Hatch about the investigation of the family histories of cases proposed for sterilization, and he intends to give me some such cases for study. A history that I am getting at present seems to be increasing the desire and efforts of Dr. Stocking (Medical Superintendent of Agnew State Hospital)...to secure the sterilization of two unfit individuals who are now at large and raising a family only to become county charges."

Thayer goes on in the letter to suggest that more field workers be hired so that the family studies could be carried out on a larger scale.

From this letter we can see two things. First, we can see the expanding role of what we now call social workers, a common phenomenon of the Progressive Era. Second, we can see the power wielded by the field workers in their compilation of family histories. Historians and others who have studied the eugenics field work that was carried out in the eastern U. S. have provided us with an almost nightmarish picture of what Miss Thayer might have done. The field workers were usually young female college students who were given some basic instruction in biology and genetic theory. They would go to economically depressed areas and proceed to assess the social value of dirt-poor families based on their impressions and available "documentation" (It should be recalled that impoverished surroundings were seen by eugenics advocates to be mainly caused by bad heredity). Individuals were labeled "degenerate" or "feebleminded" based on dirty clothing or an unkempt appearance. Children were labeled "imbecile" based on a glance from across the room. If some disorder appeared to have been present in a previous generation, it was labeled "hereditary." Individuals who had been dead for years were categorized as having been mentally deficient based on the field worker's "intuition." Single-parent or otherwise broken homes were a sure sign of hereditary degeneracy. It is unknown what action, if any, was ever taken by the State of California with regard to the people Miss Thayer was studying. They may have suffered a grave injustice.

The following two letters were written a few years later, and their text is reproduced in full here because it is extremely illustrative of the mindset that existed among many in the state medical establishment. The first is from Fred P. Clark, superintendent of the State Hospital at Stockton, to F. W. Hatch, asking for authorization to perform sterilization.

Dear Doctor: MALE, admitted April 14, 1921; native Spain; age 26; white; male; from Kern County. Is afflicted with hallucinations that he is about to be submerged in water by friends- runs away with no particular aim in view; fights and threatens to fight; saw hell- fire. Diagnosis: ALCOHOLIC PSYCHOSIS: ACUTE HALLUCINOSIS. We think this man should be operated on for for sterilization as he would likely transmit to descendants. Yours Truly, Fred P. Clark Medical Superintendent

Dr. Hatch approved this sterilization and it was presumably carried out. Today we would say that this man needed treatment for his alcoholism. Here, he is getting a vasectomy along with any treatment they might be giving him. Or perhaps he really had some other type of mental illness unrelated to drinking. At any rate, he is a young immigrant and is probably a poorly paid agricultural worker. Many of the letters collected by Laughlin indicate that the patients are giving their "consent" for the operation. This particular letter does not. We can also see the assumption that his condition is hereditary.

The second letter is from Leonard Stocking, the Superintendent of Agnew State Hospital. This is the Dr. Stocking mentioned by Miss Thayer.

Dear Doctor: FEMALE; self-committed No. 442; from Alameda County, January 22, 1921; white; native of Kansas; female; age 32 when committed; married; housewife by occupation; diagnosis: manic-depressive. One previous attack. Admitted June 8, 1918; discharged June 18, 1920. Present attack began two months ago; sudden in onset. Bodily condition: fair. No injuries; no epilepsy; depressed. Suddenly became very much confused. No liquor, tobacco, drugs. Cause of insanity unknown. After leaving the hospital the last time she became pregnant and had another child. Soon after this she had to be recommitted to the hospital, and I think further pregnancies would be a decided hindrance for her remaining stable when she again goes home. Yours truly, Leonard Stocking, Medical Superintendent.

The decision to sterilize was approved by Dr. Hatch three days later. This particular sterilization is therapeutic rather than eugenic in nature, showing that sterilizations could be performed for more than one reason. This would be keeping with Dr. Hatch's views on the subject. Like the first letter, however, this one gives no mention of the patient agreeing to the procedure. Most likely her husband gave consent. Regardless, Dr. Stocking did not feel that matter of consent was even worth mentioning - and this is on a formal request for approval! This suggests that perhaps the mechanism for high-level approval was a mere formality, and that the decision to sterilize was an "in- house" operation "open to all sorts of abuse by a zealous eugenics advocate." In some ways the eugenic sterilization program in Nazi Germany was to have more extensive safeguards for the patient than the system in California.

John R. Haynes was a doctor, social reformer and eugenic sterilization advocate. His interest in halting the reproduction of the unfit can be seen in a letter he wrote in 1916. Copies of the letter, essentially a questionnaire asking, among other things, how many sterilizations had been performed to date and why, were sent to the superintendents of all state hospitals in California, as well as any other State where Haynes thought Sterilization might be taking place. The final question in the letter asks: (Since) "few of the insane discharged as cured, remain permanently cured, should not the vast benefits accruing to Society in the prevention of the propagation of the unfit, outweigh an occasional injustice to an individual?" Hatch would surely have answered yes to this, but there is no record of a reply from him. Dr. Leonard Stocking, Medical Superintendent of California's Agnew State Hospital, replied to Haynes that not all mental patients should be sterilized upon release, just those "of a class likely to reproduce." Dr. John Reily, Superintendent of the Southern California State Hospital at Patton replied that 267 people had been sterilized to date at his institution, and that: "An occasional man or woman who would be denied the joys of parenthood, when they were entitled to same, would be a small consideration as compared with the vast benefits accruing to society in the prevention of the propagation of the unfit." There was clearly no shortage of state medical officers willing to put what they saw as the good of society over the rights of the individual.

It has so far been impossible to determine with any certainty the opinions of Governor Gillett, or the more well-known Hiram Johnson, regarding sterilization. Obviously, they signed the legislation into law, but other than that, the conditions and the degree of their support are unclear. We can, however, find a highly placed sterilization advocate outside the medical-institutional establishment in the person of U. S. Webb, the Attorney-General in California who served under both Pardee and Johnson. In an official position released on March 2, 1910, shortly after the creation of the first sterilization law, Webb mentions that while laws mandating the castration of certain criminals might not survive a legal attack, laws with a more eugenic focus and featuring the vasectomy and salpingectomy are much more secure. This combined with certain "consent" provisions make Webb confident that the laws will avoid court challenges. In this he was anticipating the 1927 Buck vs. Bell case in which the U. S. Supreme Court upheld sterilization if it was done for eugenic reasons. California was on the forefront of policy in this regard.

Webb seems to prefer that sterilizations be prescribed by doctors at state-run mental institutions rather than by the courts in the context of "punishment." Webb mentions a meeting of the National Prison Association in 1907 where it was mentioned that punitive sterilization, especially castration, "would be unsafe in the hands of the court and the modern jury and should only be applied after the investigation of experts." He goes on to say that many acts of "paternalism" by the government are limited by the legal system in United States. Here we can clearly see the Progressive Era faith in government power and the need for "experts" to solve social problems. Regarding eugenic legislation, Webb has the usual concern about the unfit:

"Most of the insane, epileptic, imbecile, idiotic, sexual perverts; many of the confirmed inebriates, prostitutes, tramps and criminals, as well as the habitual paupers found in our country poor-asylums; also many of the children in our orphan homes, belong to the class known as degenerates. For this condition to go on unchecked eventually means a weakening of our nation.

The unfit, which for Webb would appear to include a large number of disadvantaged people who were not criminals, were a threat to society. Webb goes on to commend the vasectomy as a device to preserve an individual's liberty, and to argue that traditional common law must keep up with "scientific and social advances."

As we have seen, officials of the State of California promoted sterilization out of a concern for improving the human race and thereby reducing the number of people that had to be dealt with in institutions. Like many people of the time, they saw eugenics as the new branch of science that could eliminate many sources of corruption and degeneracy. For many eugenics advocates, individual reproductive choice, at least for those deemed unfit by society, was a small price to pay.

Sterilization for eugenic purposes continued in California into the 1930's. Activity tapered off during WWII, partly due to a shortage of doctors in the state institutions. The policy essentially ended in the five-year period after the war, due to changing attitudes toward eugenics and the treatment of mental disorders, new leadership at the state institutional level, and the general discrediting of eugenics by association with Nazi policies.

Other Instances

The second Supreme Court case generated by the eugenics movement tested a 1935 Oklahoma law that prescribed involuntary sexual sterilization for repeat criminals. Jack Skinner was chosen to test the law's constitutionality. He was a three-time felon, guilty of stealing chickens at age nineteen, and convicted twice in later years for armed robbery. By the time his case was struck down by the U.S. Supreme Court in 1942, some 13 states had laws specifically permitting sterilization of criminals.

The opinion striking down the sterilization law in the case of Skinner v. Oklahoma (1942) was written by Justice William O. Douglas. He highlighted the inequity of Oklahoma's law by noting that a three-time chicken thief could be sterilized while a three-time embezzler could not. This clearly shows the bias of the eugenics laws against the poor. Said Douglas: "We have not the slightest basis for inferring that ... the inheritability of criminal traits follows the neat legal distinctions which the law has marked between those two offenses." Despite the Skinner case, sterilization of people in institutions for the mentally ill and mentally retarded continued through the mid-1970's.

Another example of the impact that the sterilization (eugenics) laws had on the lives of American citizens can be found in North Carolina. Children who enrolled in the Winston-Salem school district were given IQ tests and those who fell below desired levels were sterilized.

Dr Claude Nash Herndon (president of the Eugenics Society in 1953), in an interview in 1990 for the book *George Bush, The Unauthorized Biography* stated:

"...IQ tests were run on all the children in the Winston-Salem School system. Only the ones who scored really low [were targeted for sterilization], the real bottom of the barrel, like below 70. Did we do sterilizations on young children? Yes. This was a relatively minor operation…It was usually not [done] until the child was eight or ten years old. For the boys, you just make an incision and tie the tube…We more often performed the operations on girls than with boys. Of course, you have to cut open the abdomen, but again, it is relatively minor."

The years of 1946-1948 marked the first time that the number of sterilizations in North Carolina performed on members of the general public exceeded the number performed on inmates and patients in state institutions. With the exception of the 1950-52 biennial reporting period, the number of institutional sterilizations would never again exceed the number performed on members of the general public.

There were other notable court cases and the scandal of the 1970's regarding eugenics (forced sterilization). These included the sterilization of 12- and 14-year-old African-American sisters in Alabama, without consent, and the trial of a South Carolina doctor who refused maternity services to large numbers of welfare mothers who did not consent to his demand for their sterilization. This legacy of coerced, if not legally mandated, sterilization was felt within the mentally-challenged community as well.

Voices of Opposition

Opposition to eugenics began even as the movement was being organized into a scientific discipline. By 1910, the equilibrium model developed by Godfrey N. Hardy and Wilhelm Weinberg disproved the claim that degenerate families were increasing the societal load of dysgenic genes. The Hardy-Weinberg equation also showed that sterilization of affected individuals would never appreciably reduce the percentage of mental defectives in society. At the same time, George Shull, at the Carnegie Station for Experimental Evolution, showed that hybrid corn plants are more vigorous than pure-bred ones. This refuted the notion that racial purity offers any biological advantage or that race mixing destroys "good" racial types.

Work by a number of scientists countered the simplistic assertion that complex behavioral traits are determined by single genes. Herman Muller's survey of mutations in Drosophila and other organisms, from 1914-1923, showed variation in the "gene to character" relation: A single gene might affect several characters (traits) at one time; conversely, mutations in several different genes can affect the same trait in similar ways. The environmental contribution to behavior was pointed up by twin studies – conducted in the 1930's by Horatio Newman, Frank Freeman, and Karl Holzinger – showing that identical twins raised apart after birth had different IQs. Lionel Penrose found that most cases at a state-run institution in Colchester, England resulted from a combination of genetic, environmental, and pathological causes.

A review panel, convened by the Carnegie Institution in 1935, concluded that the vast majority of work sponsored by the Eugenics Record Office was without scientific merit and recommended a halt to its propagandizing for eugenic social programs, such as sterilization and immigration restriction. In retrospect, it is easy to recount these lines of evidence that refuted key eugenic tenets. It is much harder to understand why eugenic social programs continued unabated in the United States – until they were directly discredited by association with the Nazi eugenic program, whose "final solution" led to the Holocaust.

Many sophisticated geneticists – including some who provided refuting evidence – supported some form of eugenic program at one point or another. Although he denounced the negative eugenics of the American movement, Herman Muller remained committed to a personal brand of positive eugenics based on individual worth. Despite the fact that the Hardy-Weinberg showed that sterilization would have little effect on incidence of feeblemindedness, most geneticists still believed that affected individuals should not be allowed to reproduce. The Catholic Church opposed eugenics from the outset, and helped to ward off eugenic social legislation in much of Europe. However, the Catholic viewpoint held little sway in Protestant America. With Buck vs. Bell providing the full approval of the U.S. Supreme Court, state legislatures continued to enact new eugenic sterilization laws up until WWII.

CONCLUSION

During the 1940's the theory of eugenics came under increasing criticism because of its racial prejudices and its lack of scientific foundation. Most American sterilization laws were abandoned during the 1950's. In 1980, former psychiatric patients who had been forced into sterilization banded together for a class-action suit, demanding compensation from the state of Virginia. But a federal judge rejected their suit on the grounds that the U.S. Supreme Court had affirmed the constitutionality of sterilization back in 1927. That Supreme Court ruling was never fought, even in subsequent years. As a result, future damage claims have little prospect of success. And the victims of eugenic forced sterilization have no lobbying power to achieve out-of-court settlements.

Two exhibits have shed light on this repressed chapter of American history. The Jewish Federation of Los Angeles, in cooperation with the Goethe Institute, has shown an exhibit of photographs and documents titled "Polluting the Pure" and the Cold Springs Harbor Laboratory, a genetics research institute in the state of New York, features an online exhibit on the history of the American eugenics movement (excerpts from this online exhibit contributed greatly to this section). Between 1910 and 1940, the "esteemed" Cold Springs Harbor Laboratory on Long Island housed the Eugenics Record Office, the central research facility of the American eugenics movement. Most of the exhibit's 1,200 documents come from its archives.

The supposed objective of the eugenics movement was to "create better human beings through better breeding." Yet, it resulted in whole clans of people being labeled as genetically inferior. Most states enacted mandatory sterilization laws requiring tens of thousands of people considered "feebleminded," "indolent," or "licentious" to be sterilized against their wills. It created a subculture of people deemed "undesirables" and unworthy of existence.

As stated previously by the geneticist Thomas Hunt Morgan (in regards to determining the inheritance of behavioral and mental traits), "The main difficulty is one of definition…" I too believe that these atrocities committed in the name of science should cause our society to look at definitions. Chiefly: how is the value of a human being defined? How this question is answered, determines our success or failure as a society.

SOURCES

Overview of Colonial Laws

Bailyn, Bernard The Ideological Origins of the American Revolution (Cambridge, Mass., 1967)

Jordan, Winthrop D *White Over Black: American Attitudes Toward the Negro*, 1550-1812 Chapel Hill, N.C., 1968)

Beverley, Robert, *History of the Present State of Virginia* [London, 1705], ed. by Louis B. Wright (Chapel Hill, N.C., 1947)

Allen, Theodore, The Invention of The White Race

Nash, Gary; Red, White and Black: The Origins of Racism in Colonial America

Beckett, J.C.; *The Anglo-Irish Tradition* (Ithaca, 1976)

Jackson, Luther Porter; *Free Negro Labor and Property Holding in Virginia, 1830-1860* (New York, 1942)

Edward Waterhouse, A Declaration of the State of the Colonie and Affaires in Virginia (London, 1622), Susan M. Kingsbury, ed., The Records of the Virginia Company of London (4 vols.; Washington, D.C., 1906-1935), III

John Mason, A Brief History of the Pequot War (Boston, 1736), in Alden T. Vaughan, *New England Frontier: Puritans and Indians*, 1620-1675 (Boston, 1965)

Coombs, Norman, *The Black Experience in America* (Guttenberg Project 1990)

The Indian Removal Act 1830

Axtell, James: *The European and the Indian: Essays in the Ethnohistory of Colonial North America* (1981)

Billiard, Jules B.: ed., *The World of the American Indian* (1974)

Driver, Harold E.: *Indians of North America* (1961).

Prucha, Francis Paul: *The Great Father: The United States Government and the American Indians,* 2 vols. (1984)

Prucha, Francis Paul: *The Sword of the Republic: The United States Army on the Frontier, 1783-1846* (1969; reprint, 1977)

Utley, Robert M.: *Frontier Regulars: The United States Army and the Indian, 1866-1891* (1973).

Washburn, Wilcomb E.: *The Indian in America* (1975).

The Fugitive Slave Act of 1850

Allen, James Egart*: Black History, Past and Present,* Exposition Press Inc., Jericho, New York 1971.

Bennet Jr, Lerone: *Before the Mayflower: A History of the Negro in America,* 1919-1962, Johnson Publishing. Co., Chicago 1962.

Appiah & Gates: *Africana- The Encyclopedia of the African and African-American Experience,* 1999

Hugh Thomas*: The Slave Trade- The History of the Atlantic Slave Trade: 1440-1870, 1998*

Internet

University of North Carolina at Chapel Hill Libraries: Documenting the American South- North American Slave Narratives: (http://docsouth.unc.edu/neh/neh.html)

The Chinese Exclusion Act of 1882

Hsu, Francis L.K. (ed.) *The Challenge of the American Dream: The Chinese in the US* (Belmont CA: Wadsworth, 1971).

McClellan, Robert. *The Heathen Chinee: A Study of American Attitudes Toward China, 1890-1905* (Columbus: Ohio State U, 1972).

Miller, Stuart Creighton. *The Unwelcome Immigrant: the American Image of the Chinese, 1785-1882* (Berkeley: U. California, 1969).

Salyer, Lucy E. *Laws Harsh as Tigers: Chinese Immigrants & the Shaping of Modern Immigration Law* (Chapel Hill: U. North Carolina, 1995).

Sandmeyer, Elmer C. *The Anti-Chinese Movement in California* (Urbana: U. Illinois, 1973).

Siu, Paul C.P. *The Chinese Laundryman: A Study of Social Isolation* (NY: NYU, 1987).

Steiner, Stan. *Fusang: The Chinese Who Built America* (NY: Harper & Row, 1979).

Wong, K. Scott & Sucheng Chan. *Claiming America: Constructing Chinese American Identities during the Exclusion Era* (Philadelphia: Temple, 1998).

Daniels, Roger, *Asian America*. Seattle: University of Washington 1988.

Knoll, Tricia, *Becoming Americans*. Coast to Coast Books: Portland 1982

Takaki, Ronald. *A Different Mirror: A History of Multicultural America*. Boston: Little, Brown, and Company, 1993.

Takaki, Ronald *Journey to Gold Mountain: The Chinese in 19th-c. America* (NY: Chelsea House, 1994).

Roediger, David. *The Wages of Whiteness: Race and the Making of the American Working Class*. New York: Verso, 1999.

Lai, Him Mark, Lim, Genny and Yung, Judy. *Island; Poetry and History of Chinese Immigrants on Angel Island 1910-1940*

Plessy vs. Ferguson

Abraham, Henry J., *Freedom and the Court*. 4th ed. New York: Oxford University, 1982

Boskin, Joseph, *Urban Racial Violence*. Beverly Hills, 1976

Franklin, John Hope, *From Slavery to Freedom*. 4th ed. New York: Knopf, 1974

Fredrickson, George M. *The Black Image In The White Mind: The Debate on Afro-American Character and Destiny 1817-1914*. New York: Harper & Row, 1971

Orfield, Gary, *Congressional Power: Congress and Social Change*. New York: Harcourt Brace Jovanovich, 1975

Pritchett, C. Herman, *Constitutional Civil Liberties*. Englewood Cliffs, N.J.: Prentice-Hall, 1984

Rapier, Arthur. A. *The Tragedy of Lynching*. Chapel Hill, 1933

Stetson, Kennedy. *Jim Crow Guide: The Way It Was*. Boca Raton: Florida Atlantic University Press, 1959/1990

Woodward, C. Vann, *The Strange Career of Jim Crow*. New York: Oxford University Press, 1957

Executive Order No. 9066

Biddle, Francis. "Attorney General" manuscript, Box 4, FBP. From Greg Robinson, *By Order of the President: FDR and the Internment of Japanese Americans*. Harvard University Press, 2001.

Commission on Wartime Relocation and Internment of Civilians. *Personal Justice Denied: Report of the Commission on Wartime Relocation and Internment of Civilians*. 1982. Seattle: University of Washington Press, 1997.

Daniels, Roger. *Concentration Camps: North America*. Malabar, Florida: Kreiger Publishing Company, 1981,1989.

Daniels, Roger. *The Politics of Prejudice: The Anti-Japanese Movement in California and the Struggle for Japanese Exclusion*. 1962. Berkeley: University of California Press, 1977.

De Tocqueville, Alexis. *Democracy in America*. Anchor Books edition, 1969.

Foner, Philip S. *History of the Labor Movement in the United States* (Vol. 3). New York: International. 1964.

Ichioka, Yuji. *The Issei: The World of the First Generation Japanese Immigrants, 1885-1925*. New York: Free Press, 1990.

Korematsu, v. United States, 323 U.S. 214 (1944) (dissenting opinion).

Korematsu v. United States, 584 F. Supp. 1406 (N.D. Cal. 1984).

Miller, John J. *And Hope to Die*. Jokertown Shuffle, ed. Bantam, 1991.

O'Brien, David J. & Fugita, Stephen S. *The Japanese American Experience*. Indiana University Press, Bloomington and Indianapolis. 1991.

Robinson, Greg. *By Order of the President: FDR and the Internment of Japanese Americans*. Cambridge & London: Harvard University Press, 2001.

Takami, David. *Executive Order 9066: Fifty Years Before and Fifty Years After*. Wing Luke Asian Museum, 1992.

TenBroek, Jacobus, Edward N. Barnhart, and Floyd W. Matson. *Prejudice, War and the Constitution, Causes and Consequences of the Evacuation of the Japanese Americans in*

World War II. Berkeley, CA: University of California Press, 1968.

Weglyn, Michi. *Years of Infamy: The Untold Story of America's Concentration Camps*. 1976. Seattle: University of Washington Press, 1996.

77th Congress. Hearings. 2nd Session, Select Committee Investigating National Defense Migration.

Overview of American Eugenics (Sterilization) Laws

Adams G., 1967. *The Age of Industrial Violence* New York: Columbia University Press.

Allen, G.E. 1986. "The Eugenics Record Office at Cold Spring Harbor, 1910-1940: An Essay On Institutional History." *Osiris* (second series).

Allen G.E. 1987. "The Role of Experts in Scientific Controversy." In *Scientific Controversy: Case Studies in the Resolution and Closure of Disputes in Science and Technology*. Cambridge: Cambridge University Press.

Anonymous. ca.1750. *Onania, or the Heinous Sin of Self-Pollution and all its Frightful Consequences in Both Sexes, Considered.* London: Charles Corbett.

Brigham, C.C. 1923. *A Study of American Intelligence* Princeton, NJ: Princeton University Press.

Brigham, C.C. 1930. *"Intelligence Tests of Immigrant Groups"* Psychological *Review*.

Brooks-Dunn, J., Klebanov, P.K., and G.J. Guncan. 1996. "Ethnic Differences in Children's Intelligence Test Scores: Role of Economic Deprivation, Home Environment, and Maternal Characteristics." *Child Development*.

Carlson, Elof, "Scientific Origins of Eugenics," State University of New York at Stony Brook

Chase, A. 1977. *The Legacy of Malthus: The Social Costs of the New Scientific Racism.* New York: Alfred A. Knopf.

Cox, E.S. 1923. *White America* Richmond: White American Society.

Cravens, H. 1978. *The Triumph of Evolution: American Scientists and The Heredity-Environment Controversy, 1900-1941.* Philadelphia: University of Pennsylvania Press.

Davenport, C.B. 1911. *Heredity in Relation to Eugenics.* New York: Henry Holt.

Davenport, C.B. 1912. *Eugenics Record Office Bulletin No. 6: The Trait Book.* Cold Spring Harbor, NY: Eugenics Record Office.

Davenport, C.B. 1913. *Eugenics Record Office Bulletin No. 9: State Laws Limiting Marriage Selection in Light of Eugenics.* Cold Spring Harbor, NY: Eugenics Record Office.

Davenport, C.B. 1919. *Naval Officers: Their Heredity and Development.* Washington, D.C.: Carnegie Institution of Washington.

Davenport C.B. 1921. *Eugenics, Genetics, and the Family: Vol. I. Scientific Papers of the Second International Congress of Eugenics.* Baltimore: Williams and Wilkins.

Davenport C.B. 1923. *Eugenics in Race and State: Vol. II. Scientific Papers of the Second International Conference of Eugenics.* Baltimore: Williams and Wilkins.

Darwin, L. 1916. "Heredity and Environment: A Warning to Eugenicists," *The Eugenics Review.*

Duke, D. 1999. *My Awakening.* Mandeville, LA: Free Speech Books.

East, E.M. 1907. "The relation of certain biological principles to plant breeding," *Connecticut Agricultural Experimental Station Bulletin.*

Eggen, J.B. 1926. "Eugenic teaching imperils civilization," *Current History.*

Eugenical News. Cold Spring Harbor, NY: The Eugenics Research Association and the Eugenics Society of the United States of America.

Eugenics: A Journal of Race Betterment. 1928-31. New Haven: American Eugenics Society.

Evans, W. S. (Secretary). *Organized Eugenics.* New Haven: American Eugenics Society.

Fisher, R.A. 1930. *The Genetical Theory of Natural Selection.* Oxford: Clarendon Press.

Freeden, M. 1979. *"Eugenics and Progressive Thought: A Study in Ideological Affinity,"* History Journal.

Galton, F. 1883. *Inquiries into Human Faculty and its Development.* London: J.M. Dent and Sons.

Galton, F. 1871. *"Experiments in Pangenesis, by Breeding from Rabbits of a Pure Variety, into Whose Circulation Blood Taken from Other Varieties had Previously Been Largely Transfused,"* Proceedings of the Royal Society (Biology).

Garrod, A. 1908. *"Inborn Errors of Metabolism,"* Lancet, July 4, 1-7.

Gilman, J.M. 1924. *"Statistics and the Immigration Problem,"* American Journal of Sociology.

Goddard, H.H. 1912. *The Kallikak Family: A Study in the Heredity of Feeblemindedness.* New York: Macmillan Company.

Gobineau, J.A. 1853, *The Inequality of Races* (English translation 1967). New York: Howard Fertig Co.

Gould, S.J. 1981. *The Mismeasure of Man.* New York: W.W. Norton & Company.

Gould, S.J. 1998. *"The Internal Brand of the Scarlet W."* Natural History 102(2): 10-18.

Gould, S.J. 1987. *"Carrie Buck's Daughter."* The Flamingo's Smile: Reflections on Natural History. New York: W.W. Norton & Company.

Gould, J. 1996. *"Thrill of Sliding Goes Straight to the Bone."* New York Times, February 22.

Grant, M. 1921. *The Passing of the Great Race or the Racial Basis of European History.* New York: Charles Scribners & Sons.

Haldane, J.B.S. 1924-1932. *"A Mathematical Theory of Natural and Artificial Selection"* (9 parts). Transactions of the Cambridge Philosophical Society.

Haller, M. 1963. *Eugenics: Hereditarian Attitudes in American Thought.* New Brunswick, NJ: Rutgers University Press.

Hassencahl, F. 1970. Harry H. Laughlin, "Expert Eugenics Agent" for the House Committee on Immigration and Naturalization, 1921-1931. Ph.D. dissertation, Case Western Reserve University.

Herrnstein, R.J. and C. Murray. 1994. *The Bell Curve: Intelligence and Class Structure in American Life.* Boston: Free Press.

Hollingworth, L.S. 1926. *Gifted Children: Their Nature and Nurture.* New York: Macmillan Company.

Hollingworth, L.S. 1929. "The Production of Gifted Children from the Parental Point of View," *Eugenics Science*

Jennings, H.S. 1927. "Public Health Progress and Race Progress— Are They Incompatible?" Eugenics Science.

Jones, G. 1982. "Eugenics and Social Policy Between the Wars," *History Journal.*

Jones, G. 1986. *Social Hygiene in Twentieth Century Britain.* London: Croom Helm.

Hardy, G.N. 1908. "Mendelian Proportions in a Mixed Population," Eugenics Science.

Kamin, L. 1974. *The Science and Politics of I.Q.* New York: John Wiley & Sons.

Kellogg, J.H. 1914. *"Needed—A New Human Race."* In E.F. Robbins (ed.), *Official Proceedings: Vol. I, Proceedings of the First National Conference on Race Betterment.* Battle Creek, MI: Race Betterment Foundation.

Kellogg, J.H. 1915. "The Eugenics Registry," *Official Proceedings: Vol II, Proceedings of the Second National Conference on Race Betterment.* Battle Creek, MI: Race Betterment Foundation.

Kevles, D. 1995. *In the Name of Eugenics: Genetics and the Uses of Human Heredity.* Cambridge: Harvard University Press.

Kevles, D. and L. Hood. 1992. *The Code of Codes: Scientific and Social Issues in the Human Genome Project.* Cambridge: Harvard University Press.

Kuhl, S. 1994. *The Nazi Connection.* New York: Oxford.

Laughlin, H.H. 1923. *Report of the Second International Congress of Eugenics.* Baltimore: Williams and Wilkins.

Laughlin, H.H. 1914. "Report of the Committee to Study and to Report on the Best Practical Means of Cutting off the Defective Germ Plasm in the American Population." *Eugenics Record Office Bulletin.*

Leinneweber, C. 1981. *"The Class and Ethnic Bases of New York City Socialism, 1904-1915."* Labor History.

Little, C.C. 1928, *Proceedings of the Third Race Betterment Conference, January 2-6, 1928.* Battle Creek, MI: Race Betterment Foundation.

Lombardo, P.A. 1982. *"Eugenic Sterilization in Virginia: Aubrey Strode and the Case of Buck v. Bell."* Doctoral dissertation, University of Virginia.

Lombardo, P.A. 1985.*"Three Generations, No Imbeciles: New Light on Buck v. Bell."* New York University Law Review.

Ludmerer, K.M. 1972. *Genetics and American Society: A Historical Appraisal.* Baltimore: Johns Hopkins Press.

MacKenzie, D. 1976. *"Eugenics in Britain,"* Social Studies of Science.

MacKenzie, D. 1979. *"Karl Pearson and the Professional Middle Class,"* Annals of Science 36: 125-143.

Mehler, B. 1988. *"A History of the American Eugenics Society."* Doctoral dissertation, University of Illinois, Urbana.

Micklos, David "Eugenics Research Methods," Cold Spring Harbor Laboratory

Nashville. Montagu, M.F.A. 1942. *Man's Most Dangerous Myth: The Fallacy of Race.* New York: Columbia University Press.

Morgan, T.H. 1932. *The Scientific Basis of Evolution.* New York: W.W. Norton.

Muller, H.J. 1918. *"Genetic Variability, Twin Hybrids, and Constant Hybrids, in the Case of Balanced Lethal Factors,"* Genetics.

Myerson, A., J.B. Ayer, T.J. Putnam, C.E. Keeler, and L. Alexander. 1936. *Eugenical Sterilization: A Reorientation of the Problem.* New York: Macmillan.

Ochsner, A.J. 1899. *"Surgical Treatment of Habitual Criminals,"* Journal of the American Medical Association.

Oskaloosa Herald. June, 1913. "Goddard Talks on Feebleminded."

Pascoe, P. 1996. "Miscegenation Law, Court Cases and Ideologies of Race in Twentieth Century America," *The Journal of American History*.

Penrose, L.S. 1932. "On the Interaction of Heredity and Environment in the Study of Human Genetics (With Special Reference to Mongolian Imbecility)," *Journal of Genetics*.

Paul, D. 1995. *Controlling Human Heredity: 1865 to the Present.* New Jersey: Humanities Press.

Perkins, H.F. 1934. *A Decade of Progress in Eugenics: Scientific Papers of the Third International Congress of Eugenics.* Baltimore: Williams & Wilkins Company.

Pernick, M. 1996. *The Black Stork: Eugenics and the Death of "Defective" Babies in American Medicine and Motion Pictures Since 1915.* New York: Oxford University Press.

Peters, C.C. 1930. *Foundations of Educational Sociology.* New York: Macmillan.

Pickens, D. 1968. *Eugenics and the Progressives.* Nashville: Vanderbilt University Press.

Popenoe, P. and R. Johnson. 1918. *Applied Eugenics.* New York: Macmillan.

Putnam, H.C. 1916. "The New Ideal in Education-Better Parents of Better Children," *Addresses and Proceedings of the National Education Association.*

Putnam, H.C. 1921. "Second Report of Progress of Committee on Racial Well-Being," *Addresses and Proceedings of the National Education Association.*

Putnam, H. C. 1922. "Report of the Committee on Racial Well-Being," *Addresses and Proceedings of the National Education Association.*

Reilly, P.R. 1983. *"The Virginia Racial Integrity Act Revisited: The Plecker-Laughlin Correspondence: 1928-1930,"* American Journal of Medical Genetics.

Reilly, P.R. 1991. *The Surgical Solution.* Baltimore: Johns Hopkins University Press.

Robbins, E. F. 1914. *Official Proceedings of the First National Conference on Race Betterment.* Battle Creek, MI: Race Betterment Foundation.

Rose, S. 1995. *"The Rise of Neurogenetic Determinism,"* Nature 373: 380-382.

Searle, G. 1976. *Eugenics and Politics in Britain: 1900-1914.* Leyden: Noordhoof.

Selden, S. 1999. *Inheriting Shame: The Story of Eugenics and Racism in America.* New York: Teachers College Press.

Sharp, H.C. 1902. *"The Severing of the Vasa Deferentia and its Relation to the Neuropsychiatric Constitution,"* New York Medical Journal 75: 411-414.

Shull, G.H. 1909. *"A Pure Line Method of Corn Breeding,"* Report of the American Breeders' Association 5: 51-59.

Shultze, A.H. 1923. *"Comparison of White and Negro Fetuses,"* *Eugenics in Race and State: Vol. II. Scientific papers of the Second International Congress of Eugenics.* Baltimore, MD: Williams & Wilkins.

Snedden, D. 1931. *"When Wives Go to Business: Is It Eugenically Helpful?"* Eugenics 4(1): 19-20.

Stoddard, L. 1920. *The Rising Tide of Color Against White Supremacy.* New York: Charles Scribner's Sons.

Thorndike, E.L. 1931. *Human Learning.* New York: Century Company.

"Tomorrow's Children." 1934. Movie distributed by Video Images, Box C, Sandy Hook, CT 06482.

U.S. House of Representatives Committee on Immigration and Naturalization. 1921. Statement of Harry H. Laughlin— *Biological Aspects of Immigration.* Washington, D.C.: Government Printing Office

U.S. House of Representatives Committee on Immigration and Naturalization. 1923. Statement of Harry H. Laughlin—*Analysis of America's Modern Melting Pot.* Washington, D.C.: Government Printing Office.

U.S. House of Representatives Committee on Immigration and Naturalization. 1925. Statement of Harry H. Laughlin—*Europe as an Emigrant-Exporting Continent and the United States as an Immigrant-Importing Nation.* Washington, D.C.: Government Printing Office.

Wadlington, W. 1966. "The Loving Case: Virginia's Anti-miscegenation Statute in Historical Perspective," *Virginia Law Review*

Vecoli, R. 1960. "Sterilization: A Progressive Measure?" *Wisconsin Magazine of History*

Weinstein, J. 1968. *The Corporate Ideal in the Liberal State.* Boston: Beachy Press.

Webster G. Tarpley & Anton Chaitkin, *George Bush: The Unauthorized Biography*

Weismann, A. 1888. "The Supposed Transmission of Mutilations," *In Essays upon Heredity and Kindred Biological Problems.* Oxford: Oxford University Press.

Weismann, A. 1885. *"The Continuity of the Germ-Plasm as the Foundation of a Theory of Heredity,"* In Essays upon Hereditary and Kindred Biological Problems. Oxford: Oxford University Press.

Wiebe, R. 1967. *The Search for Order.* New York: Hill and Wang.

Wiggam, A.E. 1922. *The New Decalogue of Science.* New York: Bobbs-Merrill Company.

Wright, S. 1931. *"Evolution in Mendelian Populations,"* Genetics 16: 97-159.

Yerkes, R.M. 1916. *"Educational and Psychological Aspects of Racial Well-Being,"* Addresses and Proceedings of the National Education Association 54: 248-252.

About the Author

Dr. Edward Rhymes has come to be recognized as an international expert in the areas of Critical Race Theory, History; Race and Race Relations (as well as issues that concern today's youth). Edward Rhymes has excelled in the fields of sociology education, theology and sports. His background in sociology and theology has given him the perfect avenues to immerse himself in his love for and interest in other cultures. He has a wonderful sensitivity to all things human and believes in the God-given dignity of all humanity.

Passionate, Dynamic, Down-to-Earth and Inspiring are just a few of the words that have been used by literally thousands of participants who have attended an Edward Rhymes lecture, seminar, workshop, or course (and by those who have read his work as well). Believing that "inspiration is just as important as information," Dr. Rhymes is an articulate speaker and profound writer who continues to stimulate the hearts, minds and imaginations of his audiences. Dr. Rhymes is the Senior Consultant of Rhymes Consulting Services and currently resides in Pittsburgh, Pennsylvania with his wife, Lisa Marie and is the proud father of 4 children: Serena, Clifford, Michael and Ezekiel.

Made in the USA
Lexington, KY
30 December 2016